Art and Design Pedagog
Higher Education

Art and Design Pedagogy in Higher Education provides a contemporary volume that offers a scholarly perspective on tertiary-level art and design education. Providing a theoretical lens to examine studio education, the authors suggest a student centred model of curriculum that supports the development of creativity.

The text offers readers analytical frameworks with which to challenge assumptions about the art and design curriculum in higher education. In this volume, Orr and Shreeve critically interrogate the landscape of art and design higher education, offering illuminating viewpoints on pedagogy and assessment. New scholarship is introduced in three key areas:

- curriculum, the nature and purpose of the creative curriculum and the concept of a 'sticky curriculum' that is actively shaped by lecturers, technicians and students;
- ambiguity, which the authors claim is at the heart of a creative education; and
- value, asking what and whose ideas, practices and approaches are given value and create value within the curriculum.

These insights from the perspective of a creative university subject area also offer new ways of viewing other disciplines and provide a response to a growing educational interest in cross-curricular creativity. This book offers a coherent theory of art and design teaching and learning that will be of interest to those working in and studying higher education practice and policy, as well as academics and researchers interested in creative education.

Susan Orr is Dean and Professor of Creative Practice Pedagogy at the University of the Arts London and Visiting Professor at Bournemouth University.

Alison Shreeve is Emeritus Professor of Teaching and Learning in Art and Design at Buckinghamshire New University and Visiting Professor at the University of the Arts London and Ravensbourne, London.

Routledge Research in Education

For a complete list of titles in this series, please visit www.routledge.com

This series aims to present the latest research from right across the field of education. It is not confined to any particular area or school of thought and seeks to provide coverage of a broad range of topics, theories and issues from around the world.

Recent titles in the series include the following:

Transnationalism, Education and Empowerment
The Latent Legacies of Empire
Niranjan Casinader

Reflective Practice
Voices from the Field
Edited by Roger Barnard and Jonathon Ryan

Citizenship Education in the United States
A Historical Perspective
Iftikhar Ahmad

Transformative Learning and Teaching in Physical Education
Edited by Malcolm Thorburn

Teaching Young Learners in a Superdiverse World
Multimodal Approaches and Perspectives
Edited by Heather Lotherington and Cheryl Paige

History, Theory and Practice of Philosophy for Children
International Perspectives
Edited by Saeed Naji and Rosnani Hashim

Teacher Professional Knowledge and Development for Reflective and Inclusive Practices
Edited by Ismail Hussein Amzat and Nena P. Valdez

Art and Design Pedagogy in Higher Education
Knowledge, Values and Ambiguity in the Creative Curriculum
Susan Orr and Alison Shreeve

Art and Design Pedagogy in Higher Education

Knowledge, Values and Ambiguity in the Creative Curriculum

Susan Orr and Alison Shreeve

Routledge
Taylor & Francis Group
LONDON AND NEW YORK

First published 2018 by Routledge

2 Park Square, Milton Park, Abingdon, Oxfordshire OX14 4RN
52 Vanderbilt Avenue, New York, NY 10017

Routledge is an imprint of the Taylor & Francis Group, an informa business

First issued in paperback 2018

British Library Cataloguing-in-Publication Data
A catalogue record for this book is available from the British Library

Library of Congress Cataloging-in-Publication Data
A catalog record for this book has been requested

ISBN: 978-1-138-21941-0 (hbk)
ISBN: 978-0-367-19250-1 (pbk)

Typeset in Galliard
by Apex CoVantage, LLC

Susan

I dedicate this book to my partner Jean, my daughters Alanna and Baibin and my 'sibs' Kevin, Emma and Judith.

Alison

This book is dedicated to the memory of my parents, Mary and Rex: ordinary, extraordinary people who always believed in us and the power of education.

Contents

List of figures viii
Foreword by Professor James Elkins ix
Acknowledgements xii

PART 1
Art and design education territories 1

1 Introduction 3
2 Knowledge and knowing in practice 19
3 The construction and meaning of value(s) 39
4 Ambiguity and uncertainty in creative education 56

PART 2
Art and design education practices 69

5 The sticky curriculum in art and design: identity and engagement 71
6 Teaching practices for creative practitioners 88
7 Realising the curriculum in art and design: the role of the project 107
8 Art School evaluation: process, product and person 125
9 Drawing conclusions 142

Index 163

Figures

2.1	The Bauhaus curriculum designed by Walter Gropius	21
2.2	Knowledge and knowing in art and design	35
3.1	Studio 2017	41
4.1	BLIND LIGHT, by Antony Gormley 2007	57
5.1	The sticky curriculum in art and design	84
6.1	The Crit is a signature pedagogy	89
8.1	A student Crit 2017	128
8.2	MA Art and Science Crit 2017	130

Foreword

What is the most significant change in art and design education since 1980? That year marked the emergence of the 'anti-aesthetic', as Hal Foster (2002) called it: the idea that visual art should be primarily interested in politics and social change. The anti-aesthetic was a crystallisation of anti-modernist initiatives that had begun in the 1960s, and Foster's edited book *The Anti-Aesthetic* marked the entry of political, anti- or non-aesthetic work into the curriculum. The debate between art that asks for aesthetic response and art that hopes for intellectual or political change remains unresolved, and it provides an essential tension in contemporary art and design teaching.

It has now been almost forty years since art and design education was transformed by politics and postmodernism. It could be said that institutional critique, from Fred Wilson to Andrea Fraser (Globus and Wilson 2011; Fraser 2005), is a major development, but it is itself generally non-aesthetic, and is taught using the same points of reference – from Adorno to Buchloh – that informs the anti-aesthetic. Another change is the acknowledgement of the international art market, which is now taught as a subject to undergraduate students in studio and art history. In the field of design education, the relationship between the university studio and the industry collapses, offering a problematic to our students who seek to challenge and critique the field of play rather than simply slot into it on graduation. Curation has also emerged as a central subject in art pedagogy. In my own institution, the School of the Art Institute in Chicago, there's a room dedicated to the archives of Hans-Ulrich Obrist; that curator's archive is itself curated by students. Or perhaps the biggest change has been in the direction of art without objects, as in relational aesthetics (Rirkrit Tiravanija) or reperformance (Marina Abramović). It could also be said that gender, identity and diversity have transformed art teaching. Many institutions require sensitivity training so that students and teachers are taught about things such as personal pronouns, microaggressions and trigger words. Whilst some commentators berate students for being 'snowflakes', their artwork continues to be politised in ways that reflect contemporary students' priorities and material circumstances.

Important as these changes are, I think they can be understood within the general terms articulated beginning in 1980. The deeper development, I think, is university art education. In scattered ways the effect of the new pedagogy is already visible. I can often guess when I'm seeing an exhibition of art done by someone who has graduated from a practice-led or studio-art PhD or a course that leads to a PhD. The art is intellectual, and it often demands reading and study on the part of viewers. Typically it is graphically, iconographically and referentially complex and ambiguous. Designed objects are accompanied by theories, metrics, hypotheses and other products of the postgraduate environment. Visual art is presented as potential knowledge, as the product of cogitation, theorization, positioning and critique. This new PhD art is more clearly academic, I find, than the art that was produced beginning in the 1960s by students in the new MA and MFA programmes. At the time it was often said that postgraduate degrees would 'intellectualise' or 'academicise' art, but the new art is a different creature entirely. Andrea Fraser is a product of the Whitney Program in New York, where the students read Frankfurt School theory; the new graduates of practice-led doctoral programmes have been led through seminars on research, experiment, hypothesis, evidence and outcomes.

This difference came home to me when I was revising a book called *Art Critiques: A Guide*, which was mainly for master's-level work, and I realised there was no way to integrate the concerns of doctoral programmes. At the doctoral level, especially in design, what matters are research and knowledge. At the MFA level, what matters are critique and criticality. Doctoral programmes still have 'Crits', but they're entirely distinct from undergraduate Crits: the latter are forums for judgement; the former are collegial assessments of research outcomes. The cultures are very different, even inimical. An MFA student might be told her painting doesn't 'work' or isn't 'persuasive': those are postmodern leftovers of modernist judgements. The instructors are really telling her the work isn't good. At the doctoral level, such questions of judgement aren't pertinent. What matters is reasoning, facts, verification or falsification and knowledge. This systematic pedagogy is expanding and moving down the curriculum from the doctoral through the postgraduate and into the college level.

The change is deep, it's fundamental, and so far, it's insufficiently noticed by art historians, theorists and critics who continue to write about curation, identity, political art and other subjects as the art world shifts under their feet. The years 2005–2015 saw an outlandish proliferation of books on the PhD, none of them – not one – written by an art historian, critic or theorist. The new literature is being written by educators and administrators, and in my experience it is being ignored by people who think of themselves as theorists of the contemporary, whether they're interested in the market, curation or criticality.

The pedagogy of research and knowledge has intersected with two other developments, producing a sea of change in art and design higher education. The first of those developments is the ongoing quantification of education, begun in the UK under Thatcher and continuing in the REF, REA and Bologna accords; in the United States and in the European Union (EU), quantification is indirectly influenced by the growth of accrediting bodies and administration. The second development is the gradual movement of art and design education from independent academies and schools to universities – a development noted in the

Introduction – which increases the pressure on art departments to conform to university-wide concerns about the production of knowledge and research.

I think this academic turn, as it's called here, is producing the single most important change in art education since 1980. Orr and Shreeve's book is an outstanding contribution because it brings together all the elements of the new pedagogy: the interest in assessment (Chapter 8); the identification of art with the production of knowledge (Chapter 2); the paradox of ambiguity at the centre of art school ontology (Chapter 3); and the codification of artistic research (Chapter 7 distinguishes project based learning, problem based learning, studio based learning and enquiry based learning). In this new order, there are some remnants of the older modernist and postmodernist agendas: Chapter 3 reconceptualises modernist judgement as 'value'; and Chapter 6 explores the romantic concept of creativity. This scholarship is brought together within a theoretical framework they call 'the sticky curriculum' (Chapter 1).

The challenge for the future, as I see it, is to connect this new literature to the writing on contemporary art that is being done in art history, visual culture, art criticism and art theory. For me, 2011 was a turning point: that was the first year when it became impossible for any one person to read all the literature on third-level art and education, pedagogy, administration and assessment. (It has long been impossible for any single scholar to keep up with the literature in art history, visual culture, art criticism and art theory.) So as we look to the close of the second decade of the century, we face an especially 'sticky' task, to use one of the keywords of this book: on the one hand, the literature on third-level art and design education is un-encompassable; on the other, historians, critics and theorists continue to ignore that literature, producing a widening un-conceptualised split between pedagogy and reception.

Professor James Elkins
School of the Art Institute of Chicago

References

Foster, H., ed., 2002. *The Anti-Aesthetic: Essays on Postmodern Culture.* New York: The New Press.

Fraser, A., 2005. From the Critique of Institutions to an Institution of Critique by Andrea Fraser – artforum.com/in print. *Artforum.* Available at: www.artforum.com/inprint/issue=200507&id=9407 [Accessed February 5, 2017].

Globus, D. and Wilson, F., 2011. *Fred Wilson: A Critical Reader.* London: Ridinghouse.

Acknowledgements

We would like to thank the many people (colleagues and students) we have worked with in creative education who have inspired us to think about learning and teaching in art and design. Particular thanks go to Dr Margo Blythman, Professor Mantz Yorke and the anonymous reviewers for their insightful feedback on drafts of the text. The list of people we owe thanks and gratitude to would fill a chapter, but for those who have worked at the following institutions, you will know who you are: University of the Arts London, particularly The Teaching and Learning Exchange, The London College of Fashion and Chelsea College of Arts; Sheffield Hallam University; York St John University; Buckinghamshire New University; Glasgow School of Art; Lancaster University; and the Institute of Education University College London. We also thank participants in the Group for Learning in Art and Design; European League for the Institute of the Arts; Council for Higher Education in Art and Design; the erstwhile Subject Centre for Art, Design and Communication at the Higher Education Academy and the Creative Learning in Practice Centre for Excellence in Teaching and Learning, and to those at numerous conferences and workshops who have engaged and inspired us to write this book, we thank you and are enriched by having known you.

Finally we wanted to say thank you to each other! Without this collaboration we doubt we would have got round to putting this volume together, and working in partnership enabled new views and thoughts to emerge.

We kindly acknowledge the following for giving permission to quote from works we cite in the text:

Harman, K. & McDowell, L., 2011. Assessment Talk in Design: The Multiple Purposes of Assessment in HE. *Teaching in Higher Education*, 16(1), pp. 41–52. Published by Taylor & Francis Ltd, www.tandfonline.com extracts reprinted by permission of the publisher.

Fryer, N., 2010. From Reproduction to Creativity and the Aesthetic: Towards an Ontological Approach to the Assessment of Devised Performance. *Research in Drama Education: The Journal of Applied Theatre and Performance*, 15(4), pp. 547–562. Published by Taylor & Francis Ltd, www.tandfonline.com extracts reprinted by permission of the publisher.

We are grateful for permission to reproduce the image in Chapter 4, Antony Gormley's

BLIND LIGHT, 2007, Fluorescent light, water, ultrasonic humidifiers, toughened low iron glass and aluminium 320 x 978.5 x 856.5 cm
Commissioned by the Hayward Gallery, London
Installation view, Hayward Gallery, London
Photograph by Stephen White, London

Part 1

Art and design education territories

1 Introduction

Art and design pedagogy

In this volume we offer a rendering of creative, studio based pedagogy. Opening the door of the studio, we explore art and design education with a particular focus on the role of knowledge, values and ambiguity. This is messy and uncertain territory, and by 'helicoptering' above the field we explore commonly applicable practices and approaches to teaching, learning and assessment across art and design.

Students studying art and design in higher education are on a journey that involves identity transformation. Our students journey towards proto artist/designer status on to their graduations, where they exit into the world of professional practice. As Kinniburgh (2014) points out in the context of design, students are developing dual identities as students and professionals from the moment they embark on their studies. In this volume we consider this arc of learning from a range of perspectives. The chapters offer the weft and weave of the territory building up embroidered narratives that tussle with the challenges and paradoxes of creative teaching and learning. Dineen and Collins (2005:46) describe art and design students as explorers finding their own way 'through territory which is at least partly uncharted'. In relation to art and design, we investigate the ways that the student's journey is shaped. Studio education is not delivered. Studio education is forged.

A look at the dazzling diversity and creativity of art and design students' graduate degree shows serves to remind us that when students embark on a course in art and design, the tutors and the students do not know what the final learning destination will be. The students work with staff to co-create the learning. As Buss (2008) observes, art and design students do not follow a path; they leave a trail.

Our particular focus is on undergraduate teaching and learning, but where relevant we bring in research from the school sector and postgraduate education. Whilst there is a scarcity of research in art and design higher education pedagogy (Svennson and Edstrom 2011), we note a growing body of recent publications that are extending the scholarship in this area (Tovey 2014; Lyon 2011; Fleming 2012; Llewellyn and Williamson 2015). This development reflects recognition of the importance of researching pedagogy in the disciplines (Kreber

2009). Paradoxically, a granular examination of teaching and learning in specific disciplinary contexts can surface pedagogical insights that have resonance beyond disciplinary boundaries (Harman and McDowell 2011; Trowler 2014). In this volume we are looking at curriculum, teaching, learning and assessment in the specific territory of creative, studio based education addressing readers who research and practice in this area, but we also draw out conclusions that will have wider educational relevance. The disciplinary focus offers a lens to look at educational practices beyond art and design.

At this point it is necessary to take a moment to contextualise the ways we talk about disciplines in general and art and design more specifically. Disciplines are perhaps best explained as persisting to provide useful shorthand social groupings with which to identify oneself within academia and are likely to persist because we need to be able to refer to complex and shifting ideas about legitimised knowledge and the creation of identities within formalised pedagogic environments, including the presence of creative disciplines in the university. There are several recent books that explore pedagogy by focusing on either design or fine art (see, e.g., Tovey 2014 or Daichendt 2010). We explore art and design higher education in one volume because we believe that art and design have elements in common, namely: a flexibility in the ways that curriculum is understood and applied; an emphasis on practice and making rather than on transmission; a reliance on students working independently and the employment of part-time creative practitioners to teach (Yorke et al. 2013). However, we also recognise that it is an oversimplification to argue that art and design is one discipline. In fact Trowler (2014) argues that art and design is too broad to be defined as a discipline, containing within the term many different subjects in various stages of development:

> Some of the sub-areas of art and design, such as fine art, do count as disciplines, but others, such as design for performance, are too young and restricted to yet have developed regularised sets of discourses, ways of thinking, procedures, emotional responses and motivations.
>
> (Trowler 2014:10)

This volume is expressly concerned with the kinds of teaching and learning practices which make up the grouping of creative subjects which comprise the art and design or creative industries subjects – a large conglomerate which masks many of the differences and subtleties between and within subject areas. The range of distinctly different sub-disciplines includes textiles, fashion, furniture, product design, graphics, or communication design, advertising, fine art, photography, sculpture and media based courses. This is not an all-inclusive list. Media's disciplinary position within art and design is contested by many and seen as a distinct subject area in its own right. Design may include computer games, linking closely to computer sciences and communication, thus overlapping and extending into other disciplinary areas. As new fields of employment emerge, and as technologies evolve, so new nuances emerge and evolve in art and design courses, making it difficult to fix the precise nature of the subject areas and what and how knowledge is valued and taught within individual courses. This leads directly on to the increasing centrality of interdisciplinarity and the challenge of constructing curricula which traverse disciplines (Mendoza et al. 2007). We acknowledge notions of interdisciplinarity and fluidity between and within subject areas (Trowler 2014).

Discipline groupings can be as much about conflict as about community. A more fine-grained study of disciplinary difference is provided by looking at local work groups or teaching and learning regimes at course level (Trowler and Cooper 2002). Conflicts between subgroups in the sciences reveal structural impediments to more collaborative working between different but related subjects (Tuunainen 2005). This can also happen within art and design, as challenges to identities and beliefs about the nature of the subject and the allegiances established as an academic sometimes feel threatened by attempts to force new interdisciplinary activities into the curriculum. As one looks more closely at disciplines, subjects and the practices within them, more differences and tensions appear, and art and design is no exception.

Art and design can be likened to a spectrum of related practices. Art is the practice of an aesthetic approach to the world originally based on drawing and observation preceding the creation of artefacts which relate to, reject or respond to previously existing works of art and to life experiences from the perspective of the artist. Contemporary art encompasses many different kinds of approaches embracing the conceptual and the digital. It involves many kinds of media and skills and is increasingly co-created, transdisciplinary and working with multiple stakeholders. Art is no longer a practice for the solitary artist working in a garret with paint and easel. Design on the other hand has an applied focus which requires rethinking how objects and artefacts, or products, services and communication, might improve or embellish the way we live. 'Art and design' is a catch-all phrase which, like other disciplines, fragments into many different kinds of subject areas, each with its own distinctive ways of working, thinking and acting. At the overarching level there are similarities, and as one digs deeper it is possible to see a landscape with alliances, shared ideas, approaches or ideals in a patchwork of more closely related or distant groupings. As with other disciplines these subject groups morph and change in relation to economic, political and technological development, social practices, global enterprise and local social influences. For example, whilst there are more than 130 available fine art courses in the UK, each course will be different and represent a different cultural configuration, variation in beliefs and approaches and different connections to the world within and outside academia. From the widest to the most subtle differences in art and design there are similarities and idiosyncrasies from the macro and meso to the micro level.

The sticky curriculum

Turning to the subject of curriculum we present the idea of the ***sticky curriculum*** in art and design. Sticky is a term which has multiple meanings, and we use it advisedly to convey the challenges, conflicts, dilemmas and ambiguity in the creative curriculum. What follows is a series of definitions which contributes to the complexity of the term as we use it throughout the volume:

> The word sticky has connotations which range from something unpleasant that might be described as 'goo' which adheres where you don't want it to and becomes annoying and hard to escape. The opposite of this is true when sticky is used to describe something which is delicious like 'sticky toffee pudding' or Thai sticky rice. Most of us like the sweet stickiness of caramelised sugars, whether they are the product of caramelising the outside of a steak or concentrated sugars in sweets and deserts. ***Stickiness might be something to be enjoyed, to be cleaned away or to be suffered.***
>
> Stickiness can be a property of the weather; the very air around us might be perceived as hot and damp, or sticky, suggesting a pervasive quality, something almost universally affecting us, as opposed to the unwanted but localised blob of sticky chewing gum on the sole of your shoe. ***Widespread stickiness or local stickiness are both possible.***
>
> Sticky might also be used to describe a difficult situation, where the outcome is uncertain and reaches a point where it might go one way or another. Stickiness is therefore ambiguous, tentative, teetering, carrying possibilities and potential for one outcome or another. The sticky point might be difficult to negotiate, a barrier of some kind which holds positive or negative possibilities. Working through a sticky patch is challenging or hard work. ***Sticky situations hold the possibilities of positive or negative outcomes. Sticky situations are difficult or challenging and inherently ambiguous.***
>
> Stickiness also suggests clumping or grouping, like sticky rice, which is attracted by something pulling or gluing things together. Where this is used in social networking or in a business sense, it is bringing people together to engage in an activity or to see something of collective interest. ***This stickiness is an attraction or focus creating a social gathering.***
>
> As children most of us enjoyed making a sticky mess; it is part of the joy of getting stuck into creative play. Sticky substances were things to get your hands into, to create and make, to glue and stick, to enjoy and revel in. ***Sticky can be enjoyable and engaging with a sense of liberation and freedom to explore with materials.***
>
> Sticky might also be something which some people do not enjoy. A mess can feel like a failure and a sticky mess one from which you cannot extricate yourself – a problem which is insoluble or which leaves unpleasant traces behind even when you think you have escaped. ***A sense of failure or guilt might attach itself to a sticky situation.***
>
> Someone might demonstrate unwillingness to carry out a particular action. This suggests a reluctance to proceed or engage, a sticking point which is difficult for them where they are unwilling or reticent. ***Sticky suggests reluctance or unwillingness to proceed or holding back.***
>
> Surfaces are sticky if they adhere to other things; a property of stickiness is to hold or restrict movement, gluing things in place or preventing change.

This could be a positive outcome, if you want to hold things together, or a negative one, if you perceive this as being stuck and unable to change or develop. Stickiness as a positive or negative force for change is associated with being stuck, unable to move although you might wish to, or held down by a force which is not of your own making. ***Sticky might result in being stuck or in the serendipitous joy of things happily in position.***

Sticky substances have a tendency to stretch when they stick to different surfaces; they are elastic, mutable and in extreme cases form strands of connecting stickiness. ***Sticky can be elastic and stretchy.***

Harnessing the complex and nuanced meanings of the word sticky, we offer the idea of the sticky curriculum as a unifying theme that provides the connective tissue for the ideas explored across each chapter. The sticky curriculum offers a theory of art and design curriculum. Rather than a curriculum which is understood as content consisting of lists of topics and engagement in pedagogies which help students to learn those topics, we see the curriculum as a complex web of activities in which students forge a way to becoming a creative practitioner. The sticky curriculum presents ambiguity and unclear options which require negotiation for those working in higher education; for those translating creative practice into pedagogic activities; for those who are in a position as learner and find themselves as experts in innovative forms of knowledge and processes and for the technical teams supporting material learning opportunities. All these participants encounter the stickiness of fluctuating roles and responsibilities in studio learning environments, whether these are located in virtual spaces, in the studio, in the university or outside it. Stickiness abounds in the curriculum to be enjoyed or fought; learning to live in and through the ambiguous territories that comprise learning in art and design, those who negotiate it successfully have forged an identity as a creative practitioner creating work that embodies who they are in their creative personas. Our graduates have learnt not only skills and knowledge in its many forms but also practices which enable them to enter the diverse creative workplaces and flexible working spaces that characterise life in the creative and cultural arena post graduation.

Studio curriculum can appear to have little form or shape, but there is a sticky and complex, loose structure. Art and design curriculum comprises skills, practices and theories, and the ways that these components stick together creates a personalised curriculum for each student. Art and design curriculum is sticky because it is complex and contentious. For one student the curriculum may be viewed as a wonderful set of opportunities, whilst for another it is experienced as a chaotic mess. To summarise, we assert that art and design curriculum is sticky for these reasons:

- it is messy and uncertain;
- values stick to it in ways that are difficult to see;
- it has an elasticity, being both sticky and stretchy;
- it is embodied and enacted – it sticks to the person; and
- it is troublesome and challenging.

Creativity

Readman (2015:1) asks 'what do we talk about when we talk about creativity?' In this volume we discuss art and design education, and we explore creativity within this context. Creativity is fundamental to the practices we describe, but to avoid lengthy discussion about the meaning of creativity and the various ways in which it might be interpreted, we will briefly situate the way this term will be deployed in this volume. We note that creativity may be understood as a psychological concept (Amabile 1996); it may be considered in a sociological sense related to issues of power and justice (Bourdieu 1977) or it may be understood in a purely aesthetic sense as something largely unknowable. Creativity is variously described, with some degree of contradiction, as a learnt skill and an innate attribute. Robinson (2009) believes passionately that all of us are creative, but in common parlance people are often talked about as being creative or not creative in a much more categorical and essentialist sense. Creativity is viewed in very simplistic terms as being associated with intuition and right brain processes. For Wagner,

> [c]reativity is a beloved non-word, an almost messianic formulation; one of those public screens onto which everyone can project almost everything . . . Invoking it is de rigueur for 'alternative minds' rebelling against bourgeois 'virtues'.
>
> (Wagner 2009:1)

In this volume creative approaches are associated with curiosity and the willingness to take risks; the focus is on students creating artefacts, products and services which are distinctive contributions to the discipline. These are based on knowledge and learning; the ability to see things from a different angle or to utilize new or different tools and processes; to make connections in unexpected ways and places and to see possibilities where others might not. We do not view creativity as existing in a vacuum divorced from society inside someone's head. We view creativity as located in society and inflected through the lens of that society's values and material circumstances. What we deem to be creative is aesthetically, personally, culturally and politically determined within society. Creativity is a social activity building on and being judged by those who practise the creative arts. Viewed from this perspective creativity is a socially situated human practice which can be fostered and encouraged. Creativity can be a process, or it can be a product or manifestation of process. It is an identity position, but it can also be a hard-won skill. Creativity is impossible to define precisely and is like a butterfly that we look at from afar, making no attempt to capture for fear of destroying it in the act of capture. Like Fleming we recognise that an attempt to define creativity needs a 'tolerance of ambiguity and ragged edges' (Fleming 2012:80).

The creative turn

In the twenty-first century university there is keen interest in creative teaching and learning across the disciplines (Gustina and Sweet 2014). This has become known as the creative turn in higher education (Harris 2014). There is an appetite for the adoption of creative teaching approaches across a range of subjects. In universities today we have examples of nursing education drawing on fine art approaches, business students creating artwork and arts being deployed to enhance clinical practice for medical students (Gustina and Sweet 2014). There is interest in design thinking approaches across the disciplines, and visual literacy is becoming more important as visual information is being conveyed rapidly through a range of digital media. This is linked to wide agreement that today's graduates, from across the disciplines, need to be creative and agile (Gibson 2010). The key argument is that we need to teach creatively to support students' creative development regardless of disciplinary context.

A study of pedagogy in art and design offers the opportunity to draw out the artfulness of teaching and learning (Lupton 2013). Members of the FLΔG collective describe fine art teaching as a 'publicly performed form of art practice' (FLΔG 2014). Orr and McDougall (2014) draw out the symmetries between creative practice and educational practice. Pedagogy in art and design embodies elements of creative practice such as reflection, creativity and an interest in process. Effective teaching is serendipitous and creative, deploying the suspension of judgement, rethinking and redesigning approaches. Pedagogy needs spontaneity as well as careful planning. As Lupton (2013:161) observes if we view 'teaching as art', we acknowledge 'the role of teacher and student as co-creators while still placing the teacher at its centre'.

Wareing (2009) cautions against viewing any particular disciplinary pedagogy as intrinsically better than another, so it is important to note that we do not argue that art and design pedagogy is particular in an essentialist way, nor do we imply that art and design pedagogy is superior to pedagogies in other disciplines. We have worked and researched in the field of art and design higher education for many years, but this volume is not a eulogy to art and design education. We offer a critical interrogation of the landscape. Clearly there are elements of art and design education that echo pedagogies in other disciplines (e.g., the focus on practice is similar in nursing education, and the focus on creativity is paralleled in creative writing degree courses). We offer art and design as a lens through which to study curriculum and pedagogy, and in doing so we seek to draw together and discuss characteristics of art and design education which will be of interest to a wider readership.

The digital turn

Fifty years ago most students' art and design work would have been hand rendered. To consider design education before the digital age is difficult, and increasingly fine art students are turning to digital media to express their ideas. Given the centrality of the digital, we want to explain the absence of a chapter on this central aspect of art and design education. We challenge the idea that students choose to study in analogue or digital worlds, rejecting the binary between the material and the digital university. Drawing on the work of White (2015), we do not view the digital as some other worldly space that is not in the real world. We note the university sector's alarm concerning massive open online courses (MOOCs) and the way that this disruptive technology has yet to shake the roots of studio education. Analysing the concept of the Post Digital Art School (Deaking and Webb 2016), we look to the idea of blended spaces and practices. The digital and the analogue are entwined. Throughout the volume we braid references to the digital, reflecting the ways that digital is positioned for students today. We acknowledge that this is contested territory and that for some, materiality is felt to be superior to any digital engagement (e.g., lecturers cite the importance of the handling of fabric in fashion or the importance of the process of using materials to learn how to design furniture away from the keyboard). However, in many cases educators celebrate what colleagues at University of the Arts London refer to as the 'high tech low tech no tech' approach to creative education.

In the last few years we have moved from a situation where students were universally told to turn their phones off in classes to a situation where educators exploit the phone as a key learning tool. For example, Burns et al. (2016), in an article titled 'Every one phones out: teaching experiments with Instagram', report on a teaching approach that exploits the affordance of the mobile phone. The mobile and the laptop are as ubiquitous as the sketchbook. The emphasis on bring your own devices (BYOD) is changing the landscape of art and design spaces. Computer rooms with rows of computer terminals look dated. In the contemporary Art School, the digital is dispersed throughout our spaces and practices. The digital is part of the cultural landscape in art and design.

The art and design academic turn

A full analysis of the history of art and design in higher education and the ways that government educational policy impacts on art and design is beyond the remit of this volume. The global and political contexts for art and design education are diverse and specific across different continents. In South Africa we find examples of fine art and graphic design educators addressing post-apartheid educational policy (Behardien 2014; Gilio 2016). In China we note the expansion of art and design education where there are as many as 1,791 courses with fine art in the title (www.cucas.edu.cn), reflecting the growth of the middle class and the ambitions of the Chinese government in relation to global creative industries (Zhengrong Lu 2016). In parts of Europe Art School education has been affected by the Bologna Process, which has sought to regularise and standardise aspects of degrees across Europe. The key point is that each country will have its own particular set of issues. We reject any simplistic or colonial analysis that implies Western government contexts are universal, but it is our argument that there are some common elements that apply across a range of international contexts. Crucially, in the twenty-first century, it is more likely that art and design students will be educated in universities than in independent non-affiliated Art Schools. This may be informed by specific government policy; for example, in the UK the move to offer a university experience to 50 percent of school leavers led to the creation of new universities, many of which incorporated former Art Schools into their faculty structures. In the first half of the twentieth century, there were 180 Art Schools in the UK, and there were 28 universities. By 2011 there were 11 Art Schools and 119 universities (Beck and Cornford 2014). We respond to this seismic change by considering the role of art and design within the university sector. In this volume we refer to Art School as a term that embraces art and design faculty within the university as well as independent Art Schools.

How have art and design educators managed the transition from Art School to the university? This move has been associated with the academisation of art and design education, the so-called academic turn. For some this has been a journey from the edginess/edges of Art School Cool to the corporate heart of the university machine. Without overgeneralising what is nuanced territory, we argue that in the early years of this academisation, the focus was very much on the Art School adapting to the university. Learning outcomes were written, timetable software was used, modularity sliced the courses into credit chunks and regulations were applied. However, now we are at a new stage. Rather than being a story of adaptation *to*, we are looking to what academia can learn *from* art and design (Gustina and Sweet 2014). We see this in the ways that many universities, having merged their Art Schools into generic faculty structures, are now recasting them as Art Schools within the university, thereby recognising their strengths and their particular ways of being and doing. Art and design can be the jewel in the crown rather than being seen as the university space eaters who refuse to conform.

The relationship between art and design and academia points to fundamental questions of epistemology. It is our key argument that art and design is academic. We reject the idea of art and design being simply practical because we reject the practical/academic divide. We call on the sector to flex its idea of academic to include and embrace creative practice and ways of knowing in practice. In the UK the distinction between 'academic' and 'non-academic' subjects was partly fuelled by the dichotomy between vocational education and training and university education (similar to the split in education in Australia, with its distinct technical and vocational offerings). In the UK the Coldstream Report (Coldstream 1960) was associated with the introduction of complementary studies and the so-called academic components in degree courses in art and design, and there remains in some areas the notion that this written component is the sole validating aspect of degree-level study in art and design. The hegemony of the written word (Candlin 2000; Kill 2013) helps maintain the notion of an inferior kind of knowledge, that which manifests itself through created artefacts. However, manifest within products, processes and artworks, there is evidence of academic approaches to the discipline. Creative work has the power to embody deep, rich and complex enquiry, attitudes and responses which move the discipline/subject forward or reflect on and offer up new insights, much as an academic essay might do in history, for example. These we maintain are high-quality academic approaches achieved by students within the medium of choice, not necessarily through the written word. The growth of practice based PhDs strengthens this argument. Art and design students develop a bilingual practice communicating visually and textually (Orr et al. 2010; Llewellyn and Williamson 2015). We seek to position our research within a framework which recognises the value of creative practice within academia. Whilst some may reject the academic turn, there is less contention about the educational turn discussed by Rogoff (2008), which sets out the points of intersection and connectivity between arts practice and educational practice. This is the focus of our attention.

Part 1: art and design education territories

Chapters 2, 3 and 4 set out the volume's overarching theoretical framework offering a careful rendering of the ways we understand knowledge, values and ambiguity within the curriculum. In the second section of the volume (Chapters 5–9) we apply this analysis to the ways that teaching, learning, assessment and curriculum are enacted.

Knowledge

In Chapter 2 we address the complexity of knowledge and the way it constructs different hierarchies and preferences within the university. In the creative arts knowledge manifests itself in different formats, which are more or less accessible to conscious thought. These forms of knowledge are apprehended not only through mental activities but are social, embodied and encultured within creative practices. Creative education knowledge is mutable, situated and provisional; it has multiple dimensions and forms. This knowledge is sticky and unstable. We explore how different forms of knowledge and their associated academic practices manifest themselves in a schism between practice and theory.

Value(s)

What and whose ideas, practices and approaches are given value or valorised within art and design education? In Chapter 3 we explore the idea of value from two interconnecting perspectives. Firstly what are the taken-for-granted values that underpin art and design education, and secondly how is value assigned to students and their work? Budge (2012) argues that the idea of mystery and magic conceals the value systems that underpin art and design education, and in this chapter we excavate the values to expose the ways that art and design education is positioned and partial.

We examine the role and nature of discourse to surface the ways that talking legitimises or constrains the activities and outcomes of learning. Dialogic pedagogies create 'a kind of exchange' (Shreeve et al. 2010) between student and tutor. We use the idea of exchange repeatedly throughout the volume as a shorthand to describe the multimodal forms of communication between students and tutors in the studio. The phrase 'a kind of exchange' became the title of an article about art and design signature pedagogies following an observation by a tutor in a research study (Shreeve et al. 2010); the phrase summarised how the authors felt teaching was approached, largely through dialogue, but also through tentative exploration as opposed to didactic certainty. The phrase 'a kind of exchange' usefully encompasses the learning experienced by the tutor during exchanges with students.

Analysing the 'making' of student success and failure, we point to the ways that certain values may serve to advantage and disadvantage students. Values stick to the curriculum but often remain un-codified. Within constructions of value there are dynamic and changing power relations, and we examine the transactional interplay between staff and students that creates value(s).

Ambiguity

In Chapter 4 we look at the role of ambiguity in creative education. In higher education today, there are competing tensions between a need for clarity driven by concerns regarding accountability and transparency, which in art and design competes with the need to allow for open-endedness, playfulness and ambiguity. One of the key characteristics of the sticky curriculum is the pervading sense of uncertainty, where practice is messy and full of unknowns. Articulating a 'pedagogy of ambiguity' (Austerlitz et al. 2008), we explore the notion of safe and unsafe uncertainty (Masson 1993). We consider what can and what cannot be certain in the creative learning environment, cautioning against viewing ambiguity as an equivalent to mystery or elitism. Recognising the discomfort that arises from uncertainty, we outline ways to develop students' tolerance of the unknown. Identifying ambiguity as a threshold concept (Osmond 2009), we look at the ways that teachers work with students to scaffold transition so that students, and indeed faculty staff, can embrace ambiguity.

Part 2: art and design education practices

Sticky curriculum

In Chapter 5 we explore more fully what we constitute as a sticky curriculum and offer up examples to illustrate the experience for students, tutors and others working to support learning in creative subjects. In the sticky curriculum there are always positive and negative possibilities for students' experiences when learning. Students need to negotiate a curriculum which is not clearly set out with defined goals but offers up potential and requires exploration and commitment from the student to develop an individual path through the territory. The curriculum is therefore an opportunity for 'knowing, acting and being' (Barnett and Coate 2005:2). Curriculum is popularly understood as being about the 'what' of education – that is, *what* do students learn? In Chapter 5 we argue that creative education challenges this view of curriculum; in creative education there is a connection between skills, practices and approaches to making that embody an alternative view of curriculum, or curriculum as practice (Weller 2015) across a range of localised contexts.

Tutors have multiple roles in their working lives, even when they are full-time academics. The requirements of university quality assurance systems have become increasingly more demanding as checks and balances demand paper trails and evidence (Strathern 2000); this can be at odds with tutors' own creative practices, which seldom take place in the academy. There are therefore tensions between the boundaries of tutors' roles within and beyond the university.

For both students and those supporting learning, the stickiness of the learning environment and the complexity of changing and fluid roles of learner and teacher requires constant 'identity work' (Taylor and Littleton 2006). Within studio learning the relationship between those engaged in learning and teaching is critical as the 'kind of exchange' (Shreeve et al. 2010) at the heart of pedagogic engagement is complex, difficult and requires negotiation, sometimes obscuring the role of the teacher who manages the paradoxical roles of teaching but not teaching (Buckley and Conomos 2009). We therefore explore the identities of those engaged in higher education art and design in a sticky relationship within learning and teaching.

Teaching practices for creative practitioners

In Chapter 6 we look more closely at pedagogic practices in the creative curriculum. We develop the work on signature pedagogies in art and design (Shreeve et al. 2010; Sims and Shreeve 2012) which set out the key learning activities that characterise art and design higher education and which prepare students for careers in a professional practice (Shulman 2005). Shulman's original contention was that ambiguity characterised signature pedagogies which have evolved explicitly in response to professional practices beyond the university. We also introduce the idea of relations between teaching and practice 'worlds' and the ubiquitous use of the 'real world' to represent practices outside the university in opposition to those within it. Teachers who are also creative practitioners use a number of different strategies to convey their knowledge of practice to their students, negotiating the boundaries between the so-called real world and the educational context. We conclude with a discussion about the range of subtleties within the signature pedagogies of the subjects loosely grouped as art and design and question how changes in technology, social practices and employment are changing learning in the disciplines.

The project in art and design

The open-ended project brief is the focus of Chapter 7. It is a commonly used approach to pedagogy in art and design, but little is written about how it is used to support learning. Project based learning, problem based learning, studio based learning and enquiry based learning are all terms to describe different but related approaches to student centred learning. The nuanced differences between these terms are summarised in this chapter with a clear articulation of a need to capture the distinctiveness of project centred pedagogy in the art and design studio. Our key argument is that project centred pedagogy is a tacit part of the studio environment and that it is important to interrogate this approach to identify its full pedagogic potential.

The project in art and design enables students to co-construct a personalised curriculum. In this sense the project is generative, forward looking and serves as a learning catalyst. Projects vary in their stickiness and elasticity, and over the course of study projects will direct students' attention from a primary concern with process (the making) to a primary concern with product (the artefact). Project based learning destabilises the power relations in the studio, where lecturers can be cast as facilitators (Orr et al. 2014). We seek to reclaim the idea of project centred learning as a form of advanced teaching practice by setting out the mastery needed to adopt this approach to pedagogy successfully. This serves as a direct challenge to the commonly held view that art cannot be taught.

Assessment

Grading offers a key site to explore the sticky curriculum. Chapter 8 discusses the dominant hegemonic position in relation to grading in mainstream universities. This situates within a techno-rationalist frame that presents grading as concerned with making explicit judgements about students' work against predetermined learning outcomes. Research into art and design studio based assessment practices exposes the shortcomings of this perspective (Orr and Bloxham 2012; Orr 2007). Lecturers' interest in students' learning journeys means that grading judgements address the process of making, the product and the studentship associated with the production of work (Belluigi 2013). The interdependency of subjectivity and objectivity are surfaced, and the difficulty associated with writing learning outcomes in a creative context is explored.

Conclusion

In the final chapter we summarise the volume's key arguments, emphasising the complexity of the terrain by highlighting the paradoxes within creative curriculum. Barnett (2012) calls on universities to prepare students for uncertain times, and we propose that art and design offers teaching and learning models suited to this agenda, which has relevance across academia. The pedagogies we articulate have utility beyond the creative studio. Throughout the chapters in this volume, we *look in* to the art and design studio to explore the particularities of art and design pedagogy. In the final chapter we *look out* to the higher education sector to consider the concept of the sticky curriculum and studio based education in relation to the wider university community. We seek to offer the art and design education community a mirror with which to reflect on their pedagogies, but we also seek to reflect and refract these ideas out for wider discussion and analysis across the disciplines.

References

Amabile, T. M., 1996. *Creativity in Context: Update to the Social Psychology of Creativity.* Boulder: Westview Press.

Austerlitz, N., Blythman, M., Grove-White, A., Jones, B. A., Jones, C. A., Morgan, S., Orr, S., Shreeve, A. and Vaughan, S., 2008. Mind the Gap: Expectations,

Ambiguity and Pedagogy Within Art and Design Education. In L. Drew, ed. *The Student Experience in Art and Design Higher Education: Drivers for Change*. Cambridge: Jill Rogers Associates Ltd Publishers, pp. 125–148.

Barnett, R., 2012. Learning for an Unknown Future. *Higher Education Research & Development*, 31(1), pp. 65–77.

Barnett, R. and Coate, K., 2005. *Engaging the Curriculum in Higher Education*. London: Open University Press/McGraw-Hill.

Beck, J. and Cornford, M., 2014. *The Art School and the Culture Shed*. Kingston Upon Thames: The Centre for Useless Spendour.

Behardien, I., 2014. *'Who Are They' or 'What and How They Know': An Investigation by a Fine Art Lecturer Into the Basis of Her Own Legitimacy*. Unpublished MPhil Thesis. University of Cape Town.

Belluigi, D. Z., 2013. A Proposed Schema for the Conditions of Creativity in Fine Art Studio Practice. *International Journal of Education & the Arts*, 14(19), pp. 1–22.

Bourdieu, P., 1977. Cultural Reproduction and Social Reproduction. In J. Karabel and A. Halsey, eds. *Power and Ideology in Education*. Oxford: Oxford University Press, pp. 487–511.

Buckley, B. and Conomos, J., 2009. Introduction. In B. Buckley and J. Conomos, eds. *Rethinking the Contemporary Art School: The Artist, the PhD and the Academy*. Halifax: The Press of the Nova Scotia College of Art and Design, pp. 2–26.

Budge, K., 2012. A Question of Values: Why We Need Art and Design in Higher Education. *Art, Design & Communication in Higher Education*, 11(1), pp. 5–16.

Burns, E., MacLachlan, J. and Rees, J. C., 2016. Everybody Phones Out: Teaching Experiments With Instagram. *Spark: UAL Creative Teaching and Learning Journal*, 1(2), pp. 79–94.

Buss, D., 2008. Secret Destinations. *Innovations in Education and Teaching International*, 45(3), pp. 303–308.

Candlin, F., 2000. Practice-based Doctorates and Questions of Academic Legitimacy. *Journal of Art & Design Education*, 19(1), pp. 96–101.

Coldstream, W., 1960. First Report of the National Advisory Council on Art Education: Ministry of Education. London: National Advisory Council on Art Education.

Daichendt, G. J., 2010. *Artist-teacher: A Philosophy for Creating and Teaching*. Bristol: Intellect.

Deaking, F. and Webb, C., 2016. Discovering the Post Digital Art School. *University of the Arts London*. Available at: http://freddeak.in/my-report/?utm_source=rss&utm_medium=rss&utm_campaign=my-report [Accessed August 17, 2016].

Dineen, R. and Collins, E., 2005. Killing the Goose: Conflicts Between Pedagogy and Politics in the Delivery of a Creative Education. *International Journal of Art & Design Education*, 24(1), pp. 43–52.

Fleming, M., 2012. *The Arts in Education: An Introduction to Aesthetics, Theory and Pedagogy*. Oxon: Routledge.

FLΔG Collective, 2014. FLΔG Collective: Praxis Between the Educational Turn and the Art School. *Art, Design & Communication in Higher Education*, 13(1), pp. 57–71.

Gibson, R., 2010. The 'art' of Creative Teaching: Implications for Higher Education. *Teaching in Higher Education*, 15(5), pp. 607–613.

Gilio, S., 2016. *The Knowledge-Knower Structures Used in the Assessment of Graphic Design Practical Work in a Multi-Campus Context*. Unpublished PhD Thesis. Rhodes University.

Gustina, C. and Sweet, R., 2014. Creatives Teaching Creativity. *International Journal of Art & Design Education*, 33(1), pp. 46–54.

Harman, K. and McDowell, L., 2011. Assessment Talk in Design: The Multiple Purposes of Assessment in HE. *Teaching in Higher Education*, 16(1), pp. 41–52.

Harris, A., 2014. *The Creative Turn: Toward a New Aesthetic Imaginary*. Rotterdam: Sense Publishers.

Kill, R., 2013. Novel Apprehensions and Hybrid Utterances: Practice, Research, Language. *Art, Design & Communication in Higher Education*, 12(1), pp. 21–31.

Kinniburgh, J., 2014. Conflating Student and Professional Identities: Fostering Development of Professional Identity in First Year Architecture Australia. In *Proceedings, 17th International First Year in Higher Education Conference, Darwin*. Darwin: FYHE, pp. 1–10.

Kreber, C., 2009. *The University and Its Disciplines: Teaching and Learning Within and Beyond Disciplinary Boundaries*. Oxford: Routledge.

Llewellyn, N. and Williamson, B., eds., 2015. *The London Art Schools*. London: Tate Publishing.

Lupton, M., 2013. Reclaiming the Art of Teaching. *Teaching in Higher Education*, 18(2), pp. 156–166.

Lyon, P., 2011. *Design Education: Learning, Teaching and Researching Through Design*. Farnham: Gower.

Masson, B., 1993. Towards Positions of Safe Uncertainty. *The Journal of Systemic Consultation & Mangement*, 4, pp. 189–200.

Mendoza, H. R., Bernasconi, C. and MacDonald, N. M., 2007. Creating New Identities in Design Education. *International Journal of Art & Design Education*, 26(3), pp. 308–313.

Orr, S., 2007. Assessment Moderation: Constructing the Marks and Constructing the Students. *Assessment & Evaluation in Higher Education*, 32(6), pp. 645–656.

Orr, S. and Bloxham, S., 2012. Making Judgements About Students Making Work: Lecturers' Assessment Practices in Art and Design. *Arts and Humanities in Higher Education*, 12(2–3), pp. 234–253.

Orr, S., Dorey Richmond, J. and Richmond, D., 2010. Reflect on This! *Journal of Writing in Creative Practice*, 3(3), pp. 1–24.

Orr, S. and McDougall, J., 2014. Enquiry Into Learning and Teaching in Arts and Creative Practice. In E. Cleaver, M. Lintern and M. McLinden, eds. *Teaching and Learning in Higher Education: Disciplinary Approaches to Educational Enquiry*. London: SAGE Publications, pp. 162–177.

Orr, S., Yorke, M. and Blair, B., 2014. 'The Answer Is Brought About From Within You': A Student-Centred Perspective on Pedagogy in Art and Design. *International Journal of Art & Design Education*, 33(1), pp. 32–45.

Osmond, J., 2009. 'Stuck in a Bubble': Identifying Threshold Concepts in Design. In D. Clews, ed. *Dialogues in Art and Design: Promoting and Sharing Excellence*. York: ADM HEA/GLAD, pp. 130–135.

Readman, M., 2015. *What Do We Talk About When We Talk About Creativity?* Available at: http://teachingexchange.arts.ac.uk/latd/2015/keynotes/readman/ [Accessed September 23, 2016].

Robinson, K., 2009. Ken Robinson Says Schools Kill Creativity? *TED Talks*. Available at: www.ted.com/talks/ken_robinson_says_schools_kill_creativity.html [Accessed November 5, 2016].

Rogoff, I., 2008. *Turning e-Flux*. Available at: www.e-flux.com/journal/turning/ [Accessed August 16, 2016].

Shreeve, A., Sims, E. and Trowler, P., 2010. 'A Kind of Exchange': Learning From Art and Design Teaching. *Higher Education Research & Development*, 29(2), pp. 125–138.

Shulman, L. S., 2005. Signature Pedagogies in the Professions. *Daedalus*, 134(3), pp. 52–59.

Sims, E. and Shreeve, A., 2012. Signature Pedagogies in Art and Design. In N. Chick, A. Haynie and R. Gurung, eds. *Exploring More Signature Pedagogies: Approaches to Teaching Disciplinary Habits of Mind*. Virginia: Stylus Publishing, LLC, pp. 55–67.

Strathern, M., 2000. The Tyranny of Transparency. *British Educational Research Journal*, 26(3), pp. 309–321.

Svennson, L. and Edstrom, A. M., 2011. The Function of Art Students' Use of Studio Conversations in Relation to Their Artwork. *International Journal of Education and the Arts*, 12(5), pp. 1–29.

Taylor, K. and Littleton, S., 2006. Biographies in Talk: A Narrative-discursive Research Approach. *Qualitative Sociology Review*, 2(1), pp. 22–38.

Tovey, M., ed., 2014. *Design Pedagogy: Developments in Art and Design Education*. Oxfordshire: Routledge.

Trowler, P., 2014. Disciplines and Interdisciplinarity: Conceptual Groundwork. In P. Trowler, M. Saunders and V. Bamber, eds. *Tribes and Territories in the 21st Century: Rethinking the Significance of Disciplines in Higher Education*. London: Routledge, pp. 5–29.

Trowler, P. and Cooper, A., 2002. Teaching and Learning Regimes: Implicit Theories and Recurrent Practices in the Enhancement of Teaching and Learning Through Educational Development Programmes. *Higher Education Research & Development*, 21(3), pp. 221–240.

Tuunainen, J., 2005. Hybrid Practices? Contributions to the Debate on the Mutation of Science and University. *Higher Education*, 50(2), pp. 275–298.

Wagner, G., 2009. *Forum for Creative Europe III – 'Contra o fetichismo da criatividade' – CULTURASCÓPIO*. Available at: http://culturascopio.com/2009/03/26/forum-for-creative-europe-iii-"contra-o-fetichismo-da-criatividade"/ [Accessed September 24, 2016].

Wareing, S., 2009. Disciplines, Discourse and Orientalism: The Implications for Postgraduate Certificates in Learning and Teaching in Higher Education. *Studies in Higher Education*, 34(8), pp. 917–928.

Weller, S., 2015. *Academic Practice: Developing as a Professional in Higher Education*. London: SAGE Publications.

White, D., 2015. *Post-digital Revisited – Digital – Learning – Culture*. Available at: http://daveowhite.com/post-digital-revisited/ [Accessed August 16, 2015].

Yorke, M., Orr, S. and Blair, B., 2013. Hit by a Perfect Storm? Art & Design in the National Student Survey. *Studies in Higher Education*, 39(2), pp. 1–23.

Zhengrong Lu, 2016. More Chinese Students Pursuing Art and Design Dreams in the U.S. *World Education News and Reviews*. Available at: http://wenr.wes.org/2016/03/more-chinese-students-pursuing-art-design-dreams-in-the-u-s/ [Accessed August 24, 2016].

2 Knowledge and knowing in practice

Epistemologies in art and design

In this chapter we explore the nature of knowledge and how it is manifested in art and design subject areas. The conception of knowledge held by individuals and organisations and the metaphors used to express it help construct particular expectations and actions in higher education environments. Such implicit theories of knowledge help create discourse in higher education which might include instructional design, units of instruction, materials for instruction and instructional techniques. Whilst these terms are taken from an international journal in curriculum studies, they are not widely used in a UK context in higher education art and design. Others, like the curriculum, are used more generally to denote the content of higher education courses, but even this has associated discourses which are not sympathetic to many practitioner teachers in the sector.

The curriculum is a term which appears in general usage to have a particular association with knowledge which can be clearly codified into topics, and curriculum can suggest a content-delivery approach in higher education where topics are introduced and closely controlled by the tutor, perhaps due to echoes of compulsory education and in further education competency based approaches (Wheelahan 2010). Biggs's (2003) idea of constructive alignment advocates a constructivist approach which stresses the importance of what students do to create knowledge and meaning for themselves, but it also suggests that one can simply provide content, learning activities and assessment to 'align' so that students understand what is to be taught and tutors can assess whether they have designed activities which have facilitated students' learning through appropriate assessment techniques. The underlying assumption here is that if the curriculum is right and the delivery is right, then students will learn the correct subject matter within their time in higher education and will graduate with an appropriately assessed and graded qualification. Within a curriculum which is seen as sticky (see Chapter 1 for a definition and Chapter 5 for further discussion), where boundaries change and things are not always what they seem, where what is taught and how it is taught both create and recreate particular kinds of knowledge, the curriculum as knowledge per se becomes problematic. This is particularly so where the content (knowledge) is obscure or hard to write down and codify as it is in art and design. Such knowledge is embedded in creative practice, largely visual and material in nature and process rich. There are relatively few commonly held and used theories, and the canon is dependent on the precise discipline being studied and the particular viewpoints and beliefs of the teaching team; for those not used to studio based teaching, the content appears to be minimal.

A broader view of curriculum is expressed by Barnett and Coate (2005), who identify the general paucity of discussion about important matters relating to curriculum, which go to the heart of the purpose of higher education. They suggest that there are three aspects to curriculum which consist of knowing, acting and being. An appropriate curriculum project for the twenty-first century which engages students as participants in an educational environment has designed learning spaces to enable the development of the whole person. This is a view of curriculum more in tune with most art and design educators who see development of the student as a neophyte practitioner (Drew 2004) to be drawn into art or design through practising and developing their identity alongside appropriate skills to enable creative practice to evolve and develop.

Much has been written about the nature of knowing and of learning, from Plato onwards, but we wish to highlight the complexity of knowing within the multiple subject disciplines loosely labelled art and design, because codified knowledge within these disciplines is not highly visible. In the studio students and tutors appear to be chatting, formal lesson plans are probably brief and there are likely to be few required readings; a codified curriculum in the form of validated course documents may simply describe different kinds of projects (see Chapter 7 for further discussion of the role of the project). Students and tutors spend long periods in activities which may result in unfinished outcomes. We wish to dispel two myths about art and design, those of little rigour and simplistic pedagogies. The apparent lack of tutor activity in the studio and the need for students to explore as individuals has given rise to notions that anything goes in art and design, that teaching is very laissez-faire. A creative environment might be perceived as unstructured, messy and lacking in standards or rigorous approaches to study. In jest a senior manager (from a different discipline) once said: 'Oh of course, your students don't read books do they!' In part he was right; they might read less than students in some disciplines, but underlying this statement was a belief that knowledge, rigour and proper study lies only in the printed word or explicit scientific formulae. There is also an historic dimension to the myth. When artists taught in the Art School of the 1960s and 1970s, they might hold tutorials in the pub; they might have had very unconventional approaches to teaching. As Sander, cited in Reardon and Mollin (2009:319), recalls of teaching in the 1960s and 1970s: 'a teacher has a certain kind of charisma, walks through the class and the student soaks up the air and the smell and that is how he (sic) learns'. Such ideas linger around the Art School still. Design teachers might have employed pedagogies which were simplistic, such as 'sitting by Nellie', or watch and copy, but as Swann's seminal paper says: 'Nellie is Dead' (Swann 1986, 2002). These historic, laissez-faire approaches have gone in every place we know, and there are many innovative approaches adopted by practitioner tutors in the Art School, just as there have been since Art Schools were formed. The Bauhaus curriculum

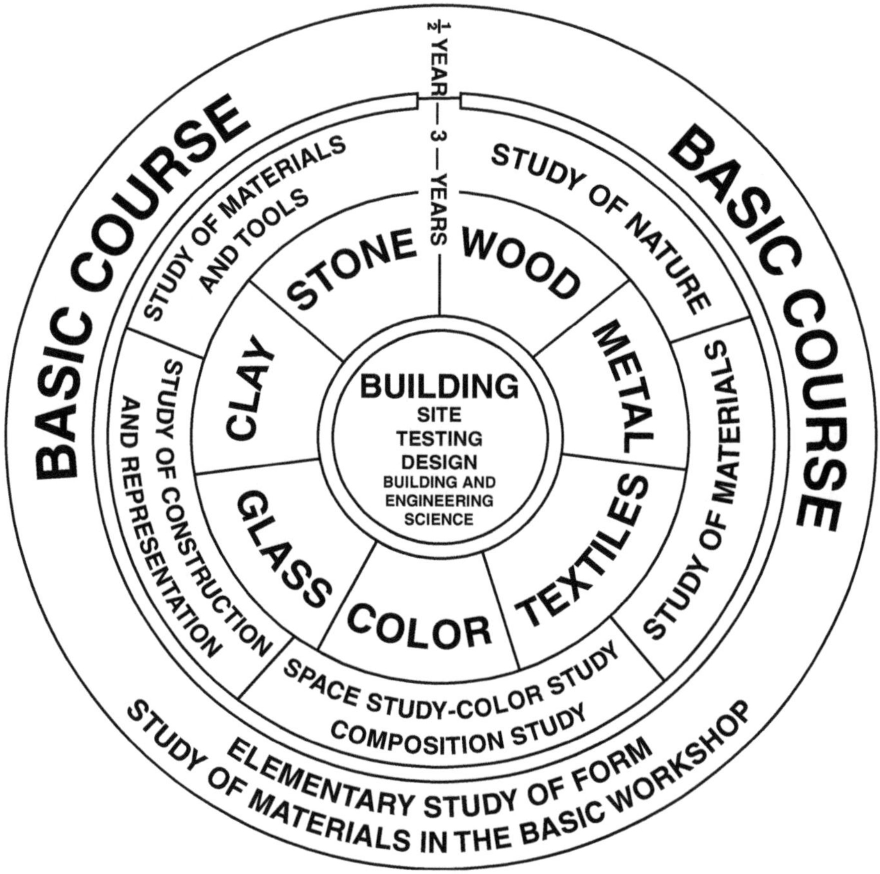

Figure 2.1 The Bauhaus curriculum designed by Walter Gropius

Wheel designed by Walter Gropius in 1922 indicates what the priorities were in the 1920s (see Figure 2.1), and much was written about studying art by the artists and designer teachers of the Bauhaus, for example, Paul Klee. These were rigorous attempts to pin down learning and teaching in art and design and the subject matter and approaches that should be used. However, the kinds of knowledge needed were complex, and we wish to advocate that these forms of knowledge and knowing, which are fundamental to art and design higher education, are also important in other disciplinary areas.

Sociocultural perspectives

In social constructivist theories of learning, practice becomes central (Lave and Wenger 1991) and might be defined as a set of activities which are shared by groups of people (Wenger 1998). Underlying this of course are commonly held beliefs, standards and expectations which all constrain individual agency. Within art and design higher education, there are overlapping sets of practices which are central to learning: the creative practice beyond the academy and the learning practices within it. Both of these sets of practices are obviously related if the objective of higher education is to develop neophyte creative practitioners. This relationship has been described by Logan (2006) in graphic design education, where she explored how the two practices overlap, shared metaphors indicate a flow of knowledge within the discipline area and an immersive educational model enables graphic design practice to be absorbed.

The critical realist critique of social constructivism is rooted in the increased vocationalism of curriculum in post compulsory education since the 1980s with dominant government agendas of marketisation (Wheelahan 2010). Wheelahan argues that access to knowledge is differential because systemic knowledge has been removed from curricula in favour of work-related practices, and this denies access to powerful knowledge for many participants in education. The emphasis on generic attributes and skills, she argues, has lessened the access to more disciplinary knowledge. However, Wheelahan's view of 'good' vocational knowledge is that it:

> comprises complex and difficult bodies of knowledge that individuals acquire in the process of becoming a member of a community of practice, which they then use as *a tool to transform practice and create new knowledge*.
>
> (p. 104, emphasis added)

In art and design the knowledge base beyond the university frames what is taught within the university, but there is an emphasis on students challenging and creating new forms of creative outcomes and therefore new knowledge which emerges from within the university at undergraduate level. Wheelahan's concern about the missing form of knowledge is that of the abstract and codified elements or perhaps a love of knowledge in its 'pure' forms not simply allied to vocations. By inference we might suggest that this underlying codified knowledge is likely to be recognised in written and symbolic forms (maths and science perhaps), that which denotes the 'academic' rather than applied. There appears to be an absence of 'structured systems of principled knowledge' (p. 111) in vocationally oriented curricula.

It is questionable whether such a structured form of knowledge underpins art and design disciplines. There is however much theorising about art, see for example, Harrison and Wood (2003), a massive tome of selected writings, debates and interviews about art practice in the twentieth century, and also theorising about design. The academic journal, *Design Studies*, was first published in 1979, and its mission is to provide 'an interdisciplinary forum for the analysis, development and discussion of fundamental aspects of design activity, from cognition and methodology to values and philosophy' (www.journals.elsevier.com/design-studies/ accessed 28/10/16); *Fashion Theory*, first published in 1997, indicates a relatively newly theorised specific design discipline entering the realm of academic theory. Both journals recognise the interdisciplinary nature of their theoretical studies, drawing on other disciplines to provide insights into the subject. Many different disciplines across the wider range of art and design can be theorised in this way, depending on the sub-discipline or area of study. Theory may be based on the relatively 'new' discipline of cultural studies, on art histories, social theory and psychology as well as science and technology. In design pedagogy there are tutors drawing on theory of design to help students use a more informed and questioning approach to the design process, for example, employing 'critical design' (see Mazé and Redström 2009 for a discussion of approaches to design). These theoretical perspectives can provide new ways to understand and also create new art and design practices, but the primary medium of art and design is visual and material, which does not lend itself to easily articulated underlying comprehensive and universal theories.

Art and design could be argued to constitute a form of abstract knowledge in its own right, or indeed a visual language, but one which is heavily dependent on cultural historical context for its form and definition (Eisner 1994). Simply engaging in art and design practice requires one to learn how to communicate using the techniques and processes available, and art is only deemed to be art by the gatekeepers of social convention. But art and design disciplines have a particular currency and meaning for those who engage in them. They are not simply vocational. Fine art in particular has a challenging relationship to current 'employability skills' debates, but there is a relationship between practice within and beyond academia. For some disciplines the idea of not being tied to the commercialised version of the discipline is very important for academics. They are not dependent on reproducing practice but are intent on creating in academia students who question what the discipline is and might be. The use and access to powerful knowledge from an art and design perspective might be to foster an ability to see or realise the 'not-known' and 'subjects-yet-to-come' (Atkinson 2015:44) and to look beyond the surface gloss and pleasure of the activity to question more deeply what the discipline is capable of becoming and who the protagonists are to become.

However, the understanding and manipulation of form, colour, space, line, tone, plane, proportion, volume, mass, rhythm, texture and pattern could be argued to provide the core language of art and design. The translation of art and design principles into learning and teaching was embodied in the work of the Bauhaus in the 1920s and the Basic Design Movement in the UK through the 1950s and 1960s, and these approaches to the subject are practical but describe particular pedagogic structuring of knowledge related to art and design (Llewellyn and Williamson 2015; Daichendt 2010). Within universities there will always be selection and translation of knowledge to construct the curriculum (Bernstein 2000), and over time this changes with geographic, political, social and structural pressures on the educational environment. Houghton's historical analysis of the Art School curriculum (Houghton 2016) identifies six different approaches to learning and teaching which have been influenced by prevailing conceptions and, therefore, discourses of art in a Western global context. He terms these the apprentice curriculum, the academic curriculum, the formalist curriculum, the expressive curriculum, the conceptual curriculum and the professional curriculum. Rather than having clear ideological breaks between these different conceptions, Houghton identifies that many are held concurrently in present-day practices, which lead to curricula 'riddled with contradictions' (p. 118). These competing and messy conceptions of the subject offer up a sticky picture of the curriculum and one which is likely to have local variation.

Art and design is fundamentally concerned with making or creating, frequently drawing on other disciplines to offer up ways of changing and reflecting on the production and consumption of its creative outputs. It does not mean, however, that theory cannot be embodied in the outcomes of creative learning or inform approaches to pedagogy. Work may reference other kinds of work, in homage or critique, or embody complex responses to the world, concepts and ideas which are intellectually challenging, although not codified through words. This form of vocationalism is not simply reproducing process; at its best it challenges and creates a new form of dialogue able to contribute to 'society's conversation' (Wheelahan 2010:37) and indeed to change the way that we perceive and take part in society (e.g., new products, performances and solutions to pervasive problems like pollution and climate change).

Looked at more critically, what students are learning and therefore the knowledge base for design practices (like Logan's graphics study cited previously) might be usefully broken down into more distinctive and potentially more accessible forms of knowledge. The philosopher Gilbert Ryle (2009, first published 1949) explored two forms of knowing: 'knowing how' and 'knowing that', also picked up by Cross et al. (1981) in relation to art and design, as being two distinct and importantly different kinds of knowledge. When applied to art and design curricula in higher education 'knowing how' might be argued to be the predominant form of knowledge. It is this kind of procedural knowing, being able to do certain kinds of things, which underpins the creative practices of artists and designers. When students are learning how to do graphic design, for example, they are practising the ways in which designers work, with support and guidance from their tutors who are more knowledgeable and experienced graphic designers, but not copying what designers are already producing (see Logan 2006).

The characteristics of 'know how' include skill and expertise, qualities associated with a good or perhaps professional performance. Novice practitioners may make mistakes or stumble in carrying out their tasks, whereas more skilled or expert practitioners either incorporate mistakes, making adjustments and using the mistake creatively, or demonstrate fluency through the performance. The idea of mistakes leading to creative readjustment is a commonly held tenet in art and design education, where students are encouraged to see a mistake as an opportunity to travel down a different route, to view alternative solutions or ideas to develop the practice in their own direction, not simply to mimic or replicate existing practices (see also Chapter 3). So 'know how', or performing the practice of creative professions, is not simply copying but developing the general practice or procedure of the profession, within boundaries of acceptable competence, which are socially created, usually within the university and informed by practices beyond it. The boundaries of acceptable competence, or the rigours of the discipline, are controlled both by the tutors within the university and within the creative cultural arena of practitioners beyond it through a constantly changing culture based on the knowledge of the (changeable) practice norms, although always mediated through the pedagogic frame or context in the university (Bernstein 2000).

As well as knowing how, students are also inducted into 'knowing that'; they acquire information. This consists of preexisting 'truths' which may be information which is 'academic' knowledge or may relate to practice based knowledge, for example, the way that business communities work, how to calculate a fee for a piece of work, which tax laws may apply, what printers may charge and which printers are best for specific kinds of work. 'Truths' may relate to the world of practice itself, as in the previous examples, in which case they are most likely to be taught in the studio environment; or 'truths' may pertain to the cultures and histories of art and design, and frequently, but not always, taught through lectures and the written word, thus embodying the practice/theory divide associated with 'knowing how' and 'knowing that', a point which we will return to later in the chapter:

> Learning how or improving in ability is not like learning that or acquiring information. Truths can be imparted, procedures can only be inculcated, and while inculcation is a gradual process, imparting is relatively sudden.
>
> (Ryle, 2009:46)

Thus, as Ryle suggests, the process of learning in art and design is just that, an immersion over time in the practice of the creative discipline studied. However, even such a clear dichotomy in knowledge and its implied pedagogic traditions indicated by Ryle's terms, 'knowing how' and 'knowing that', is not as neat and tidy as one might imagine when applied to creative arts. Ryle's work was an attempt finally to blow apart the Cartesian dualism of mind and body seen as two separate and non-related spheres; the arenas of mental and material practices had long been perceived as separate and unconnected. Bringing these together and expanding the dichotomy offers other dimensions of knowledge which are important to creative practice and to learning.

A possible subset of 'knowing that' might be described as 'knowing why'. Reasons why things work or don't work is helpful in carrying out the practice. Underlying rules help structure knowledge and inform practice. For example, it helps to know that you have to adjust the stitch length and tension according to the fabric you are sewing to create an unpuckered seam on a dress. However, as with all rules in art and design, they are there to be questioned and exploited. If you want to have a puckered seam on a dress, you will know how to achieve it if you know why a seam might pucker in sewing. Knowing why also has the potential to link theory to practice.

'Knowing that' and its subset 'knowing why' has a related dimension, 'knowing about' (Bruner 1996 in Duguid 2005). 'Knowing about' might imply that one can know about a practice without being able to produce a skilled performance (e.g., as a critic might), and knowing about aspects of practice may be an important piece of knowledge to work on collaborative projects or across different disciplines to achieve major works of art or performance, such as an opera, for example (Wenger-Trayner et al. 2015). 'Knowing about' might also be a precursor to knowing how or may be an important empathetic position to adopt when designing with and for others, for example, in designing mobility aids.

Experiential knowing

In painting there was a long tradition of studying the work of 'the masters' through the medium of paint and drawing. Such a form of study was undertaken to better understand the production of the artwork or, to put it another way, to get inside the head (and/or hands?) of the painter. Artists sometimes make studies of other artists to gain insights into the handling of paint, its application, colour mixing, composition or construction. Such studies are not simply copies or replications but are undertaken with the intention of understanding or creating knowledge about the artist and his or her work. 'Knowing about' is undertaken through a process allied to the original medium and is visual, tactile and kinaesthetic. It produces 'knowledge about' but in forms not articulated through the written or spoken word. It produces procedural knowledge, knowing how something was done, but also insights into the thought processes of the producer. Exploration of artists' knowledge becomes evident when eavesdropping on a fine art studio teaching session where students are undertaking their own creative practice. Tutors will talk to them and pick up cues from the ongoing process. Discussion will trigger references to the tutor's knowledge of others' artistic practice. Suggestions will be made to look at the work of such an artist or to query whether the student has seen a particular example of film, performance or exhibition. Here, the tutor is making links on behalf of the student who is challenged to position her work in the canon or to relate ideas or concepts to her own developing outcomes. This knowledge is knowledge about ideas, often complex and abstract ideas, but another form of embedded knowledge which is critical to developing as an artist. Such knowing cannot be set out neatly as 'fact' or 'truths' but is much more conditional, speculative, tentative and ambiguous. The lecturer's knowledge bank is triggered by the student work. It is frequently specific knowledge directed at an individual student rather than to groups. Nevertheless, it is important in terms of personal development of a creative practice and in continued renewal and extension of the practice as a whole. 'Knowing about', 'knowing how' and 'knowing that' can therefore encompass different forms of knowing, and such forms of knowing are also central to learning in art and design higher education.

Amongst these different forms of knowing, Polanyi's now-famous idea of tacit knowledge (Polanyi 1967, 2012), that which we know but cannot tell, holds an important place in art and design. Polanyi explored the ways in which we know our 'personal knowledge' about everyday activities, such as riding a bike. These ways of knowing, he claimed, were not subject to articulation but were understood implicitly. When we try to break down and explain exactly what we know and how we are doing things such as riding a bike, it breaks up the fluency of the action, and we struggle to find the words to explain what and how we are doing it. This ability to 'know more than we can tell' he termed tacit knowledge. As we 'tell', or proclaim or profess through words and language, knowledge which is not readily accessible to language is often hidden from view and remains tacit. The idea of tacit knowledge in skilled craft production was also explored by the critic Peter Dormer (1994) in his book which studied excellence in craft practice and making. The level of skill demonstrated by traditional and modern craft producers is not easily conveyed when trying to help students to learn. Nuances lie in the way that a tool is held, a material feels or a process is carried out. Sometimes these nuances may be brought to the level of awareness by a teacher, but often they are not. It is not only creative disciplines which use tacit knowledge. In a study of city stock brokers Fenton-O'Creevy et al. (2011) found that emotions and 'gut feelings' were acknowledged by many traders, and the most successful were those who reported using their 'gut feeling' as well as the explicit knowledge of markets. The authors refer to the use of emotion in decision-making in this example; affective responses are part of the (hidden) personal knowledge we hold in relation to the world.

Thus tacit knowledge is the knowledge gained through experience which usually remains unspoken or unarticulated. Where disciplines work through visual and material outcomes as their primary medium, the means of communication is through the work produced and is supported by the articulation of spoken and sometimes written commentaries. The multimodal communication which is exemplified by 'the kind of exchange' in studio encompasses all forms of articulation including verbal, visual, embodied and emotional exchanges. One might argue that there is an inherently built in bias towards that which is unspoken in the creative arts. In a series of early investigations into studio learning and teaching in textiles and fashion, Shreeve (1998) identified ways in which tacit knowledge underpinned the learning environment. In a discussion of a set of student projects, three tutors rank the work and discuss their reasons for placing the work in a particular order of merit. One tutor says of a particular fashion design, 'Well, you can see it being cut'. Embodied in this phrase is a whole disciplinary set of knowledge about how garments are constructed and manufactured and how to 'read' a flat design drawing. Beneath that layer of knowledge a student understands how to convey the intention of the construction to create a garment. This knowledge is experiential knowledge, largely tacitly held. It is complex, multidimensional and accessible only in part to explicit description and analysis.

Metaphors, as identified by Logan in her study, are one way in which tacit knowledge moves towards the explicit. The metaphor stands for something which is challenging to articulate. Metaphors reposition the unfamiliar in familiar terms, likening the inexpressible to something more readily grasped and illuminating obliquely that which is hard to express directly. In the research described here, tutors and students use metaphorical terms to describe project work and its qualities. They use phrases such as 'it has an authority', or it is 'strong' or 'weak' or the designs 'work'. Learning the appropriate use of such terminology to describe the quality of a project is to use metaphorical language in a particular community of practice, here within the fashion design learning environment. When students also use the metaphors appropriately, it is an indication that they have understood and are becoming part of the community of practice which is higher education in a creative subject. These kinds of language usage are common within the professional sphere as well as the educational sphere and refer to a whole range of processes, knowledge and understanding required to become a creative practitioner.

Duguid (2005) argues that tacit knowledge is more than simply un-codified explicit knowledge which could, with further work, be articulated. He, as Polanyi before him, maintains that there is knowledge which remains stubbornly inaccessible to articulation. Duguid implies that this kind of knowledge resides within communities of practice and in complex networks of practices which are differentiated from each other. As practice lies at the heart of art and design, we must assume that the tacit knowledge inherent in practice is also something which the pedagogies of higher education seek to develop, through a variety of means, but primarily through doing or carrying out aspects of the practice. To some extent the tacit knowledge elements may be acquired through legitimate peripheral participation in a community of practice (Lave and Wenger 1991) or may be supported through conscious efforts of the tutor to indicate cues or obliquely illuminate aspects of practice.

Multiple modes of knowing

Different kinds of knowing were explored by Blackler (1995), who identified five different forms of knowing apparent in the business organisational literature, where the discourse of the 'knowledge economy' was prevalent in the 1990s. These forms of knowledge included that which he identified as embodied, embedded, embrained, encultured and encoded or located in bodies, routines, brains, dialogue or symbols. This exploration of different ways in which knowledge can be conceived and experienced hints at the complex richness of learning experiences we all undergo as part of our social lives. We are exposed to and absorb knowledge in many ways, sometimes unconsciously, sometimes through deliberations or interactions, but always as part of social worlds. Blackler's paper goes on to argue that these forms of knowledge cannot 'sensibly be conceived as separate, one from the other' (p. 1032).

When considered in relation to creative art and design subjects, one might argue that these different forms of knowing are evident and supported through the traditional studio pedagogies of the disciplines embodied in the studio culture or learning through doing and making. Embodied knowledge is essential to understanding material properties, for example, in a silversmith making a bowl or annealing a piece of metal. Cues which are visual, auditory and tactile enable the creation of an artwork, and knowing through such embodied practices is the way in which artefacts are created. Embedded knowledge exists within the community of practice of silversmiths in routine procedures, the way things are done and talked about, and students have to learn such embedded knowledge. Embrained knowledge might be most easily recognised as facts, figures or theories; knowing that a particular metal melts at a certain temperature, for example, or enamelling requires certain processes for success. Encultured knowledge about new technologies and materials, who is doing what and how, where the discipline is travelling, all exist within socially transferred networks. Encoded knowledge, such as information in books or, more selectively perhaps, through culturally significant images or artefacts, channel knowledge in particular formats. All forms of knowledge are therefore important for the rounded development of novice practitioners.

As knowledge is socially constructed and not solely residing in people's heads, or in books or in computer networks, but in complex social organisations and activities, Blackler argues that knowledge is also mediated, that is, through systems of language, communication and control (and we include universities within such systems). It is also situated within a time and place and particular social context or a particular community of practice in some instances. It is provisional in that knowledge is constantly created, developed, recreated and adapted and also pragmatic in that it is purposive and related to activities and actions. Viewed in this way knowledge becomes much more than a list of topics to be studied and is a much more sympathetic way of conceptualising knowledge in the art and design curriculum. Such a knowledge base is harder to pin down in writing and much more fruitful to regard as an ongoing and developing practice or, as Logan identified, an overlapping practice with the professional world of the artist and designer. Thus knowledge in the curriculum might be regarded as sticky, stretching and changing, moving with the changes in the outside world and subject to changes in technologies, materials, ideas and conventions. Furthermore, if the richness of knowledge as embodied, embedded, embrained, encultured and encoded is taken to imply the wholeness of knowing within a person, the logical conclusion is to see learning as developing people or, in Marton et al.'s (1993) terms, changing as a person. Such a complete approach to knowing and learning implies that an ontological perspective to learning (Dall'Alba 2009; Dall'Alba and Barnacle 2007) is more appropriate or that Barnett and Coate's (2005) threefold vision of curriculum – knowing, acting and being – is central to learning creatively.

This emphasis changes the focus from knowledge for its own sake and learning becomes focused on people and their identities. In Wenger's (1998) terms there is a social ecology of membership within a community of practice which requires engagement, imagination and alignment. To belong to a community of practice, the member has to adopt an identity of belonging and participation or, in Dall'Alba's terms, an ontological positioning, being part of the community. Within a higher education art and design curriculum, there is then a requirement to think not only about the epistemologies, the kinds of knowing and knowledge we impart or inculcate, but about how people are learning to become certain kinds of people and how identities are being formed (see Chapters 5 and 6). The pedagogies we use are important and inextricably linked to the practice based knowledge being developed. Individual identities are central; how do students learn to identify with particular kinds of artists and designers, and how do they envisage themselves becoming part of the community of practice which they would like to belong to? How do students know what and how many communities of practice might be open to them?

The curriculum, sticky with complex knowledge, subject to change and provisional in nature is also subject to changes from within the higher education system, specifically, from the students themselves. Where students are developing their own identity as artist or designer, they are beginning to respond to the subject, to own it and to make it their own (see also Chapter 5).

It could be argued that the whole raison d'être of a creative arts education is to create new knowledge in the form of innovative artefacts, performances or products and services. Where new knowledge is the expected outcome of learning there is no specific right answer, and at the beginning of a project students and tutors do not know the outcome or result. Through encouraging innovation and creativity tutors are guiding students through the practices and existing knowledge of the discipline but also encouraging them to try out new routes and question received wisdom (we develop further discussion on this topic in Chapter 7). In some cases the student becomes the holder of the new knowledge and is more expert than the tutor. In these cases the centre of power (which is knowledge according to Foucault – see Ball 2013) moves from the established tutor practitioner to the student and may disrupt the order of the studio. Sometimes this also makes assessment difficult as the normalised boundaries for the production of art or artefact is challenged (discussed in Chapter 8). Where innovation is successful tutors also learn, and practice based knowledge is enhanced. Where innovation is not accepted by the community, the ideas and changes may not be recognised and absorbed. Thus power and control are also linked to knowledge in the academy, and where assessment and recognition are held by tutors in a position of power, the valorisation of knowledge is controlled by a small community (see Chapters 3 and 8). Beyond the university similar systems of recognition and valorisation are also practiced, whether by critics, audiences or industrialists, new knowledge is either accepted and embedded into systems and communities or is ignored.

Knowledge seen as a complex mix which involves apprehension in many different senses and forms requires a view of learning which is multidimensional; information takes many forms including written text, images, moving images and material objects. Students are working in complex multimodal discourses (Kress and van Leeuwen 2001). Whereas many subject areas rely heavily on the written word for learning in the university, the creative arts predominantly rely on more visual and kinaesthetic modes. However, with the increasing use of virtual learning environments and social media, the world is becoming much more attuned to visual communication, and more students would benefit from understanding and being able to read the visual constructs now common in everyday life. Metros and Woolsey (2006) argue that it is an institutional imperative in the United States for all students to be taught about visual communication and to be able to understand and read images.

Practice and theory – conflict and necessity

Visual literacy, a term developed to describe the fluency of understanding visual material, or fluency in visual language, is a key aspect of art education but, in our experience, one which is seldom articulated. To really understand and be fluent in visual terms requires a deeper understanding of the cultural contexts of art and design production and its social consumption. Although the primary means of communication is visual and students are trained and develop as visual practitioners, it is the additional ability to analyse and manipulate cultural meanings which can provide students with a more critically rounded ability to practise their art (Grove-White 2003). Because much of this analysis is actually articulated through words and theories, a division has arisen within the higher education culture which is embodied by the practice/theory split. Art and design is not the only subject area where this happens; nursing also has a similar tension in higher education. Where carrying out the practice is seen as the primary function or reason for being in higher education, many students and some tutors also question why they should have to write or study theory as well. Herein lies the difference between 'knowing how' and 'knowing that', which is probably exacerbated by individual learning preferences.

Historically in the UK this practice/theory split was embodied by the Diploma in Art and Design (DipAD) set up by the Coldstream Report of 1960 and considered the equivalent of degree-level study. This required 15 percent of the curriculum to consist of history of art and complementary studies – a move which was not universally welcomed (Tickner 2008). Further reforms moved many small Art Schools and technical colleges into the Polytechnics (from 1965), and the introduction of a central awarding body (Council for National Academic Awards [CNAA]) introduced BA honours degrees in art and design in 1974 (Llewellyn and Williamson 2015). These more academic subjects, it was claimed, differentiated the award and made it distinctly degree level rather than the technical education level it had been considered previously as a National Diploma in Design (NDD). This is an example of the discourse of particular kinds of knowledge being privileged over others, an example of Foucault's theories of power in action and a problematic in the critique of social constructivist approaches to education (Wheelahan 2010). There remains still in some places the notion that working with one's hands, or doing vocational education, is an inferior form of study to that carried out by using only one's brain (demonstrated through written text and symbols) in the university. Similar distinctions were also made in the United States and in Australia around the same time, and to some extent are still evident. Wheelahan (2010) and others argue that it is detrimental to the project of higher education that academic knowledge has been displaced in preference to vocational knowledge, but art and design is vocational and, we would argue, is based on a particular kind of social constructivist approach in higher education which seeks not simply to replicate knowledge but to extend and develop it.

The split between theory and practice has also been attributed to the incorporation of the Art School into the university, characterised as two separate 'worlds' (Prentice 2000) with their own histories and traditions.

> The art school tradition is rooted in professional practice and a commitment to experiential learning, while theoretical knowledge underpins the tradition of academic research on which the reputations of universities are founded.
> (p. 524)

The Art School tutors were largely practitioners, and their 'public output was visual, rather than written texts' (p. 524). Prentice thus identifies the key differences between these kinds of knowledge bases as conflicted, and although practice based research is much more widely accepted and common now, there is still a tension between the mode of knowledge and the means of communication in art and design higher education. This is exemplified by the ongoing (for nearly half a century!) debate about the nature of academic research in art and design and the form doctoral research should take. Kill (2013) explored the nature of doctoral submissions and the multiple and complex possible relationships between the artefact and the written word, in practice based research, from the divorced to the hybrid. These tensions exist at all levels within university based art and design courses which coexist with a majority of academic subjects where the primary means of communication is written. Or as Kill suggests, there is 'logobias' within university cultures, where standard or normalised practice rests on the written word. In an earlier article she explores how the tensions and binary divisions between aspects of the art and design curriculum have arisen, giving substance to the belief that art and design students can't write – a position which she challenges (Kill 2006).

For some students who have excelled in so-called practical subjects at school, they are disappointed to find that they have to write essays when they study art and design. There is no reason why art and design students should not both enjoy and excel at written forms of communication, as many demonstrate each year through their dissertations. We suspect the main challenge to the theory/practice divide is actually to enable students (and some of their tutors too) to see the relevance and significance of theory to practice rather than to see it as a separate subject which takes them away from the practice work they enjoy. Practice/theory binaries are frequently emphasised by having different groups of tutors for theory and practice and in teaching these in different locations, usually a lecture space and a studio with their (different) associated pedagogical approaches. The persistence of a division between practice and theory may help to disguise differences in student attainment. Pandering to the belief that art and design students can't write could provide an excuse not to develop better approaches to learning and teaching. In a small-scale study of fashion design, students undertaking their dissertations in their final degree year, Tynan and New (2009) argue that confidence and ability in English appear to be the determining factors for students who undertook an industrial placement year and who appeared to be better prepared to write their dissertations, not the fact that they undertook placement, which was their first hypothesis. When examined in more detail, the prior experience of students, rather than their on course experience, meant that they were predisposed to tackle new learning opportunities, but their final performance was not significantly different to those who had not taken a placement year. By maintaining a discourse of 'difficulty' with writing and a schism between practice and theory, institutions may be doing a disservice to students who find solace in the schism and fear writing rather than tackling it with support.

In recent years in the UK, there has been an emphasis on helping bridge the theory/practice schism through different approaches to enabling writing in higher education. Melles and Lockheart (2012) discuss a changing landscape and the introduction of different kinds of literacies. That is, the conventions and forms of acceptable academic writing are changing and evolving constantly, and the learning and execution of forms of writing should be taught explicitly rather than be left to chance. When this is done students can be supported to become fluent, or literate, in ways that are acceptable to those assessing their outputs. The Writing Purposefully in Art and Design (Writing PAD) project in the UK (see http://writing-pad.org/HomePage) has been a successful initiative which has enabled tutors who teach theory to rethink the ways in which they teach writing. In some institutions the hegemony of the written dissertation has been superseded; practical responses with annotation and referencing have been allowed. These, however, are not easy options but must demonstrate complex arguments, ideas and responses (academic 'theory') in exactly the same way an extended essay might do.

The difference between carrying out or 'practising' and learning about your practice through theory was exemplified by a part-time tutor in Shreeve (2008). This tutor had spent many years working in the broadcast industries, primarily in television. He felt that he really understood his practice as a broadcast technician and editor, from working his way up on the shop floor, carrying out a number of different roles and living the life. He had come into teaching because he had 'fallen out of love' with the practice, but he still considered himself to be a broadcast practitioner. He had begun to study for a master's course in political communication and was bringing his expertise and experiential knowledge to bear using theoretical understandings combined with his previous knowledge to gain new insights. He described this as being engaged in his practice in a different way. He had stepped outside the practical experience and was looking at the practice more objectively, something he described as 'keeping up with my professional practice but in a different way than I have hitherto' (p. 90). He also used this interest and awareness of the professional roles in his teaching, describing how he extended students' technical knowledge into a much broader awareness of what it meant to be part of the professional practice world:

> They've done the technical stuff and I sort of mess with their heads and start talking about the politics of editing, and group dynamics, and group

> behaviour, how to, you know, power in the cutting room, relationships within the cutting room, hierarchy within production. How do you protect yourself, where is the money, all of those things!
>
> (p. 115)

Here is an example of the complexity of practice knowledge and the integration of different forms of knowing which, in a good studio teaching environment, are brought forth for students, preparing them to think more deeply and consciously about issues embedded in practice and issues which might lend themselves readily to the application of theory. The variable experiences within teaching situations, however, and the wide range of experiences tutors themselves have mean that standardised sets of theoretical knowledge are unlikely to be offered across different courses in different institutional contexts in the same subject area. This is most probably the situation in many disciplines and may account for variation in performance indicators, but the knowledge embedded in learning situations is a cultural phenomenon, and each micro culture is going to be different.

The often perceived split between theory and practice needs to be challenged in art and design higher education. The common adage that nothing is as practical as a good theory links the two poles of practice and theory together, and we see these as a continuum. Knowledges in all their forms span the two poles, from the more implicit and tacit elements of practice to the theoretical or more explicit forms of knowledge. There is theoretical knowledge embedded in the enactment of creative practice, but the extent to which this is consciously used is dependent on individuals and whether their engagement in higher education has enabled the theoretical to be fundamental to their growing understanding of the discipline.

To illustrate the complexity of knowledge and the interrelationship to ways of knowing identified by Blackler (1995) discussed earlier in the chapter, we offer the reader Figure 2.2. Here the forms or ways of knowing sit between the extremities of tacit and explicit knowledge and have stronger or weaker affinities to both ends of the spectrum. Similarly they are linked to practice and theory, representing two different kinds of knowledge in the art and design curriculum. Over all these aspects is the unknown, or yet to be known, the search for the new which characterises creative pedagogy.

For most students entering the workplace is a daunting challenge and increasingly important as large debts incurred during their studies weigh heavily. Being able to take advantage of different forms of knowledge and knowing and being able to bridge any perceived gap between creative practice and theory opens up more opportunities as this graduate describes:

> Investing time in my VMC [Visual Material Culture] Dissertation meant that when I went out into the advertising industry I could surprise people with theories they hadn't even considered. . . . I now help them take academic theories and apply them to business challenges. VMC was terrifically important to me.
>
> (Sam Shaw, graduate, quoted in Bucks New University Art and Design prospectus 2014)

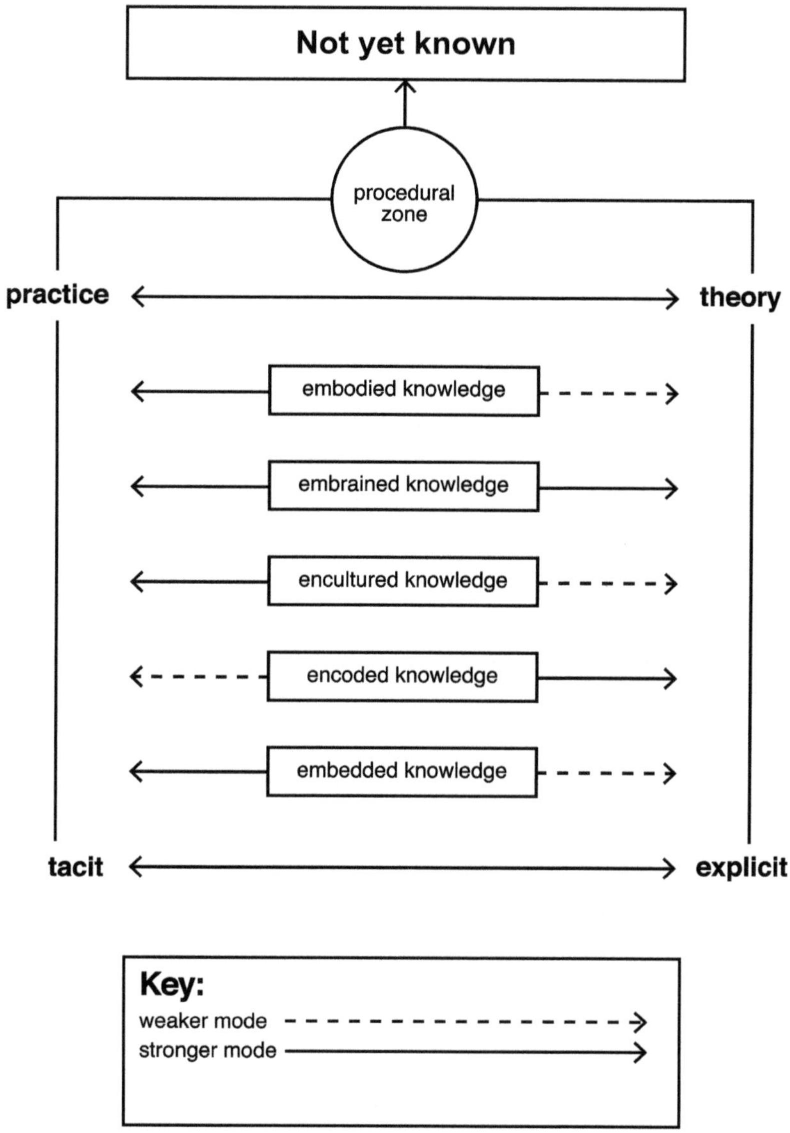

Figure 2.2 Knowledge and knowing in art and design

Conclusion

Our conception of knowledge plays an important part in our understanding of the creative curriculum and the approaches to pedagogy which enact the curriculum. Where we understand knowledge as being something which is multifaceted and multidimensional rather than something which resides in a person's head, the way that learning such knowledge is undertaken requires a different approach. Knowledge which resides in individuals, communities, networks, bodies and objects requires a much wider acceptance of multiple modes of apprehending and internalising this knowledge. The university becomes less the centre and control of learning and more a fulcrum or catalyst where learning is facilitated through access to many forms of knowledge and through many different systems and locations of delivery.

Recognising that knowledge is not standardised, consistent and open to simple written explanations requires us to reconsider issues of consistency across courses and subject areas. Where transparency, that is, the simple rendering of subject content and experience into lists, is increasingly called for from regulatory bodies, in a creative curriculum we should perhaps be celebrating the diversity of experiences. Like cooking, a dish may consist of similar ingredients but may taste very different depending on who has made it, where it is eaten and with whom. Where multiple forms and combinations of knowledge are gained through different experiences, knowing how, knowing why, knowing that, knowing about and where knowledge is apprehended through different senses and accessed through different systems, languages, networks and discourses, learning becomes a potentially rich field requiring total engagement of learners and teachers.

Knowledge demonstrated through art and design curricula varies with time, social configurations, prevailing philosophies and theories positioned in dominant sociopolitical discourses. It also resides in the objects created by students. If powerful knowledge offers the ability to engage in 'society's conversation' (Wheelahan 2010:1), then those students who become artists and designers are engaging through the ways that they change the world around us: in performances, communication and the visual and material aspects of life. As Ashwin (2014) states, it is 'the importance of knowledge in transforming our relations with the world and the ways in which knowledge is transformed as we engage with it' (p. 126). This relational approach to knowledge is a social one which is demonstrated through the new artefacts that art and design students produce, although of course, not all the new ideas and products actually reach a mass audience. Knowledge changes people, and people change knowledge.

Knowledge and knowing then is a messy and complicated business. It is multifaceted, changing and located in different places and systems; it is inherently sticky. As a practice based discipline area, art and design offer insights into the ways in which learning in universities might usefully be thought of as sticky and knowledge forms complex landscapes requiring different forms of learning. It is also a site of contestation and creation of new knowledge which has the potential to change the discipline, even at an undergraduate level. This requires changes in power relations in the learning environment to enable new forms of practice to be acknowledged. More variable and responsive approaches to learning would help develop people who are comfortable with change and communicating through multiple forms of information, including an increasingly visual world of social media.

References

Ashwin, P., 2014. Knowledge, Curriculum and Student Understanding in Higher Education. *Higher Education*, 67(2), pp. 123–126.

Atkinson, D., 2015. The Adventure of Pedagogy, Learning and the Not-known. *Subjectivity*, 8(1), pp. 43–56.

Ball, S. J. ed., 2013. *Foucault and Education: Disciplines and Knowledge*. London: Routledge.

Barnett, R. and Coate, K., 2005. *Engaging the Curriculum in Higher Education*. Maidenhead and New York: Open University Press/SRHE.

Bernstein, B., 2000. *Pedagogy, Symbolic Control and Identity: Theory, Research, Critique*. Lanham and Oxford: Rowman & Littlefield.

Biggs, J., 2003. *Teaching for Quality Learning at University*. Maidenhead: Open University Press/SRHE.

Blackler, F., 1995. Knowledge, Knowledge Work and Organizations: An Overview and Interpretation. *Organization Studies*, 16(6), pp. 1021–1046.

Bruner, J., 1996. *The Culture of Education*. Cambridge, MA: Harvard University Press.

Cross, N., Naughton, J. and Walker, D., 1981. Design Method and Scientific Method. *Design Studies*, 2(4), pp. 195–201.

Daichendt, G. J., 2010. *Artist Teacher: A Philosophy for Creating and Teaching*. Bristol and Chicago: Intellect.

Dall'Alba, G., 2009. Learning Professional Ways of Being: Ambiguities of Becoming. *Educational Philosophy and Theory*, 41(1), pp. 34–45.

Dall'Alba, G. and Barnacle, R., 2007. An Ontological Turn for Higher Education. *Studies in Higher Education*, 32(6), pp. 679–691.

Dormer, P., 1994. *The Art of the Maker: Skill and Its Meaning in Art, Craft and Design*. London: Thames and Hudson.

Drew, L., 2004. The Experience of Teaching Creative Practices: Conceptions and Approaches to Teaching. In A. Davies, ed. *Enhancing Curricula: Towards the Scholarship of Teaching in Art, Design and Communication*. London: CLTAD, pp. 106–123.

Duguid, P., 2005. 'The Art of Knowing': Social and Tacit Dimensions of Knowledge and the Limits of the Community of Practice. *The Information Society*, 21(2), pp. 109–118.

Eisner, E., 1994. *Cognition and Curriculum Reconsidered*. New York: Teachers College Press.

Fenton-O'Creevy, M., Soane, M., Nicholson, N. and Willman. P., 2011. Thinking, Feeling and Deciding: The Influence of Emotions on the Decision Making and Performance of Traders. *Journal of Organizational Behavior*, 32(8), pp. 1044–1061.

Grove-White, A., 2003. Theory and Practice in Photography: Students' Understandings and Approaches to Learning. *Active Learning in Higher Education*, 4(1), pp. 56–73.

Harrison, C. and Wood, P., 2003. *Art in Theory, 1900–2000 an Anthology of Changing Ideas*. Malden, Oxford and Carlton: Blackwell Publishers Ltd.

Houghton, N., 2016. Six Into One: The Contradictory Art School Curriculum and How It Came About. *International Journal of Art and Design Education*, 35(1), pp107–120.

Kill, R., 2006. Coming in From the Cold: Imperialist Legacies and Tactical Criticalities. *International Journal of Art & Design Education*, 25(3), pp. 308–317.

Kill, R., 2013. Novel Apprehensions and Hybrid Utterances: Practice, Research, Language. *Art, Design & Communication in Higher Education*, 12(1), pp. 21–31.

Kress, G. and van Leeuwen, T., 2001. *Multimodal Discourse: The Modes and Media of Contemporary Communication*. London: Hodder Education.

Lave, J. and Wenger, E., 1991. *Situated Learning: Legitimate Peripheral Participation*. Cambridge: Cambridge University Press.

Llewellyn, N. and Williamson, B. eds., 2015. *The London Art Schools*. London: Tate Publishing.

Logan, C., 2006. Circles of Practice: Educational and Professional Graphic Design. *Journal of Workplace Learning*, 18(6), pp. 331–343.

Marton, F., Dall'Alba, G. and Beaty, E., 1993. Conceptions of Learning. *International Journal of Educational Research*, 19, pp. 277–300.

Mazé, R. and Redström, J., 2009. Difficult Forms: Critical Practices of Design and Research. *Research Design Journal*, 1(1), pp. 28–39.

Melles, G. and Lockheart, J., 2012. Writing Purposefully in Art and Design: Responding to Converging and Diverging New Academic Literacies. *Arts and Humanities in Higher Education*, 11(4), pp. 346–362.

Metros, S. and Woolsey, K., 2006. Visual Literacy: An Institutional Imperative. *Educause Review*. Available from: http://er.educause.edu/~/media/Files/Article-Downloads/ERM0638.pdf. [Accessed February 13, 2017].

Polanyi, M., 1967. *The Tacit Dimension*. London: Routledge & Kegan Paul.

Polanyi, M., 2012. *Personal Knowledge: Towards a Post-Critical Philosophy*. Chicago: University of Chicago Press.

Prentice, R., 2000. The Place of Practical Knowledge in Research in Art and Design Education. *Teaching in Higher Education*, 5(4), pp. 521–534.

Reardon, J. and Mollin, D., 2009. *Ch-ch-ch-changes: Artists Talk About Teaching*. London: Ridinghouse.

Ryle, G., 2009. *The Concept of Mind: 60th Anniversary Edition*. Abingdon and New York: Routledge.

Shreeve, A., 1998. Material Girls. In P. Johnson, ed. *Ideas in the Making: Practice in Theory*. London: Crafts Council, pp. 41–48.

Shreeve, A., 2008. *Transitions: Variation in Tutors' Experience of Practice and Teaching Relations in Art and Design*. Unpublished PhD Thesis. Lancaster University.

Swann, C., 2002. Nellie Is Dead., 1986. Designer, April; Reprinted. *Art, Design & Communication in Higher Education*, 1(1), pp. 50–58.

Tickner, L., 2008. *Hornsey 1968: The Art School Revolution*. London: Frances Lincoln Ltd.

Tynan, J. and New, C., 2009. Creativity and Conflict: How Theory and Practice Shape Student Identities in Design Education. *Arts and Humanities in Higher Education*, 8(3), pp. 295–308.

Wenger, E., 1998. *Communities of Practice*. Cambridge: Cambridge University Press.

Wenger-Trayner, E. et al. eds., 2015. *Learning in Landscapes of Practice: Boundaries, Identity, and Knowledgeability in Practice-Based Learning*. Abingdon and New York: Routledge.

Wheelahan, L., 2010. *Why Knowledge Matters in Curriculum: A Social Realist Argument*. London and New York: Routledge.

3 The construction and meaning of value(s)

Introduction

> Art schools are a particularly contradictory site. They are a location for the perpetual production of key ideologies.
>
> (Pollock 2011:149)

> Each studio culture features a different set of values, beliefs and actions.
>
> (Strickfaden and Heylighen 2010:122)

The 'anything goes' espoused values of the Art School can lead us to misrecognise the value systems within which we work. As Pollock (2011) and Strickfaden and Heylighen (2010) point out, the apparent openness of creative opportunity can conceal rigid but largely tacit structures of power relations and value systems. Power relations are at play as much in the Art School as in other sectors of society in spite of the apparent freedom of expression and creative imperatives of the discipline (Barrow 2006).

Society's ideas about creativity and education are culturally and historically saturated, so any analysis of art and design in the university needs to include a careful excavation of the values and assumptions that sit, often hidden, within our creative educational discourses. Exploring dominant definitions of worth is a way to uncover value systems (Lamont 2012). Art School values are not natural, universal or permanent. The twenty-first-century art and design education values that are currently so taken for granted to be barely noteworthy are likely to look quaint, offensive or irrelevant in 100 years' time. For example, current ideas about sustainability are likely to evolve and change as technologies for circular economy and zero waste develop. An arts project today might utilise waste from a skip or a dump, whilst in the future the art might be premised on pre-cycling rather than recycling. Elkins reminds us that 'academies emphasize some art and marginalize other art' (Elkins 2001:44). This was powerfully demonstrated in an anecdote shared with one of the authors during a research interview with a senior fine art lecturer who reported that there was a moment in his Art Department many years ago where a newly appointed sound artist wanted to fail all the painting students because he couldn't see the point of painting anymore (Orr 2011).

A further illustration is offered by Dash (2011), who describes feeling out of step with the avant-garde favoured by his Art School tutors in the 1970s and his sense of relief and recognition when he came across and then worked with the Caribbean Artists Movement.

Elkins (2001) reminds us that today's diverse graduate show will look homogeneous to viewers fifty years from now. The ways that the work looks similar today is hidden from view, but one only has to imagine design work in the 1960s to know that current design work has a set of aesthetical values that will look very much of its time from a future vantage point. For example, we can see the influence of space travel on design and fashion in the late 1960s. Values are historical, temporal, provisional and in a state of flux representing a time and a place. For example, if one charts the rise of Brit Art, a moment in the Art School that Madoff (2009:43) refers to as 'the golden period of Goldsmiths', one marks the passage of a set of ideas about art that worked its way from the margins to the centre. The changing power relations as Brit Art became more successful and more valuable (and more part of the establishment) is also a journey that charts the gradual process of legitimisation as the work's value and currency moved from the edge to the canon (Lamont 2012). Even before its place at the centre was assured, there was new art bubbling up in the margins of the Art School to topple its position at the centre. The work's value is dynamic and in flux.

The Crit is a key site for the creation of value, and for those readers less familiar with art and design education we offer a short description of this aspect of pedagogy. Moran states that 'the crit is a public revealing of a private activity' (2009:35). When students are developing their creative work, whether it be in response to a brief or the self-initiated pursuit of their own artistic practice, there will be points over the term or semester where the students will present their work to tutors and fellow students in the studio or in a virtual environment and the work will be discussed and evaluated (see Figure 3.1). In most cases the tutor will facilitate the feedback conversation about the work on display. This feedback exchange is referred to as a Crit in the United States and the UK and as the Jury in parts of Europe. At the end of the term or semester, the students will submit their final work for grading. The final grading element may also be in the form of a Crit, or the work may be marked in the student's absence. The submission of work is often accompanied by the student's development work in the form of sketchbooks, prototypes and a reflective commentary, the latter increasingly offered in blog post format. Crits are diverse and multipurpose, but their key commonality is discourse around student work (Crippa 2015).

Within the university Crit judgements are made about students' creative art and design work. The idea of measuring student work against stated standards in the creative arena is challenging given that there can be no model or predetermined answers. There are a number of ways to respond to this. We might seek to make a purely personal aesthetic response to the student work that attempts to 'park' the wider context within which the work is made. Fleming (2012) refers to this as a heartfelt or so-called pure response to the work. Alternatively we may explicitly seek a 'judicious intervention' by situating the work within its cultural/politic setting to understand the ways the work informs and is informed by the

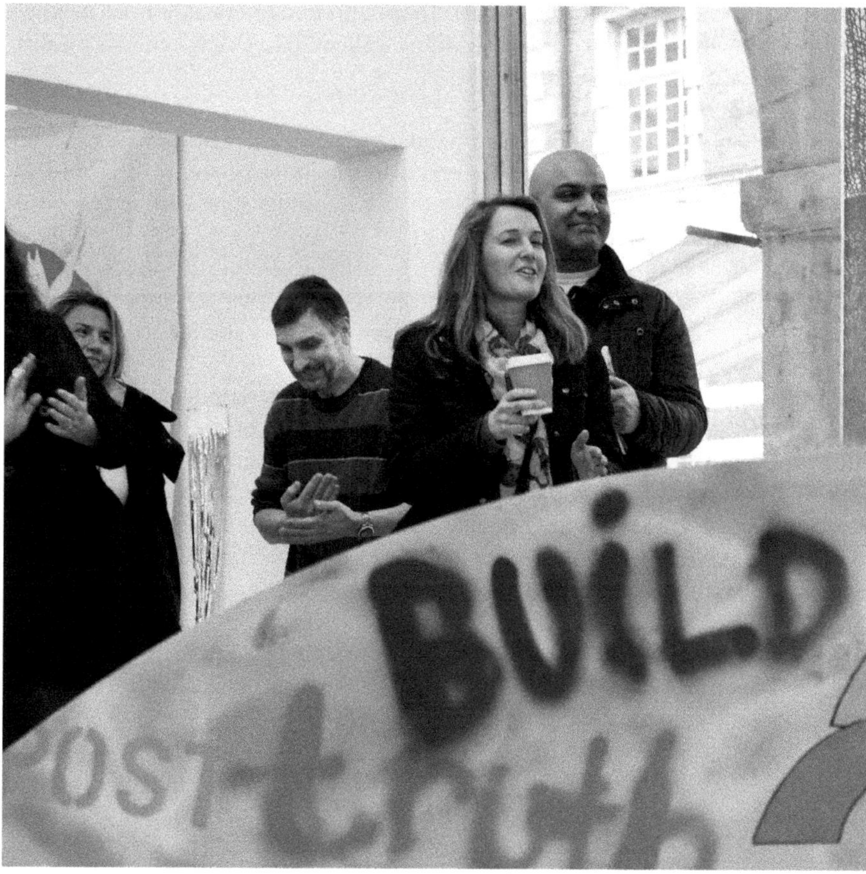

Figure 3.1 Studio 2017
Photograph by Valentina Schivardi

milieu within which it is created and the people who made it and are responding to it (Fleming 2012:4). In contrast an artist or designer tutor judging student work may take the view that could be typified as 'I am an artist; if I say it is good art it is good art'. In opposition to this would be the view that whilst there can no model answers, there *are* agreed parameters for inclusion and exclusion in the categorization of art and design. In this case grading teams need to establish consensus about how these categories are applied in practice. For Lamont (2012) these approaches are connected and overlapping. The (e)valuation of work is not removed or separate from society, but equally any judgement about work is made by a human being with the subjectivities this brings with it. Whilst an analysis of the idea of valuation can sound abstract and remote, it is important to note that it is a continuous process in art and design education that is not confined to the end of term Crit. Nor is it definitively captured in the written grading scheme.

Valuation is manifest and enacted through practices and dialogue; it is 'a social and cultural process' (Lamont 2012:6). In art and design education we produce meaning and worth in practice and in doing (Allen 2011). A system of (e)valuation typically has three elements:

1 a number of criteria about which people can agree or disagree;
2 a negotiation about these criteria and who the judge is; and
3 the establishment of relational values (i.e., comparisons within the set of work to be evaluated) (Lamont 2012).

These elements of evaluation are explored in an integrative way in this book. A focus on values underpins this chapter, and this analysis is applied to the grading and assessment practices explored in Chapter 8.

Readers who have worked in more than one art and design department (in the same country or internationally) will be able to comment on the ways that certain Art Schools manifest particular values and mores. This might be called the chemistry of a particular Art School (Baldessari and Craig-Martin 2009) that results from a particular constellation of people, time, space and possibilities. The extract that follows with its reference to the bar serves to locate the moment described in Western twentieth-century Art School practices:

> We just hung out in the bar, and that worked. You know, it's like all the planets surrounding you have to line up in the right way: the right students, the right moment, the right time, the right faculty, the right city. Everything just aligns for a few moments.
>
> (Baldessari and Craig-Martin 2009:47)

This extract makes one think about the students who might find themselves in the wrong moment, the wrong time and the wrong city. Different Art Schools are situated within structures of values that privilege and disadvantage students in different ways. In this sense Elkins (2001) and Pearson (2009) remind us that rural Art Schools are less valued and subsequently their students and their work are sometimes not as valued as Art Schools situated in a metropolis. The Art School is produced by its context whether this is rural, urban, rich or poor. Each art and design faculty has a cultural milieu which accrues or is denied currency. We use the word currency because it usefully denotes what is current as well as what is valued.

Addison notes that in art and design 'the design of curriculum is always conditioned by the values and aims of an educational institution' (Addison 2014:217). Curriculum isn't innocent – it reflects the values of those who produce it and the wider context within which it is produced. This is illustrated powerfully in fierce debates in Western art and design education systems where students are challenging what they call the 'pale, male, stale' art and design curriculum (Asquith 2015). Students are calling to decolonize the curriculum to bring in new voices and alternative narratives that reflect queer and post-colonial contexts for learning. This is not about adding some Black or Lesbian, Gay, Bisexual, Transgender, Queer (LGBTQ) creative practitioners to the existing mainstream curriculum (although this is to be welcomed). This movement is more concerned with de-othering the new voices and changing the centre ground. Pollock refers to this as 'pivoting the centre' (Pollock 2011:156). Thus a Black, Asian and Minority Ethnic (BAME) curriculum is just as much about challenging views of whiteness in the curriculum as it is about bringing in Black experiences. This connects to the idea of the globalised Art School and the globalised curriculum: 'Art schools need to embrace the narratives of their international professors and students, or they will betray them once again by colonizing them through whiteness' (Pujol 2009:11). Values are often a tacit and unexamined element of art and design education. Their presence crashes to the surface where there are examples of value clash. For example, building on ideas explored in Chapter 2, we note that in contexts where art and design departments are located inside larger multidisciplinary universities, there can be a clash of values and cultures between the art faculty and the wider university (Budge 2012). One arena where this plays out is in relation to the ways that knowledge is communicated. Written text is highly valued and credentialised as the basis of knowledge creation in the academy. Creative practice is highly valued in art and design education. This means that art and design practice based research outputs can be misunderstood if the wider university is more familiar with monographs, articles, books and journals. In these contexts creative practice may not be valued or valorised. Indeed artistic practice may not even be recognised as representing or communicating knowledge at all. The Art School may be deemed 'other' because knowledge in practice is not in readily recognisable academic forms. The Art School in this context may struggle to be recognised as academic. This is complicated by art and design commentators who themselves reject the very idea of academicisation in relation to Art Schools (De Duve 2011). Whilst Pollock (2011:149) argues that there is a 'structural contradiction which is at the root the collision of two professions – artist and teacher the collision of two ideologies', we take the view that as well as collision there are alignments, fusions and serendipitous opportunities that complicate this oppositional perspective. For example, cross-cultural values mix and mingle to create new affordances through the current focus on interdisciplinarity. This hybridity is central to our conception of the creative education practitioner.

Many art and design educators lament the conjoining of Art Schools and universities polarising into the idea that the university has 'murdered' the Art School (Heron 2011). The wider university is commonly regarded as having a risk-averse, bureaucratic, compliance set of values that is regarded as a constraining force for art and design colleagues. But this is to present the values of higher education in a purely negative light. Some changes have been welcomed. One example that highlights this and reveals the ways our ideas of the acceptable changes over time is the description of the admissions interview at one Art School in the 1970s. A prospective student is asked if he thought his work was precious. When the student said no, the admissions tutor responded by throwing the portfolio out of the window (Gomperts 2011). This anecdote surfaces the machismo of the 1970s Western Art School and points to values that are best left in the past.

Another site for value clash is the relation between art and design faculty and industry. As Logan (2008) points out, 'The need to negotiate between the values of the two communities [industry and education] can alter teacher/learner relationships and problematise criteria for evaluating student achievement' (Logan 2008:15). Is the Art School distinct from the 'real' world, or is it part of the 'real' world? At this point it is essential to note the differences between the external stakeholders for the disciplines of art and design. At its simplest art education is in dialogue (consensual and dissenting) with aspects of the art world and/or the art market, whilst design education is more commonly in dialogue (consensual and dissenting) with the design industry. Sometimes the values of these stakeholders will clash. For example, in the fashion industry discriminatory practices linger in relation to the (non)use of Black models or models of unusual body shape. These values would be an anathema in some progressive Art School fashion education contexts. In Chapter 6 there is further analysis of the idea of the real world as something external to the Art School.

Some design and fashion educators seek to emulate and inculcate tough industry and art market values, whilst others seek to provide a place of refuge from these values. At times the Art School can be 'a coddling environment' (Madoff 2009:273) that is likened to a womb (Abramović 2007). From this perspective art and design educators may take the view that they are 'educating art away from life' (Archer 2011:111). At other times the Art School can be more like a Darwinian space where students are offered the opportunity to sink or swim (Pollock 2011). In this case students will need to 'embrace this proposition with social-Darwinist steeling of the nerves' (Sekula 2011:117).

So art and design education can offer protection from the world whilst at the same time preparing students to be part of the world. Educational and professional values mix and mingle. The key point is that there is a mutual co-construction; education and industry influence each other. Alumni forge the art world, and the art world forges the Art School. The student, the Art School, the university and the world of art and design creative sector are not islands. They connect and collide in a state of constant flux. Thus the Art School is best understood as a contradictory site of contestation and challenge in its relation to the external context (Pollock 2011). Birnbaum asks this question:

> Should the art school turn itself into a monastery that protects students from the evil forces outside or should it invite the market in and become a lively bazaar? It seems to me that the answer is neither and both.
>
> (Birnbaum 2009:238)

Exchanging value

> The core pedagogic approach of the [Art School] is conversation and critique.
>
> (Lauterbach 2009:92)

> [Design students] adjust their approach, outlook and the expression of it to those befitting educated members of society.
>
> (Barrow 2006:358)

In Chapter 1 we introduced the phrase 'a kind of exchange' (Shreeve et al. 2010). The word exchange is freighted with meaning. In any art and design Crit, there is an exchange or dialogue about the work. But let's explore the idea of art and design education as a place to create and *exchange* value. Thus the Crit becomes a place of exchange, a place to create and deny value. In art and design it is rarely the case that the student work is judged without reference to its creator. What this means is that the studio becomes a place or means to create (or deny) human value. The work and the student are part of the exchange. This links to the idea of the Art School as an incubator for the art world or design industry where students may themselves become commodities in the market (Massouras 2015).

In the context of design Mewburn points out that 'conversation is a process of enculturation into studio practices' (2011:364). Studio talk links to the reproduction of values (Svennson and Edstrom 2011) where the Crit plays a role transmitting lecturers' mores and values (Percy 2004). To put it simply, students imbibe values as part of the studio conversation (Logan 2013; Llewellyn and Williamson 2015).

Daily exchange and conversation offers students insight into the value their work and their practices are accruing (or failing to accrue). Broadening out the idea of 'studio talk' to draw in Critical Discourse Theory (Gee 2012), we view discourse as a set of ideas about value creation and the denial of value. The role of talk in studio pedagogy is explored by Mollin (2009), who devotes a book chapter to 'the verbal nature of teaching art' and Harman and McDowell (2011), who research design lecturers' studio based assessment talk.

Studio talk does not only offer a means to represent value. Studio talk helps to *constitute* the work's value and the tutors' values (Crippa 2015). The Crit conversation offers a place to share and co-construct meanings. This perspective on the studio is premised on the idea of language as contingent, dynamic and slippery. Meanings are not fixed or transmitted. This is an interpretative conception of language where meanings are created and contested in communities. Students and their work are 'languaged' into being. To illustrate this, Webster (2005:284) offers a Foucauldian rendering of the Architectural Design Crit and notes that a student in her Western based study presents a design that incorporates principles of feng shui. In her Crit this student is told 'that Feng Shui was "mystical mumbo jumbo" and was not relevant to Western Architecture'. One of the authors of this volume has visited a Chinese university architecture department where parts of the campus explicitly draw in principles of feng shui. The globalised and connected nature of today's higher education exposes value conflicts and the ways that our values locate to place and time.

Art School cool and paradoxical values

In this section we present five commonly held idea(l)s in Western Art Schools. We analyse each one in turn to excavate meanings and to shore up their paradoxical foundations. We offer these as illustrative examples; readers will be able to reflect on core values within their own contexts to identify the extent to which these examples have resonance across international and interdisciplinary contexts. The five examples we select are these:

1 You can't teach art.
2 Students need to take risks.
3 Students need to understand the importance of failure.
4 In the Art School anything goes because art and design education is transgressive.
5 Art and design education is about deschooling.

1. You can't teach art

> I don't think you can teach art at all.
>
> (Birnbaum 2009:233)

> The point of art being teachable or not still remains one of the primary pedagogic issues everywhere. It has certainly plagued Latin American art schooling.
>
> (Camnitzer 2009:208)

There is something alluringly contradictory about discussing the idea that art cannot be taught in a volume about art and design teaching. Elkins (2001) explores this in his book about fine art pedagogy that is titled *Why art can not be taught*. The idea that art and design is a discipline that is unteachable is less frequently referred to in the context of design education, so we will focus on fine art. The conflicted nature of this idea is revealed by an artist educator who commented, 'I've always been kind of painfully aware that when I'm teaching, I'm not' (Baldessari and Craig-Martin 2009:49). Colless (2009) poses the art teacher as a trickster. He says that to 'teach art is to teach a non-subject, a subject that is and is not teachable' (p. 103). This then is the 'performative paradox' of teaching art (Buckley and Conomos 2009:17). Teaching is revealed and concealed. The paradox here is that whilst art educators say that what they are doing cannot be called teaching, their published narratives often portray elements of pedagogic practice that sound very much like teaching (Reardon and Mollin 2009). Thus Armleder (cited in Reardon and Mollin 2009) comments, 'I'm not directive in any way. I would never tell a student he'd [sic] better do something' (p. 25). Later in the same interview, he comments, 'I'm in exactly the same position as the student' (p. 27), but then he says, 'Because of my long-term practice I have some kind of knowledge . . . I'm very happy to share' (p. 28). The transmission of knowledge clearly situates this commentary within a pedagogic frame. The artist Abramović (2007:18) offers her view of teaching: 'To me teaching is transmitting my own experiences of what I know and have learnt'. These extracts point to a teacherly approach of sharing expert knowledge. Barrow (2006) unveils the directive nature of studio pedagogy when he describes design based assessment practices:

> The design lecturer is in a position to track the development of the students' thoughts, encouraging him or her to renounce those thoughts that do not conform to the discipline and to retain those that do.
>
> (p. 367)

Barrow argues that the conversations amongst students and their tutors over time serve to converge the habitus of the students in the direction of the tutors' habitus. In Barrow's view successful students learn to regulate and benchmark their behaviour and practices against the behaviour and practices of the tutors. This viewed is shared by Strickfaden and Heylighen (2010) in their account of the acculturation of architecture students into the mores and values of architectural professional practice. In Crippa's (2015:140) analysis of London Art School Crits, she notes that whilst these Crits aspire to openness and experimentation, in practice they establish 'tight parameters' and value systems within which students may feel forced to position themselves if they are to be successful. There is a lot that is learnt in the studio even when, apparently, nothing is taught. Paradoxical (non)teaching is hinted at by the sculptor Magdalena Jetelová when she writes: 'I squeeze the students like lemons until they work out what they want to do' (cited in Bourgeois 2007:130).

Students need to take risks

The idea of risk taking as a valued student behaviour has been prevalent in Western art and design education for many years (Atkinson 2012). Patterson and Sharman (2014) offer a beautifully rendered examination of student risk taking in the context of design. Their viewpoint is clear: 'Our studios without risk are not the studios we value' (p. 10). Patterson and Sharman describe an example of a risky project at their Art School where a visiting alumnus had been asked to give the students a project. The brief to students opened with this statement: 'Within your groups you have thirty hours to visually communicate the word 'Notoriety' in any form you wish.' What follows is an account which reminds us that whilst we exhort our students to take risks, students can stretch *our* risk comfort zones when they then go on, as they did in this case, to stage a fake robbery or a fake kidnapping. The students' work was reported in the national press and came to the attention of law enforcement! The acceptance of risk taking as a valorised practice is so mainstream within art and design education that the paradoxes and contradictions that underpin this value are rarely surfaced. Bell (2013) reminds us that there is an inherent paradox at the centre of our exhortation to students to take risks. If all risk taking is rewarded and valued, what is the risk? As Bell points out perhaps the riskiest of all design approaches would be to not take risks or to stay 'inside the box' so to speak.

Patterson and Sharman (2014) refer to the tensions students can feel between wanting to 'play it safe' to secure good marks and the need to take risks. Related to this, Jackson (2013) explores the ways that this value can intersect with student attainment in a UK based design case study where he discusses the students who represent 'the squeezed middle', that is, those students who don't get very high or very low grades. In his research he explores why these students, some of whom arrive at university with a strong profile of achievement, do not excel, and his research identifies that these students are often risk averse, which is a student value that will stop them getting high marks. Risk-averse behaviours and dispositions put these students at a disadvantage. What this means is that the students' personal or learnt values put them at a disadvantage in an environment which values risk taking. This surfaces the ways that art and design value systems can collide with student value systems. Perhaps the best way to respond to this paradox is to flex and enhance our innovation and creativity by taking more risks teaching our students (Lupton 2013; Gibson 2010).

Students need to understand the importance of failure

> Failure forms an important dimension of art and design and is inherent in creative endeavours.
>
> (Fremantle and Kearney 2015:309)

Connected to the idea of risk taking, art and design education valorises the idea of failure as essential to learning. For Fremantle and Kearney (2015:313) failure is a 'badge of great artistry'. This is a view of pedagogy 'not preoccupied with succeeding but with trying' (Allen 2011:18). Bauer (2009:222) proposes that failure is a prerequisite for innovation. From this perspective the objective of the Art School is to 'take the terror out of error' (Mörsch 2011:106). Like risk taking the idea of failure can be appealing, but the paradox here is that failure is usually discussed from some consequent 'in the future' vantage point of success. Thus failure is only valued if it is entwined with some form of recognisable success. The idea of failure is further complicated in the section that follows when we explore the idea of the failing student.

In the Art School anything goes because art and design is transgressive

> It seems to be almost obligatory, if you're an artist teaching in an art school, to be at odds with the bureaucracy.
>
> (Corris cited in Reardon and Mollin 2009:94)

The idea that there are no rules in the Art School and that this is to be celebrated is a commonly espoused value. This connects to the idea of the Art School as a place of intellectual emancipation. Creativity and the idea of subversion are linked

(Gibson 2010). Within this conception art and design education is perceived as value neutral, a place of possibility and realisation (Baldessari and Craig-Martin 2009). This places the Art School in some otherworldly place of infinite possibility. A cursory examination of this idea surfaces tensions: a jewellery student who wants to work in gold but finds his part-time job in the local supermarket doesn't pay enough for him to afford this or a fashion student who would prefer to create a final collection in a hard-to-source expensive fabric but can't afford it. Clearly there are material constraints in relation to creative possibility. In addition there are culturally based limitations. Students have differential access to internships and work experience connecting to their access to networks and cultural capital. One student may be able to secure a prestigious placement in New York Vogue through family networks, whilst another does not have this opportunity.

For Ewing (2009:161) the Art School is viewed as a transgressive space of 'radical openness', and Cliff and Woodward (2004) argue that design lecturers seek to inculcate an '"anti" world view' (p. 282). This is about the Art School as a place of resistance, a place where rules are there to be challenged and subverted. However, it is clear that the students are only supported if they break the right kind of rules. For example, setting fire to the Art School, stealing from staff or assaulting a tutor or a student would clearly be the wrong type of rule breaking.

Universities do have rules, and many of these rules are tacitly accepted in the day-to-day life of art and design higher education. There are fixed submission dates, agreed protocols for late submission, rules about grading practices, plagiarism rules, fixed term dates, fee payment arrangements and degree classification. Students and staff are working within an environment that poses a number of constraints. This challenges the idea of unlimited choice and openness. Values of conformity and regulation compete with values of emancipation and freedom (Allen 2011).

Art and design is about deschooling

> They come here . . . with a kind of . . . baggage of various influences: schooling . . . the domestic situation . . . when they get here, there's another kind of moulding that's taking place.
>
> (Design lecturer cited in Cliff and Woodward 2004:280)

There are differences in the ways that students are admitted to art and design courses in universities according to the country within which students apply. In the UK judgements are made about prior qualifications, but there is typically a greater focus on judging the quality of the portfolio. In some design faculties in Australia the focus is on the students' secondary school achievement, and portfolios are not part of the selection process. However, in all cases, there is a focus on some form of predetermined entry standards that students have to meet. In spite of the emphasis on prior learning at point of entry once students are admitted, there is a popular view that they need to unlearn all that has gone before. This approach can be traced back to Bauhaus, where a culture of 'unlearning' was promoted (Massouras 2012), and it is still a prevalent view in university art and design education. The Art School concept of unlearning is complex but is typically characterised as a view that students' prior knowledge is invalid (Mewburn (2011). In language that can appear evangelical, new students at Art School need to 'see in a new way, free from previous restrictions' (Katz 2011:38). Some Art School tutors want a blank sheet or a tabula rasa to work with. The central paradox here is that art and design tutors are not usually required to unlearn at any point in their careers. Their experiences are viewed as an asset (see the previous teacher extracts). As discussed later in this volume, Rancière (1991) points to the importance of starting where the students are rather than denying the value of their existing learning assets.

The valued student

Art and design education helps establish who as well as what is valued. We now turn to consider the ways that values serve to credentialise or 'punish' certain identity positions to explore the ways that students' identities are fashioned into being in the studio: 'Giving someone a first – it's like saying that they're far better than anyone else' (cited by a fine art lecturer in Orr 2007:111). In an interview based study fine art lecturers, when asked to talk about the attributes of first-class artwork, talked about the characteristics of students who get high grades (Orr 2007). Thus a question that unambiguously asks for comment about student work is responded to with commentary on the students who make this work. In this study students who were deemed 'first class' were described as being those who understood the 'rules of the game' and were self-reflective. These were students who were capable of arguing their points (and had the confidence to do so). They were in the studio a lot, thereby keeping in regular dialogue with tutors. These students were able to articulate the ways that their work fitted in the bigger picture of the art world beyond university. Interestingly they were seen as students who were not chasing good grades.

These attributes and behaviours point to the ways that lecturers are grading studentship and the link between the students' cultural capital, values and assessment. Creative education is about identity formation; it 'requires not only knowing something but *being* something' (Stevens 1995:112, emphasis added). High grades are premised on a good fit between the student, the student's work, the art/design arena and the lecturers' values. This view of studentship is echoed by a Swiss fine art educator Armleder, who comments that 'you can see they're engaged; they can discuss their work, and it means something to them' (cited in Reardon and Mollin 2009:33).

Any discussion of the ideal or successful student needs to be accompanied by a consideration of those students who are deemed to be failing; the necessity of one constructs its inverse. It is important to note that this is not the valorised failure referred to earlier in the chapter. This is about students who fail to master the Art School. According to the fine art lecturers referred to here, students who fail in fine art do not adopt agreed ways of working; they fail to listen to, respond to, and learn from feedback. They are rarely in the studio and do not turn up for progress Crits. These students don't appear to 'get the rules' and are less able to evidence their process or situate their work within the contemporary field of reference. They fail to interact with tutors and are, ironically, deemed to be grade chasing (Orr 2007). The ways these students are described has much in common with Logan's (2013) study where failing students were typified as under-participating. These students are out of step with prevailing departmental values pointing to an absence of recognised cultural literacy.

Austerlitz et al. (2008) offer the stereotype of the ideal student as one who is relentlessly pursuing their practice and who is always in the studio until it closes. Whilst this image of the ideal student may seem value free, it masks the ways that this opportunity 'to be' may not be available to all students. For example, some students may be carers or parents. Some students may need to work. Some students may not have the money for the bus fare to college or the money to print off the work to a high standard. They may need to use hessian rather than silk. Lecturers need to ensure that their values do not prevent them seeing quality work and studentship in a range of circumstances. There is a need to flex and stretch our picture of the ideal student so it is diverse and inclusive. We need to recognise that some valorised behaviours and approaches are materially out of reach for some of our students. The idea of the ever present student is a masculinised idea of the student unencumbered with children, financial constraints or responsibility. In the twenty-first century Art School, we need greater recognition of the societal networks of advantage and disadvantage within which our Art Schools are located.

Payne (2015) reminds us that it is important that we do not simply reward students for being cultured or because they remind us of what we were like when we were students. Hay and MacDonald (2008:160) talk about teachers 'having a perception of a student "locked in your brain"'. These 'locked-in' perceptions can be a place where values lurk and remain unexamined. These assumptions are hinted at when a photography lecturer remarks: 'I gave them high marks but the students deserved high marks 'cause they would bust their butt. The school was open twenty four hours and they were there at three in the morning' (Orr 2007:88). This demand for presenteeism looks dated given the digital working environments that students inhabit on and off campus.

Whilst the characteristics listed here are of interest, they risk individualising success and failure by removing the students from the cultural setting and socio-political context. Students who are deemed to be failing are inscribed with essentialised and fixed characteristics that are the opposite of the ideal student. Here we turn to Bourdieu's 'ideology of giftedness' (Bourdieu 1977). Bourdieu argues that we misrecognise failure. He exhorts us to do more to surface the relationship between the students' work and the cultural field to recognise that success is differentially available to students given their cultural capital. Failing needs to be situated within its wider sociocultural setting. This nuance is reflected in the title of a book called *Failing students in higher education* (Peelo 2002). Implicitly this title suggests that *universities* might be failing the students.

An example of a lecturer forensically examining her value assumptions is offered in Behardien's (2014) highly reflexive research interrogating fine art education values in the context of post-apartheid South Africa. In her research she asks 'what kind of knower I privilege in my curriculum and pedagogy' (p. 5). Behardien explores her own approaches to tutoring and the Crit to identify why and how some students' work and approaches are legitimated. She notes that some students have the 'right kind' of dispositions and cultural capital that matches the dispositions and cultural capital valued by the academy and the art world.

Conclusion

The idea of the sticky curriculum helps us surface and engage with the idea of value(s) to support inclusion and diversity. Values stick to the curriculum. This chapter has unpacked some of the ways that values underpin art and design education. Benson and Napier (2015:212) note that in the context of the United States, 'American Midwestern design students are often unaware of how their values, perspectives, and worldviews affect their process of designing'. Art and design educators and students need to surface and examine their values to establish whose interests are being served. This is uncomfortable territory where there can be a gap between espoused and tacit values.

Students sometimes report that they feel like detectives trying to deduce the values or aesthetics of the teachers they work with. This is manifest in students' anxiety about who is grading their work and how the teachers' creative practices align with or clash against the students' ways of making. This can be difficult for students to navigate. As art and design educators we need to be alert to any assumption that values are universal or stable. Rogoff (2011) argues that art and design pedagogy needs to recognise and accommodate its partiality; this is true, but we need to go further. We need to be reflexive enough not only to recognise but also to counter and reject some of this partiality if we are to work towards emancipatory education.

References

Abramović, M., 2007. Marina Abramovic. In V. Bourgeois, ed. *Art Mistresses: Between Classroom and Studio.* Germany: Salon, pp. 6–19.

Addison, N., 2014. Doubting Learning Outcomes in Higher Education Contexts: From Performativity Towards Emergence and Negotiation. *International Journal of Art & Design Education*, 33(3), pp. 313–325.

Allen, F., ed., 2011. *Education: Documents of Contemporary Art.* London: Whitechapel Gallery.

Archer, M., 2011. Educating Art Away From Life. In F. Allen, ed. *Education: Documents of Contemporary Life.* London: Whitechapel Gallery, pp. 111–113.

Asquith, S., 2015. *Art School Curriculum: Pale, Male, Stale?* Available at: http://shellyasquith.tumblr.com/post/108163042838/event-art-school-curriculum-pale-male-stale [Accessed July 3, 2016].

Atkinson, D., 2012. Contemporary Art and Art in Education: The New, Emancipation and Truth. *International Journal of Art & Design Education*, 31(1), pp. 5–18.

Austerlitz, N., Blythman, M., Grove-White, A., Jones, B.A., Jones, C.A., Morgan, S., Orr, S., Shreeve, A. and Vaughan, S., 2008. Mind the Gap: Expectations,

Ambiguity and Pedagogy Within Art and Design Education. In L. Drew, ed. *The Student Experience in Art and Design Higher Education: Drivers for Change*. Cambridge: Jill Rogers Associates Ltd Publishers, pp. 125–148.

Baldessari, J. and Craig-Martin, M., 2009. Conversation: John Baldessari and Michael Craig-Martin. In S. H. Madoff, ed. *The Art School (Propositions for the 21st Century)*. Cambridge, MA: MIT Press, pp. 41–52.

Barrow, M., 2006. Assessment and Student Transformation: Linking Character and Intellect. *Studies in Higher Education*, 31(3), pp. 357–372.

Bauer, U., 2009. Under Pressure. In S. H. Madoff, ed. *Art School (Propositions for the 21st Century)*. Cambridge, MA: MIT Press, pp. 220–226.

Behardien, I., 2014. *'Who Are They' or 'What and How They Know': An Investigation by a Fine Art Lecturer Into the Basis of Her Own Legitimacy*. Unpublished MPhil Thesis. University of Cape Town.

Bell, S., 2013. *The Promise of the Short Text: Writing Risk Into Visual Arts Practice, Coventry University*. Unpublished PhD Thesis. Coventry University.

Benson, E. and Napier, P., 2015. Connecting Values: Teaching Sustainability to Communication Designers. *Design and Culture*, 4(2), pp. 195–214.

Birnbaum, D., 2009. Teaching Art: Adorno and the Devil. In S. H. Madoff, ed. *Art School (Propositions for the 21st Century)*. Cambridge, MA: MIT Press, pp. 231–246.

Bourdieu, P., 1977. Cultural Reproduction and Social Reproduction. In J. Karabel and A. Halsey, eds. *Power and Ideology in Education*. Oxford: Oxford University Press, pp. 487–511.

Bourgeois, V., 2007. *Art Mistresses: Between Classrooms and Studio*. Germany: Salon-Verl.

Buckley, B. and Conomos, J., 2009. Introduction. In B. Buckley and J. Conomos, eds. *Rethinking the Contemporary Art School: The Artist, the PhD and the Academy*. Halifax: The Press of the Nova Scotia College of Art and Design, pp. 2–26.

Budge, K., 2012. A Question of Values: Why We Need Art and Design in Higher Education. *Art, Design & Communication in Higher Education*, 11(1), pp. 5–16.

Camnitzer, L., 2009. In Latin America: Art Education Between Colonialism and Revolution. In S. H. Madoff, ed. *Art School (Propositions for the 21st Century)*. Cambridge, MA: MIT Press, pp. 201–215.

Cliff, A. F. and Woodward, R., 2004. How Do Academics Come to Know? The Structure and Contestation of Discipline-specific Knowledge in a Design School. *Higher Education*, 48(3), pp. 269–290.

Colless, E., 2009. Unnamable. In B. Buckley and J. Conomos, eds. *Rethinking the Contemporary Art School: The Artist, the PhD and the Academy*. Halifax: The Press of the Nova Scotia College of Art and Design, pp. 101–105.

Crippa, E., 2015. From 'Crit' to 'Lecture-Performance'. In N. Llewellyn and B. Williamson, eds. *The London Art Schools*. London: Tate Publishing, pp. 133–150.

Dash, P., 2011. Indiscipline: Foreday Morning. In F. Allen, ed. *Education: Documents of Contemporary Life*. London: Whitechapel Gallery, pp. 74–77.

De Duve, T., 2011. When Form Has Become Attitude – And Beyond. In F. Allen, ed. *Education: Documents of Contemporary Life*. London: Whitechapel Gallery, pp. 60–68.

Elkins, J., 2001. *Why Art Cannot Be Taught: A Handbook for Art Students*. Champaign, IL: University of Illinois Press.

Ewing, L., 2009. Remixing the Hive. In B. Buckley and J. Conomos, eds. *Rethinking the Contemporary Art School: The Artist, the PhD and the Academy*. Halifax: The Press of the Nova Scotia College of Art and Design, pp. 159–163.

Fleming, M., 2012. *The Arts in Education: An Introduction to Aesthetics, Theory and Pedagogy*. Oxon: Routledge.

Fremantle, C. and Kearney, G., 2015. Owning Failure: Insights Into the Perceptions and Understandings of Art Educators. *International Journal of Art & Design Education*, 34(3), pp. 309–318.

Gee, J. P., 2012. *Social Linguistics and Literacies: Ideology in Discourses*. London: Routledge.

Gibson, R., 2010. The 'Art' of Creative Teaching: Implications for Higher Education. *Teaching in Higher Education*, 15(5), pp. 607–613.

Gomperts, A., 2011. Thin Air: The Psycho-Vocalic Discoveries of Alan Smithson. In F. Allen, ed. *Education: Documents of Contemporary Life*. London: Whitechapel Gallery, pp. 145–148.

Harman, K. and McDowell, L., 2011. Assessment Talk in Design: The Multiple Purposes of Assessment in HE. *Teaching in Higher Education*, 16(1), pp. 41–52.

Hay, P. and MacDonald, D., 2008. (Mis)appropriations of Criteria and Standards-referenced Assessment in a Performance Based Subject. *Assessment in Education: Principles, Policy & Practice*, 15(2), pp. 153–168.

Heron, P., 2011. Murder of the Art Schools. In F. Allen, ed. *Education: Documents of Contemporary Life*. London: Whitechapel Gallery, pp. 139–141.

Jackson, M., 2013. The Squeezed Middle: An Exploration of Creativity, Conformity and Social Class on the Academic Achievement of Undergraduate Students Within a UK Art School. *International Journal of Art & Design Education*, 32(3), pp. 345–351.

Katz, V., 2011. Black Mountain College: Experiment in Art. In F. Allen, ed. *Education: Documents of Contemporary Life*. London: Whitechapel Gallery, pp. 38–42.

Lamont, M., 2012. Toward a Comparative Sociology of Valuation and Evaluation. *Annual Review of Sociology*, 38(21), pp. 2–30.

Lauterbach, A., 2009. The Thing Seen: Reimagining Arts Education for Now. In S. H. Madoff, ed. *Art School (Propositions for the 21st Century)*. Cambridge, MA: MIT Press, pp. 85–97.

Llewellyn, N. and Williamson, B., eds., 2015. *The London Art Schools*. London: Tate Publishing.

Logan, C., 2008. Metaphor and Pedagogy in the Design Practicum. *International Journal of Technology and Design Education*, 18(1), pp. 1–17.

Logan, C., 2013. Living Artists: Identity, Independence and Engagement in Fine Art Learning. *Art, Design & Communication in Higher Education*, 12(1), pp. 33–48.

Lupton, M., 2013. Reclaiming the Art of Teaching. *Teaching in Higher Education*, 18(2), pp. 156–166.

Madoff, S. H., 2009. *Art School (Propositions for the 21st Century)*. Cambridge, MA: MIT Press.

Massouras, A., 2012. Bauhaus: Art as Life. *Times Higher Education*, p. 1. Available at: www.timeshighereducation.com/features/culture/bauhaus-art-as-life/419839.article [Accessed November 18, 2016].

Massouras, A., 2015. The Art of Art Students. In N. Llewellyn and B. Williamson, eds. *The London Art Schools*. London: Tate, pp. 37–48.

Mewburn, I., 2011. Lost in Translation: Reconsidering Reflective Practice and Design Studio Pedagogy. *Arts and Humanities in Higher Education*, 11(4), pp. 363–379.

Mollin, D., 2009. Re: The Verbal Nature of Teaching Art. In J. Reardon, ed. *Ch-ch-ch-Changes: Artists Talk About Teaching*. London: Ridinghouse, pp. 15–19.

Moran, M., 2009. Aesthetic Platforms. In S. H. Madoff, ed. *Art School (Propositions for the 21st Century)*. Cambridge, MA: MIT Press, pp. 32–37.

Mörsch, C., 2009. Take the Terror Out of Error. In F. Allen, ed. *Education: Documents of Contemporary Life*. London: Whitechapel Gallery, pp. 106–108.

Orr, S., 2007. *Making Marks: The Artful Practice of Assessment in Fine Art*. Unpublished Doctoral Thesis. Institute of Education, University College London.

Orr, S., 2011. 'Being an Artist You Kind of, I Mean, You Get Used to Excellence': Identity, Values and Fine Art Assessment Practices. *International Journal of Art and Design Education*, 30(1), pp. 37–44.

Patterson, Z. and Sharman, I., 2014. *Valuing Risk in the Creative Campus*. Available at: www.research.ed.ac.uk/portal/files/16554651/Valuing_Risk_on_the_Creative_Campus.pdf.

Payne, J. C., 2015. Investigating the Role of Cultural Capital and Organisational Habitus in Architectural Education: A Case Study Approach. *International Journal of Art & Design Education*, 34(1), pp. 9–24.

Pearson, G., 2009. The Outskirts of Town: A Peripheral Centre for Art, Agency, and Academia. In B. Buckley and J. Conomos, eds. *Rethinking the Contemporary Art School: The Artist, the PhD and the Academy*. Halifax: The Press of the Nova Scotia College of Art and Design, pp. 164–181.

Peelo, M., ed., 2002. *Failing Students in Higher Education*. London: Open University Press.

Percy, C., 2004. Critical Absence Versus Critical Engagement: Problematics of the Crit in Design Learning and Teaching. *Art, Design & Communication in Higher Education*, 2(3), pp. 143–154.

Pollock, G., 2011. Art, Art School, Culture. In F. Allen, ed. *Education: Documents of Contemporary Life*. London: Whitechapel Gallery, pp. 149–152.

Pujol, E., 2009. On the Ground: Practical Observations for Regenerating Art Education. In S. H. Madoff, ed. *The Art School (Propositions for the 21st Century)*. Cambridge, MA: MIT Press, pp. 1–14.

Rancière, J., 1991. *The Ignorant Schoolmaster: Five Lessons in Intellectual Emancipation*. Redwood: Stanford University Press.

Reardon, J. and Mollin, D., 2009. *Ch-ch-ch-changes: Artists Talk About Teaching*. London: Ridinghouse.

Rogoff, I., 2011. Academy as Potentiality. In F. Allen, ed. *Education: Documents of Contemporary Life*. London: Whitechapel Gallery, pp. 132–133.

Sekula, A., 2011. School Is a Factory. In F. Allen, ed. *Education: Documents of Contemporary Life*. London: Whitechapel Gallery, pp. 115–118.

Shreeve, A., Sims, E. and Trowler, P., 2010. 'A Kind of Exchange': Learning From Art and Design Teaching. *Higher Education Research & Development*, 29(2), pp. 125–138.

Stevens, S., 1995. Struggle in the Studio: A Bourdivin Look at Architecture Pedagogy. *Journal of Architectural Education*, 49(2), pp. 105–122.

Strickfaden, M. and Heylighen, A., 2010. Cultural Capital: A Thesaurus for Teaching Design. *International Journal of Art & Design Education*, 29(2), pp. 121–133.

Svennson, L. and Edstrom, A. M., 2011. The Function of Art Students' Use of Studio Conversations in Relation to Their Artwork. *International Journal of Education and the Arts*, 12(5), pp. 1–29.

Webster, H., 2005. The Architectural Review: A Study of Ritual, Acculturation and Reproduction in Architectural Education. *Arts and Humanities in Higher Education*, 4(3), pp. 265–282.

4 Ambiguity and uncertainty in creative education

Introduction

In 2007 the artist Antony Gormley presented an installation at the Hayward Gallery in London, titled BLIND LIGHT (see Figure 4.1). The work consisted of what can best be described as a foggy box the size of a large room. One entered the box to 'unsee', to 'unknow' and to make the familiar strange. The disorientation created by this work offered an intimacy and a playfulness. The darkness and fog brought light and insight. The mist reduced the distance amongst strangers whose typical needs for personal space were compromised by our inability to see (avoid) each other. This installation offers us a valuable metaphor for the ideas explored in this chapter. To access this artwork one needed to put to one side ideas about how art is typically encountered. The foggy box was an ambiguous space, and it is our argument that there are parallels between the experience of the spectator entering this work and those engaged in learning and teaching in art and design. The foggy box offers us a way to visualise the ambiguity of the Art School. In both cases there is the need to encounter ambiguous practices and/or work. Furthermore there is, there can be, a delight in ambiguity; we can stand in it; we can embrace it; we can 'carry the wonder with [us]' (Bentz and Shapiro 1998).

Uncertainty

Uncertainty lies at the core of art and design teaching and learning. Danvers (2003) describes indeterminacy as a central characteristic of art and design teaching, asserting that uncertainty is a positive force in creative education. Belluigi (2013) reinforces this by arguing that uncertainty can be productive and supportive to learning. Signature pedagogies in visual education point to the open-endedness of creative production (Shreeve et al. 2010; Svennson and Edstrom 2011), and for Dineen and Collins (2005:46) ambiguity and uncertainty are 'prerequisites for creativity'.

The terms ambiguity, uncertainty and indeterminacy are used frequently in art and design higher education. The meanings of these words have blurry boundaries that overlap. Indeterminacy can refer to the quality of being vague or being poorly defined. Uncertainty can hint at the element of chance in an uncertain

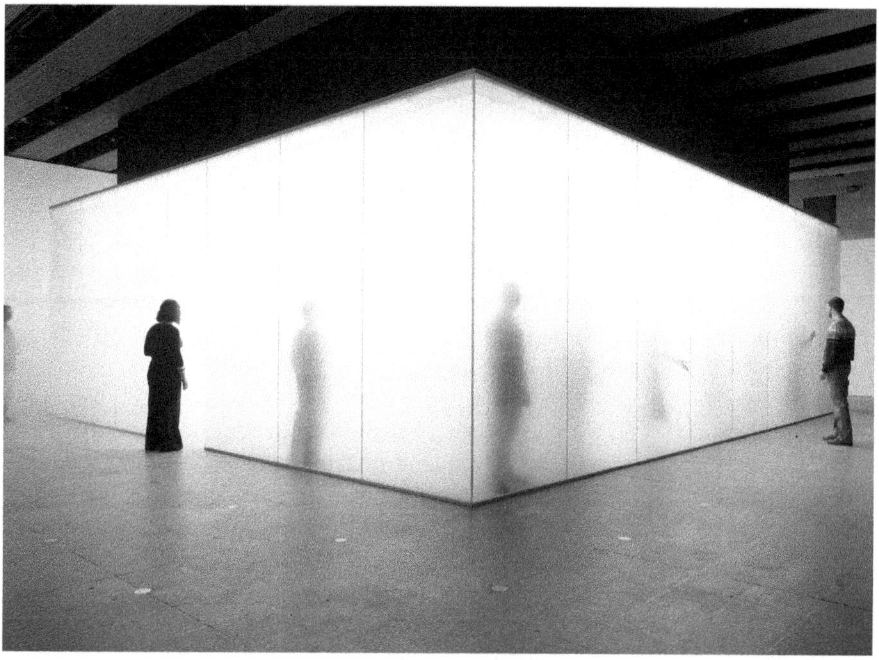

Figure 4.1 BLIND LIGHT, by Antony Gormley 2007

Fluorescent light, water, ultrasonic humidifiers, toughened low iron glass and aluminium
320 x 978.5 x 856.5 cm
Commissioned by the Hayward Gallery, London
Installation view, Hayward Gallery, London
Photograph by Stephen White, London
© the artist

outcome. Ambiguity, like indeterminacy can refer to inexactness, but it can also refer to being open to more than one interpretation, which is not the same as indeterminacy. The synonyms for these terms include the following: vagueness, doubtfulness, enigma, inconclusiveness, puzzle, obscurity, unclearness, imprecision, indistinctiveness, undefined, indefinite, unspecified, unstipulated, and borderless. Collectively the antonyms of these words include: certainty, clarity, clearness, definiteness, explicitness, lucidity, security, sureness, determined, exactness, fixedness, and measurable (www.oxforddictionaries.com).

A consideration of both sets of words side by side immediately points to the apparent allure of certainty that contrasts with the elusive riskiness of its inverse – uncertainty. Indeed a mistrust or fear of uncertainty has been 'a central feature of modern day thinking' (Tsoukas 2005:292). Responding to this we seek to present ambiguity in the context of art and design education as having its own allure and utility. Brassett and Rhodes (2013:1), in a keynote at a conference entitled 'What is the Point of Art School?' state: 'We embrace uncertainty and foster praxis,

[as] things to be defended and celebrated in art school'. Barnett (2010:123) writes that universities should aim to help students live with uncertainty, but it is also the job of the university to 'assuage that uncertainty' and enable students to 'live through uncertainty'. In the context of the Art School, Bogh (2009) states that arts education needs to both stabilise and destabilise. How are these contradictory objectives reconciled? Brassettt and Rhodes (2013:1) explain:

> The art school has always been a place where it is safe to be edgy, where the certainties of the world are questioned and their opposites championed. However, when the world is chaotic and the sureties of our lives have dissolved, what then? For us, chaos has always been an opportunity for creative innovation, rather than a problem that needs either mitigation or solving. Surely we can be sure of uncertainty.

In a chapter co-authored with seven other art and design educators in 2007 titled 'Mind the gap: expectations, ambiguity and pedagogy in art and design education' (Austerlitz et al. 2008), we set out the challenges students may encounter when they arrive at university to study art and design. We explored the ways that an art and design education aims to 'disturb the students with strangeness' (Barnett 2010:124). In this work we explored the ambiguity of art and design education from three perspectives: that of the students, that of the lecturers and that of the students' parents (with a particular focus on a parent who is unfamiliar with higher education in general and with art and design in particular). The gap referred to in the title referred to the gap in understanding, the gap in expectations and the gap between what a student or parent may expect and what the lecturer may expect. We recognise that there is a temptation to fill this gap by attempting to 'explain everything'. Indeed Peters (2010:107) reminds us that '"[l]et me explain" are words that come all too easily to the teacher's lips'. It is our argument that 'explaining everything' is a futile endeavour that would potentially limit and box in the creativity of art and design education.

It is our contention that there is a need for spaces and gaps that allow for creativity. In these spaces students can actively '*find* an explanation' (Peters 2010:108, authors' emphasis) rather than passively listen to the teacher's explanation. The gaps in understanding are not simply voids waiting for clarity to be poured in; they are not an absence of clarity; they are the *presence* of ambiguity; indeed they are a prerequisite for a 'pedagogy of ambiguity' (Austerlitz et al. 2008:130). Thus we theorise this need for a lack of clarity – turning it from an absence to a presence so it is not only defined in the negative. The presence of ambiguity can foster what Paul Bailey at the University of the Arts London refers to as pedagogic 'productive confusion' (Bailey 2014: personal communication).

The fog of transparency: BLIND LIGHT

As stated the so-called gap in art and design education can be a gap in understanding, expectation or transition requirements. At this point we dig deeper into the gap by considering the role of transparency in higher education. The central idea is that if everything is clear, why are there any gaps? Much has been written about the centrality of the twin concepts of transparency and accountability (see, e.g., O'Neill 2002; Nowotny 2016). Current educational priorities valorise explicitness (Hall 2010), and ambiguity and uncertainty are viewed as 'irritations within a target driven culture' (Dineen and Collins 2005).

Transparency is the antithesis of ambiguity, but its widespread appeal in contemporary education merits consideration. Transparency can appear to empower students. For example, applicants to universities now have access to a very wide range of data intended to aid student choice. Full disclosure about a course is intended to make its content and assessment approaches 'clear' to students so that they make informed decisions about where, what and how they study. However, recent research (Diamond et al. 2014) looking into applicants' experience of engaging with these data reported that:

> having too much information can sometimes hamper effective judgement and decision-making, causing stress and reducing the ability to function effectively . . . providing additional sources of information does not necessarily lead to better informed people.
>
> (p. 5)

Similarly, in the field of marking and grading, there has been a huge increase in the volume of written information about assessment given to students. In Chapter 8 we will discuss the ways that transparency is viewed as a means to open up education for all by setting out the hidden curriculum and the un-codified rules of engagement. We report that outcome based assessment promised, but crucially did not deliver, transparent assessment (Ecclestone 1999). However, in spite of these shortcomings, for many people transparency is irresistible. In contemporary higher education clarity is viewed as a force for good that shines a light into the dark corners of the (often perceived as elitist) academy.

As a result, Art Schools have, over the last two decades, codified the practices of Art School pedagogy in course outlines, assessment criteria, learning outcomes and regulations. What is interesting about this is that transparency and text merge into one. The examples given underline that when transparency is called for, what is typically being asked is that a process or approach is captured in written form. The capturing of practices and policies of art and design education in text is assumed to aid clarity and transparency. How could one argue against such a thing? The idea of transparency as an un-problematised force for good is a Foucauldian truth in the university (Orr 2005). In this context the quest for transparency is predicated on the idea that an art and design education will, if a light is shone at it, reveal itself with precision and clarity. The gap will disappear. However, it is our contention that art and design cannot be fully revealed in this way. There is an ontological 'gap' at the centre of art and design education. Thus Valentine and Ivey (2009:157) refer to the very impossibility of getting near to the 'transparent communication of indeterminacy' in design. This underlines the paradoxical challenge facing anyone who seeks to clarify the nature of ambiguity in art and design education.

Returning to Gormley's box it is clear (!) that if we removed the fog and shone a light at the work, the work would no longer exist. By making it transparent we unmake it. The casting of light on the art changes the art. This then is what Tsoukas (2005:13) refers to as the 'tyranny of light'. Transparency unmakes. However in today's political context with its emphasis on low trust and accountability, it is hard to argue against clarity because to do so can sound like obfuscation. The erosion of government's trust in the university (Massy 2007) means that high levels of accountability are taken for granted. The hegemonic idea of transparency is that it simply illuminates the darkness, but the process of exposure changes everything. The dangers of transparency are reviewed by Strathern (2000) in an aptly titled paper called 'the tyranny of transparency'. Strathern (2000:310) asks the beguiling question: 'what does the quest for transparency conceal?' This question is addressed by O'Neill (2002), who introduces the idea of the fog of transparency. O'Neill points out that in a regime of transparency, we can be so eager to unpack all the rules that in the case of higher education, we can end up giving students so much written information about every aspect of their course that they would not be able to find the answer amongst the thousands of words offered; instead we offer them a fog of transparency or the fog of more.

The pursuit of transparency is premised on the idea that language is an un-sticky conduit that can convey knowledge in an unproblematic way and that language itself is transparent. This view of language can be traced back to Descartes, who presents language as a conveyor of information from person to person. However, taking a view of language as co-constructed and socially positioned, we work from the position that meaning co-evolves (Lillis 2008); meaning is made. Words come into meaning in interpretative communities. Recognising the stickiness of language, it becomes apparent that an educator who is trying to set out with clarity what a course or assignment consists of will always encounter a range of interpretations and perspectives when this information is shared with course teams and students. All words have a certain elasticity, and assumptions that suggest otherwise can lead to confusion. Course documents do not communicate in an unproblematic way; they need to be actively engaged with because language can never be completely explicit. For Burke (2002:65) 'the term transparency conceals that all texts are socially constructed and read by different subjects in different ways'. At worst students can be 'held to ransom by a discourse of transparency' (Lillis and Turner 2001:63/64) because an emphasis on transparency can lead to lecturers being afraid to recognise publically the intangible, elusive and opaque nature of some learning situations (Gordon 2004). In a visual practice based education there are non-linguistic elements that defy verbal or written explication.

Complicating this view of ambiguity as a necessary and welcome part of art and design education, we turn to the slippage between ambiguity and poor organisation. Feedback from art and design students suggests that they find their courses less well organised in comparison to students studying other subjects (Orr et al.

2014). There has been speculation about why this might be so (see, e.g., Yorke and Vaughan 2009). The key questions to ask are: what are the characteristics of a well-organised course, and why might art and design courses be less able to deliver this in comparison to other disciplines?

However much we seek to problematise the concept of clarity, it is important to note that in any university course, there are fixed elements that can be clearly communicated to students. For example, a well-organised course will have clear and publically available factual information concerning dates and structure. Any information given about an assignment on the virtual learning environment will match with the information handed out and talked about in the studio. The days and start and finish times for all activities can be clear, and the information can be readily available. Hand-in dates for the submission and return of work can be published. There is no creative advantage to ambiguity in any of these examples. When these elements of a course are secure, stable and clear, then the pedagogy of ambiguity can start to shape up. Students will be free to take risks and explore their creativity with confidence. They are not, in their lexicon, needing to 'sweat the small stuff'. So the question remains: are there any disciplinary based reasons why art and design courses may be less well organised than other subjects? There are three areas to consider in response to this question.

Firstly, as we explore in Chapter 5, the curriculum itself is ambiguous. Whilst curricula in all disciplines are contested and dynamic, Elkins (2001) observes that there is almost no agreement about what constitutes a core curriculum in art and design. A practice based art and design course cannot be organised by setting out key content coverage. Students work individually and collaboratively on projects that are emergent, and as a result their learning needs may not be apparent at the start of a given unit or module. For example, they might need to access certain skills workshops that need to be offered at short notice to address a learning need. Secondly the art and design curriculum could be described as an opportunistic curriculum. It needs to be responsive and agile. Thus if successful designers are unexpectedly 'between jobs' and available at short notice, they will come in at a time that suits them to talk to students. Equally an exhibition or competition opportunity may arise that course teams want to incorporate. Whether or not these short-notice opportunities delight the students (*'new opportunities great!'*) or frustrate the students (*'this clashes with my part-time job'*) will very much vary from student to student and their individual circumstances and perspectives. Thirdly it has been shown that higher education art and design is highly dependent on part-time staff (Yorke 2014). This brings many advantages. Practising artists bring currency and externality to the academy, but a part-time member of staff may not have the detailed knowledge about a course that a student may expect. For example they may not have co-written the assignments and projects and may struggle to respond to students' questions and requests for clarification. Equally they are less likely to respond to emails or be present on campus when they are not actually teaching students. Part-time tutors are likely to have other work commitments and are not paid to be available to respond to emails when not on site. Our key point is that there are particularities that make it challenging to deliver a well-organised course, but a pedagogy of ambiguity is not a cover for poor course organisation. A foundation of basic organisational clarity offers a bedrock for creativity.

We now turn to an exploration of ambiguity in relation to equality and diversity. Ambiguity is not to be conflated with elitism. To unpack this we return to the word gap and situate this word in the literature in relation to attainment outcomes. In higher education today there is an increasing recognition of the attainment gaps (also referred to as attainment differentials) based on social class, ethnicity and gender (Singh and Cowden 2016; Dhandi 2008). This so-called gap talk research (Gillborn 2008) surfaces persistent inequalities in education. In the UK Black and Minority Ethnic undergraduates are less likely to be awarded a 2:1 or a first-class degree when compared to white students, even when previous qualifications attained are controlled for (Steventon et al. 2016). Work to reduce these attainment differentials does not stigmatise or blame the learner for these gaps. As we explored in Chapter 3, attainment needs to be understood in relation to the wider social, cultural and political context. Cousin (2016) points out that when we discuss attainment differentials, it is essential that we avoid making generalisations about groups of students; she comments that 'there is nothing that typifies all BME students except vulnerability to racism and discrimination' (p. 205). A wariness of the implied individual deficit implicit in the idea of gap has led some to reject the use of the phrase attainment gap, preferring the term attainment differentials (Steventon et al. 2016). It can be uncomfortable for universities and Art Schools to admit openly to these attainment differentials, but an open discussion is vital if these inequalities are to be addressed.

If ambiguity is conflated with mystery or elitism, it could serve to disadvantage students. The reflexive employment of ambiguity in art and design education seeks to address rather than ignore attainment differentials. Working in post-apartheid South Africa, Behardien's (2014) study of fine art identity positions and assessment practices (discussed in Chapter 3) surfaces the hidden values in higher education fine art. She explores the ways that fine art lecturers privilege certain curriculum and pedagogic positions in ways that are not codified and may serve to exclude. Her work suggests that there is gap work to be done. The ambiguity imperative sits with a concomitant focus on trust, integrity, equality and diversity. If a student is applying to an Art School where the rules of engagement are not clear and there are hidden assumptions about access to culture, then this is a form of ambiguity that serves as a barrier to participation (Burke and McManus 2009). Richards and Finnigan (2014) offer useful case studies that illustrate ways that diversity and inclusion can be supported in art and design higher education settings.

Teaching ambiguity

Students have differing levels of tolerance in relation to uncertainty. One student's safe uncertainty is another student's chaotic nightmare. Fear allows little space for uncertainty (Nowotny 2016) and levels of peak anxiety; that is, the level of anxiety that is productive and creative rather than disabling, varies from student to student (Belluigi 2013). Unknowing can cause 'turbulence' for students (Valentine and Ivey 2009:157). Masson (1993) explores the cultural contexts that may affect the ways that people deal with and respond to uncertainty, and he argues that the ways we respond may be culturally determined. The key question to explore is who thrives and who just survives.

How best will we equip our students to thrive after graduation in the twenty-first century? As Barnett (2010) recognises, today's graduates need to understand multiple perspectives holding competing views simultaneously. As they graduate they will work and live in a 'landscape of infinitely elastic production' (Madoff 2009:x) where they will need to regard confusion as a natural state of affairs (Barnett 2010). These students need ambiguity for life. This might be what Ewing (2009:161) refers to as 'a kind of multidimensional thinking, what I call spherical thinking or thinking the whole'. A sticky and ambiguous curriculum prepares students for a sticky world post graduation.

If we recognise that it is important to help students learn to value ambiguity because they are 'effective prerequisites for creativity' (Belluigi 2013:10), then what are the implications for teaching? Supporting students to a place of 'authoritative uncertainty' will, particularly in the case of the creative industries, prepare graduates for the 'uncertain circumstances' of employment (Valentine and Ivey 2009:156).

This then is the end point: a position of productive ambiguity. Conceptualising a tolerance of ambiguity and uncertainty as a threshold concept in creative disciplines (Osmond 2009) means that we need to consider ways to help students transition into the Art School. To do this we provide safe environments that support risk taking which have 'an accepting and respectful climate' where students will feel 'psychologically and physically comfortable to explore uncertain, ambiguous avenues for their learning' (Belluigi 2013:9). As well as providing a supportive environment, lecturers can adopt pedagogic approaches that focus students' attention on any given project's uncertainty and impermanence (Valentine and Ivey 2009). Instead of minding the gap we need to build 'learning bridges' that can overcome stuck-ness and support students' transitions to new threshold concepts (Savin-Badin 2008:76). To build up students' tolerance of ambiguity, we offer students multiple 'little leaps into the not-known' (Atkinson 2012:11). During induction and through the course of study, ambiguity can be part of the conversation with students, and they can be given learning situations where they are asked to think about how uncomfortable they feel. This normalises the discomfort experienced by the students and surfaces the desirability of moving students up the scale of ambiguity within the sticky curriculum.

In Chapter 7 we explore the role of the project brief in art and design education. A well-written brief will enable students and lecturers to share an 'open ended, self-questioning approach to creativity, dissent, speculation and risk taking' (Buckley and Conomos 2009:18). The project can 'generate and make use of situations in which indeterminacy prevails' (Danvers 2003:53). A well-designed project assignment will employ purposively vague language to allow for divergent answers. It will *write in* ambiguity; there will be a gap at the centre of the brief (Hall 2010). An effective and creative brief poses questions to which no one answer can be given. It will give a vehicle to ask students questions that the lecturers do not know the answers to. The open-endedness of these project briefs seeks to echo the ambiguity that may be encountered post graduation (Valentine and Ivey 2009). Projects range from very open-ended to very constrained. This range is illustrated in the 224 examples of design education assignments presented by Paim et al. (2016). Within the 224 examples are projects that ask students to 'document dog' (p. 166); to 'research the graphics of a formerly colonized or occupied state/country when it becomes independent' (p. 182) and to photograph an object in a range of environments.

All studio practice assignments sit on what might be called a tight/loose spectrum that is calibrated to offer students an ecology of clarity and creativity. Examples of this ecology are explored further in Chapter 7, where we emphasise how important it is to balance these two elements. In all contexts, we need to find ways to 'contain uncertainty' (Barnett 2010:124) and manage students' panic in cases where some students in a studio can feel overwhelmed, while others are thriving. Students should be 'encouraged to progressively extend the arena of possibilities within which they operate, not to seek enduring solutions or answers' (Danvers 2003:50).

Expertise

The ambiguous studio decentres the expertise of the teacher. Earlier in the chapter we explored the ways that uncertainty can be viewed as something that the university offers and can take away, and we identified that lecturers can scaffold ambiguity in reflexive ways to support learning. However, in arguing that ambiguity may be fashioned and scaffolded to support learning, it is important to note that we are not presenting the lecturer as a Prospero conjuring up ambiguity for the benefit of others. The lecturers themselves are positioned in the ambiguous studio. To explore this we turn to the idea of the 'ignorant school master' (Rancière 1991). As we explore in Chapters 5 and 7, art and design pedagogy decentres traditional ideas of expert and novice. When a student responds to a brief and takes it in ways that are unanticipated by the lecturer, what is the lecturer's knowledge base in relation to that of the student? The lecturer needs to feel comfortable with the idea that the students' learning will take them beyond the lecturer. The lecturer, like Rancière's ignorant school master, is taken to a place of unknowing and can use this unknowing to support the students' learning. Rancière, citing the pedagogic principles expounded by Jacotot, says that teachers need to reject the traditional role as one who explicates superior knowledge and must instead adopt a position of shared ignorance. The teacher supports students on their own self-determined learning journeys. As Peters (2010:100) observes, 'Ignorance does not (or should not) stop one from being a [art and design] teacher, indeed a proper understanding of ignorance might make one a very good teacher indeed'. This leads us to a position in which 'one can teach what one doesn't know' (Rancière 1991:15). This is tolerating ambiguity and teaching ambiguity. As an undergraduate student reported in Orr et al. (2014:34), the lecturers 'are not telling you the answer because there is no answer'.

Rancière points to the need for teachers to connect with what the students know, to find the place where the students know and to support them from that place to new learning. Interestingly this view of the student is in opposition to the idea that Art School students need to 'unlearn'.

Osmond's (2009) research suggests that a toleration of uncertainty in design education is truly transformatory for students, and her work underlines that encouraging students to embrace uncertainty is a worthwhile endeavour. Nowotny (2016), in a wonderfully titled book *The cunning of uncertainty*, suggests that understanding uncertainty as a creative and productive process can help students cross disciplinary boundaries. This is an effective way to be mindful of the gap when a student makes the transition into art and design higher education.

Conclusion

To conclude, can we (re)insert ambiguity into this chapter? Can we purposively leave this chapter messy, sticky, open, foggy and unresolved? Can we leave the reader to speculate and fill in the answers? We want our students to feel able to sustain themselves through 'periods of working "in the dark" . . . not sure of what is happening' (Danvers 2003:53). Can we work in the dark as well? Can we model a tolerance for uncertainty (Belluigi 2013)?

What else can we do? If we capture the ambiguity, we have lost the ambiguity. This is the central paradox. We are working with epistemological uncertainty (Barnett 2010). Our key point is that there is a tension between creativity and clarity and that we need to come to an accommodation of the latter to allow for the former. We need to live with the stickiness and discomfort of not knowing all the answers, but to support students' learning, we also need to establish clear frameworks and structures. These dilemmas cannot be 'cleared up'. We need to tolerate the fog and its uncertainty. We need to go further; we embrace uncertainty. Earlier in this chapter we cite Atkinson (2012), who calls on us to create opportunities for students to make small leaps into the unknown. To support our students' small leaps we draw attention to Welsh (2009), who in a polemical consideration of the future of the Art School in the twenty-first century, exhorts us to leap into the void. As educators, teachers and researchers, we need to make the big leap into the gaps.

References

Atkinson, D., 2012. Contemporary Art and Art in Education: The New, Emancipation and Truth. *International Journal of Art & Design Education*, 31(1), pp. 5–18.

Austerlitz, N., Blythman, M., Grove-White, A., Jones, B. A., Jones, C. A., Morgan, S., Orr. S., Shreeve, A. and Vaughan, S., 2008. Mind the Gap: Expectations,

Ambiguity and Pedagogy Within Art and Design Education. In L. Drew, ed. *The Student Experience in Art and Design Higher Education: Drivers for Change*. Cambridge: Jill Rogers Associates Ltd Publishers, pp. 125–148.

Barnett, R., 2010. *Being a University*. Oxford: Taylor & Francis.

Behardien, I., 2014. *'Who Are They' or 'What and How They Know': An Investigation by a Fine Art Lecturer Into the Basis of Her Own Legitimacy*. Unpublished MPhil Thesis. University of Cape Town.

Belluigi, D. Z., 2013. A Proposed Schema for the Conditions of Creativity in Fine Art Studio Practice. *International Journal of Education & the Arts*, 14(19), pp. 1–22.

Bentz, V. and Shapiro, J., 1998. *Mindful Inquiry in Social Research*. London: SAGE Publications.

Bogh, M., 2009. Borderlands: The Art School Between the Academy and Higher Education. In B. Buckley and J. Conomos, eds. *Rethinking the Contemporary Art School: The Artist, the PhD and the Academy*. Halifax: The Press of the Nova Scotia College of Art and Design, pp. 64–75.

Brassettt, J. and Rhodes, N., 2013. *Workshop: Kill the Art School – Central Saint Martins – University of the Arts London*. Available at: www.arts.ac.uk/csm/csm-culture/events/whats-the-point-of-art-school/workshop-kill-the-art-school/ [Accessed July 25, 2014].

Buckley, B. and Conomos, J., 2009. Introduction. In B. Buckley and J. Conomos, eds. *Rethinking the Contemporary Art School: The Artist, the PhD and the Academy*. Halifax: The Press of the Nova Scotia College of Art and Design, pp. 2–26.

Burke, P. J., 2002. *Accessing Education Effectively Widening Participation*. London: Trentam Books.

Burke, P. J. and McManus, J., 2009. *Art for a Few: Exclusion and Misrecognition in Art and Design Higher Education Admissions*. London: NALN.

Cousin, G., 2016. Issues, Controversies and Debates: Concluding Thoughts. In G. Steventon, D. Cureton and D. L. Clouder, eds. *Student Attainment in Higher Education: Issues Controversies and Debates*. London and New York: Routledge, pp. 204–208.

Danvers, J., 2003. Towards a Radical Pedagogy: Provisional Notes on Learning and Teaching in Art & Design. *International Journal of Art and Design Education*, 22(1), pp. 47–57.

Dhandi, M., 2008. *Understanding Disparities in Student Attainment: Black and Minority Ethnic Students' Experience*, pp. 1–50. Available at: http://www2.wlv.ac.uk/equalopps/mdsummary.pdf [Accessed February 25, 2017].

Diamond, D. A., Roberts, F., Vorley, T., Birkin, G., Evans, J., Sheen, J. and Nathwani, S., 2014. *Provision of Information Advisory Study and Literature Review*. Report to the UK Higher Education Funding Bodies by CFE Research.

Dineen, R. and Collins, E., 2005. Killing the Goose: Conflicts Between Pedagogy and Politics in the Delivery of a Creative Education. *International Journal of Art & Design Education*, 24(1), pp. 43–52.

Ecclestone, K., 1999. Empowering or Ensnaring?: The Implications of Outcome-based Assessment in Higher Education. *Higher Education Quarterly*, 53(1), pp. 29–48.

Elkins, J., 2001. *Why Art Cannot Be Taught: A Handbook for Art Students*. Champaign, IL: University of Illinois Press.

Ewing, L., 2009. Remixing the Hive. In B. Buckley and J. Conomos, eds. *Rethinking the Contemporary Art School: The Artist, the PhD and the Academy*. Halifax: The Press of the Nova Scotia College of Art and Design, pp. 159–163.

Gillborn, D., 2008. Coincidence or Conspiracy? Whiteness, Policy and the Persistence of the Black/White Achievement Gap. *Educational Review*, 60(3), pp. 229–248.

Gordon, J., 2004. The 'Wow' Factors: The Assessment of Practical Media and Creative Arts Subjects. *Art, Design & Communication in Higher Education*, 3(1), pp. 61–72.

Hall, J., 2010. Making Art, Teaching Art, Learning Art: Exploring the Concept of the Artist Teacher. *International Journal of Art & Design Education*, 29(2), pp. 103–110.

Lillis, T., 2008. *Student Writing: Access, Regulation, Desire*. London and New York: Routledge.

Lillis, T. and Turner, J., 2001. Student Writing in Higher Education: Contemporary Confusion, Traditional Concerns. *Teaching in Higher Education*, 6(1), pp. 57–68.

Madoff, S. H., 2009. *Art School (Propositions for the 21st Century)*. Cambridge, MA: MIT Press.

Masson, B., 1993. Towards Positions of Safe Uncertainty. *The Journal of Systemic Consultation & Management*, 4, pp. 189–200.

Massy, W. F., 2007. *Honoring the Trust: Quality and Cost Containment in Higher Education*. Bolton, MA: Anker Publishing Company.

Nowotny, H., 2016. *The Cunning of Uncertainty*. Cambridge: Polity.

O'Neill, O., 2002. BBC:Radio 4. Reith Lectures 2002. *A Question of Trust*. Available at: www.bbc.co.uk/radio4/reith2002/lecture4.shtml [Accessed July 25, 2014].

Orr, S., 2005. Transparent Opacity: Assessment in the Inclusive Academy. In C. Rust, ed. *Improving Student Learning: Diversity and Inclusivity*. Oxford: Centre for Staff and Learning Development, pp. 175–187.

Orr, S., Yorke, M. and Blair, B., 2014. 'The Answer Is Brought About From Within You': A Student-Centred Perspective on Pedagogy in Art and Design. *International Journal of Art & Design Education*, 33(1), pp. 32–45.

Osmond, J., 2009. 'Stuck in a Bubble': Identifying Threshold Concepts in Design. In D. Clews, ed. *Dialogues in Art and Design: Promoting and Sharing Excellence*. York: ADM HEA/GLAD, pp. 130–135.

Paim, N., Gisel, C. and Bergmark, E., 2016. *Taking a Line for a Walk: Assignments in Design Education*. Leipzig: Spector Books.

Peters, G., 2010. Ignorant Artists/Ignorant Teachers. In T. Claes and D. Seth, eds. *Frontiers in Higher Education*. Amsterdam: Rodopi Press, pp. 99–112.

Rancière, J., 1991. *The Ignorant Schoolmaster: Five Lessons in Intellectual Emancipation*. Redwood: Stanford University Press.

Richards, A. and Finnigan, T., 2014. *Embedding Equality and Diversity in the Curriculum: An Art and Design Practitioner's Guide*. York: Higher Education Academy.

Savin-Badin, M., 2008. Liquid Learning and Troublesome Spaces. In R. Land, H. Myer and J. Smith, eds. *Threshold Concepts Within the Disciplines*. Rotterdam: Sense Publishers, pp. 75–88.

Shreeve, A., Sims, E. and Trowler, P., 2010. 'A Kind of Exchange': Learning From Art and Design Teaching. *Higher Education Research & Development*, 29(2), pp. 125–138.

Singh, G. and Cowden, S., 2016. Intellectuality, Student Attainment and the Contemporary Higher Education System. In G. Steventon, D. Cureton and D. L. Clouder, eds. *Student Attainment in Higher Education: Issues Controversies and Debates*. Oxon: Routledge, pp. 82–97.

Steventon, G., Cureton, D. and Clouder, L., 2016. *Student Attainment in Higher Education: Issues, Controversies and Debates.* London and New York: Routledge.

Strathern, M., 2000. The Tyranny of Transparency. *British Educational Research Journal*, 26(3), pp. 309–321.

Svennson, L. and Edstrom, A. M., 2011. The Function of Art Students' Use of Studio Conversations in Relation to Their Artwork. *International Journal of Education and the Arts*, 12(5), pp. 1–29.

Tsoukas, H., 2005. *Complex Knowledge: Studies in Organizational Epistemology.* Oxford: Oxford University Press.

Valentine, L. and Ivey, M., 2009. Sustaining Ambiguity and Fostering Openness in the (Design) Learning Environment. *Art, Design & Communication in Higher Education*, 7(3), pp. 155–167.

Welsh, J., 2009. Transitions, Dialogues, Interuptions, Pregnant Pauses, and Leaps Into the Void: Recent Experiences in Norwegian Higher Art Education. In B. Buckley and J. Conomos, eds. *Rethinking the Contemporary Art School: The Artist, the PhD and the Academy.* Halifax: The Press of the Nova Scotia College of Art and Design, pp. 206–214.

Yorke, M., 2014. The Impact of Part-time Staff on Art & Design Students' Ratings of Their Programmes. *Journal of Higher Education Policy and Management*, 36(5), pp. 557–567.

Yorke, M. and Vaughan, D, 2009. 'I Can't Believe It's Not Better': The Paradox of NSS Scores for Art & Design. *Higher Education Academy.* Available at: www.adm.heacademy.ac.uk/library/files/adm-hea-projects/glad-nss-project/nss-report170310.pdf [Accessed February 3, 2017].

Part 2

Art and design education practices

5 The sticky curriculum in art and design

Identity and engagement

Introduction

We have discussed various aspects of learning and teaching in art and design and focused particularly on knowledge and knowing, values and ambiguity (Chapters 2–4). We have indicated already that we perceive university learning in these disciplines as something which is inherently sticky; that is, it is characterised by ambiguity in learning, multiple kinds of knowledge which are present often simultaneously and which change rapidly, including tacit knowledge and practices which might be taken for granted within existing learning communities. We also described values which are constructed, co-constructed and structured to include or exclude some students, however unwittingly. Values help recreate reflections of the creative practitioner, but learning in the university also promotes innovation, new identities and new ways of working. Students are encouraged to create new and innovative products, processes, communications and responses to the world. We have suggested that many situations in art and design pedagogy are sticky. In this chapter we will explore more thoroughly what we perceive as the sticky curriculum and the impact this has on individuals.

For us the curriculum is a complex entity, including historical canons, icons of practice which provide exemplars for students, technologies and techniques, but also multiple practices (Weller 2012) requiring ways of being and becoming within the creative milieu of our complex worlds. Courses create cultures or microcultures with their own characteristics and practices, that is, teaching and learning regimes (Trowler and Cooper 2002), or to put it another way, they create sticky curricula that are varied, unpredictable and challenging for those engaging as learners and teachers. There is an ontological dimension to the curriculum (Dall'Alba and Barnacle 2007) as identity work is carried out. In this view of curriculum, the students, tutors, technicians and others who support learning bring their identities and ways of being into the learning process. They all engage with particular kinds of knowledge linked to the discipline specialism they are learning, and their roles and responsibilities change as knowledge is absorbed, challenged and created in creative subjects. The construction or legitimisation of particular forms and kinds of knowledge is, as Ashwin (2014) argues, a site of struggle as 'different voices seek to impose particular versions of legitimate knowledge, curriculum and student understanding' (Ashwin 2014:124).

For students this engagement in creative curricula is a mixture of 'knowing, acting and being' (Barnett and Coate 2005:2) enabled by an educational designed environment. Here students are encouraged to build disciplinary identities for themselves based on values, skills, practices, beliefs, an awareness of the world beyond the university and their projected and envisioned place within it. Inevitably this environment is shaped by political, social and personal agendas and always framed by what has gone before and what is introduced or valued by society in the present, embodied in those who help facilitate learning within the university (Belluigi 2016). This curriculum provides affordances for student actions and creative practices rather than prescribed routes. There may well be skills development offered, 'how to' activities which build up a repertoire, the number of these depending on the sub-discipline studied. Increasingly students may be locating their own skill sets from software or YouTube on the Internet, acquiring just-in-time knowledge and tools to realise creative ideas. The space where learning takes place (virtual or real) will shape affordances too; if making a vast collaborative sculpture is possible when the space offers up that opportunity, this might well be experienced; otherwise, this opportunity will be absent. Materials, tools and processes are potential affordances and play a part in the variable curriculum experienced by students across and within the creative disciplines. So also is access to industry, work experience, live projects, international travel and study; all of which are valued in different measure as part of the creative curriculum and may or may not be available to students due to prevailing trends, practices and budgetary constraints. The affordances offered through the curriculum constitute the curriculum, but there also has to be engagement by learners, for without the enactment of curriculum, it remains only a possibility for learning.

Engagement and non-engagement

This view of curriculum (as with Barnett and Coate 2005) presupposes that students will engage with the learning activities which are offered, but this is not always the case (Mann 2001). Logan (2013) describes the kinds of qualities which tutors expect in their fine art students, including 'diligence', 'hard work', 'motivation', 'focus' and 'responsibility' (p. 38). Students are expected to be committed to the subject and to their peers and tutors who are engaged in learning in a studio environment. The commitment to hard work is common throughout art and design as 'the work' is the centre of the creative practice. The 'work' is also synonymous with the person of the student and is an integral part of their professional identity. As one student says in Logan's study, 'Your work is you' (p. 44). These ideas are explored further in Chapter 8.

Students may develop an identity of participation or non-participation (Wenger 1998) in the community of practice which the course represents. Students who do not demonstrate the behaviours and attitudes expected by tutors are likely to be those who are failing (as discussed in Chapter 3) or who hold strong convictions at odds with the prevailing cultural ethos of the course. Engagement is therefore seen as a prerequisite for success, requiring adjustment of the self and presenting a sticky set of values and actions to negotiate. Deakin Crick (2012) suggests that engagement in learning is involvement in a system of systems; that is, there are personal, social and global networks which all interact, not simply single aspects which create or prevent engagement with learning. Such a complex view of engagement is also mirrored by a rich learning environment, or curriculum, which inseparably links knowledge, identity of participants, social practices and discourses in art and design. This is a sticky curriculum, complex, rich, mutable, negotiable and variable, linked to practices beyond the university, and sometimes this creates a difficult place in which students, tutors and those who support learning have to negotiate their interactions around learning and teaching.

In terms of the experienced curriculum, the wide range of definitions of sticky which we associate with learning and teaching in art and design (see Chapter 1) manifest themselves in multiple ways. The complexity of knowledge, including tacit knowledge in professional learning, has been discussed earlier, as have the values inherent in art and design. These are not static, monolithic or unchangeable, but there are hegemonies which extend across the sector, and these might not be the same values as students entering higher education have been used to (Austerlitz et al. 2008). Ambiguity, as we have seen, pervades the learning situation, providing space for individual creation and interpretation. The potentially positive or negative perceptions of situations are inherent in the learning environment, where projects and activities may be interpreted by individuals as rich in potential or as a vague morass (more on this in Chapter 7). For some the experience is positive, and they feel very much at home and in fact need to become at home with ambiguity to succeed (Osmond 2009). The ambiguity or stickiness provides opportunities for success or failure and much rests on the individual who is required to create their own response and, indeed, to become an artist or designer. Thus individuals need to develop confidence and self-efficacy to successfully negotiate the curriculum (Zimmerman et al. 1992).

Negotiation is a sticky activity, and students will need determination. Each encounter with tutors and peers has an affective dimension which requires work on the part of the participants, a point which we return to later in this chapter. The characters present in the learning environment include students' peers, those on the course who are ahead in terms of time spent in higher education, tutors, technicians and others supporting learning, such as learning centre staff. The presence of multiple individuals requires teamwork and co-operation whilst developing and maintaining 'a personal handwriting', or ownership of the creative output. Many projects (particularly in the field of design education) now require students to work in teams, with the community, or professional bodies, work which requires confidence and negotiation of potentially sticky positions. The paradox of individual recognisable contribution to teamwork and working with the success of the team in mind is present in such projects (Orr 2010). Such built-in stickiness can be a deliberate strategy to develop and extend students' learning potential as stickiness in the curriculum offers the possibility of creative responses, presenting thought-provoking challenges.

Creative disruption

In many cases the stability of teaching environments is deliberately disturbed to create space which fosters new ways to 'exchange' (Shreeve et al. 2010). Examples include working across different years within one course, where students will participate in Crits or engage in extra-curriculum projects. There may be structural curriculum change to enable cross-disciplinary working on shared live projects, those with partners outside the university (see Chapter 6 for further definition of live briefs). For example, the Global Studio has an international dimension using technology (Ghassan and Bohemia 2015). In the Global Studio tutors set a framework and theme, but the project is student led. Small groups of students at two different global locations act as both client team and designer team, exchanging views to develop design solutions in a given time frame for their locality. Such projects enabled by new technologies help develop students' 'intercultural sensitivity' (p. 228). Similarly, Unit X, a module which ran across art and design disciplines as a common unit within the curriculum, described by Cocchiarella and Booth (2015), created a 'vertical studio' designed 'to establish new working conditions between tutor, student and place' (p. 327). These kinds of projects disrupt the norms of learning in the university, encouraging the roles of learner and teacher to be subverted.

There is increasing interest in the co-creation of curriculum in higher education (Bovill 2013). In many respects students have always constructed their own curricula in art and design as they are making choices constantly about what route to follow and how to become a creative practitioner, but these decisions are usually made within specified boundaries. The student's role in the production of an individualised curriculum is explored in Chapter 7. True co-construction of curriculum is a very sticky place to be for all participants but can be transformative (Bergmark and Westman 2016). In this kind of co-construction the students make decisions about what and how subjects are studied as well as being active participants in learning. Bovill (2014) suggests that this kind of co-construction changes the tutor's role and requires them to be a 'facilitator of learning' (p. 22). Our view is that the teacher's role is not diminished as a facilitator but remains powerfully educative (see Chapter 7). Enabling totally transformative co-curriculum planning is likely to be 'experienced as vulnerable, troublesome, uncomfortable, and sometimes even threatening' (Bergmark and Westman 2016:33). In an art and design curriculum, the co-construction usually takes place within tutor-controlled frameworks, seldom requiring students to tackle the underlying core principles of what might be learnt and how it might be learnt but enabling them to follow routes which are self-identified. This paradoxically offers power through self-determined actions but also obscures the learning that often takes place. Students therefore might find it hard to articulate or even recognise the learning and structured curriculum designed by the tutor, making learning in art and design sticky for students to acknowledge.

Other opportunities to create the curriculum and offer up different and challenging learning opportunities, or to create 'stickiness', might lie outside the formal, that is, assessed, curriculum. Evaluation of such a project (Smith 2015) found that co-production in the learning activity increased autonomy for all participants. Here students, tutors and technicians worked together under the leadership of students in a 'third-space' project specifically designed to enable co-production in learning. The change in roles of all participants led to ambiguity but also recognition that autonomy increased for students: 'It is possible that co-production afforded them the opportunity to become more professional workers, or more questioning students – a growing autonomy emerging due to the elastic roles taken by the tutors' (Smith 2015:31). For the technicians in this collaborative project, it increased their job satisfaction and created more meaningful approaches from students to the technical resources they controlled:

> it's a different story this kind of collaboration I think is what really makes things change. And actually the little things you start to work on together, it just opens up other doors for other students, it's not just for this project. . . . I think this is the way that in university we should work, like technician, academic, student working together in projects.
>
> (Smith 2015:46/7)

Opportunities for collaborative learning are frequently taken up through competitions and non-assessed opportunities that arise with partners in the community and in industry who are keen to have new and fresh ideas which students can bring to a situation. Managing these can be a challenge to a planned, structured curriculum, albeit one which has unknown outcomes as it disrupts 'normal' studio life and adds to the complexity and sticky nature of learning opportunities planned by the tutor.

Formal and informal components

Stickiness in the curriculum is also present because of tensions within and between formal and informal elements of the learning environment. The growth of the written elements of curriculum could be said to represent the formal curriculum. In the UK the Quality Assurance Agency requires courses to demonstrate that they meet the benchmark statements for different subject areas. These statements are compiled by panels of experts in the field and include learning outcomes which denote the kinds of abilities students are expected to achieve at different levels of their study. When validating new programmes of learning, universities require academics to demonstrate where and how students are going to be supported to achieve these learning outcomes. However, like many written approximations of complex practices, there is room for interpretation and variation in mapping out the curriculum; the documents are sticky. These documents might be described as the formal curriculum, a road map which guides the detailed planning of learning, but certainly does not encompass everything a student might learn through engaging in the curriculum.

The non-reified aspects of learning in the curriculum, sticky elements because they are harder to pin down, are less formally acknowledged. Values and tacit knowledge which are difficult or impossible to articulate constitute the inherent tacit dimension within professional practice (Eraut 2000; Polanyi 1967). The sticky curriculum composed of the formal (reified) and informal (hard-to-identify or non-assessed) aspects of knowing and being both coexist in higher education, again adding to the stickiness of the curriculum. Particular discourses, or literacies, whether verbal, written or visual, are all present, and the latter are particularly hard to articulate.

Relations in the learning environment

Atkinson (2015) suggests that the dominant models of education sit within the known, structured by hegemonic rules of assessment and audit with defined outcomes and roles of teacher and learner. Through art practice he posits an alternative, 'more uncertain pedagogical adventure' focusing on 'a subject yet to come' and where the 'not-known' is central to the endeavour. Within this art based scenario, Atkinson sees pedagogic work as 'an on-going process of intra-relating, a series of material entanglements through which what we call teachers and learners emerge' (Atkinson 2015:43). In this view of education subjectivities are important and central to the exchanges which pertain to learning and teaching. These descriptions characterise many approaches in the art and design higher education curriculum, where relations between participants are fluid and circumstances create and construct different roles and expectations.

The relationships amongst roles in the project cited (Smith 2015) are indicative of complex fluctuation and elasticity of roles and responsibilities in creative learning and teaching. Smith identifies changes in relations and the expectations of roles of learner, teacher and technician and of the kind of knowledge expected to emerge from such interactions. Through changes in relations amongst participants, the learning environment became sticky. This flux in relations within the learning and teaching environment can enhance creative education, but this demands a certain kind of performativity from tutors who, as well as deliberately disrupting the environment, may have to disrupt their own identities or subjectivities in action. Relations are central to learning in the university (Ashwin 2009). The traversing of sticky situations, being able to swap roles and allow emergent roles to evolve, is pervasive in studio environments, which demonstrate flexibility in pedagogies and epistemologies (Cennamo 2016). Tutors may move from the ignorant school master (Rancière 1991) to guide, to instructor, as mediator or enforcer, given changing contexts and environments and 'intra-actions' (Atkinson 2015:48).

Boling's (2016) description of being a studio teacher provides an insight into the complexity and reflexive nature required:

> Lecture-based teaching can be tiring, but studio teaching can be exhausting. When I am not responding to one student, I am working to draw out

> another one, maintaining sustained attention on all parts of the classroom as I do so. There is little distance between me and my students, so their actions and reactions to what happens in class affect me, in my perception, more than they would in my non-studio classes. In the studio, I inhabit a position of co-responsibility for problem solving together with my students, but I have to assess their progress and their products separately from my own input. This requires me to monitor myself all the time I am teaching, as well as when I am assessing my students' performance. Have I modelled and demonstrated design thinking to scaffold their development, or have I usurped their position in our partnership? The right balance is different for every student at every stage, so this equation has to be re-figured continuously. The students surprise me constantly. When I do not structure their actions in advance they go further and faster than I was used to in pre-studio versions of this course. Unlike a course in which my interactions with students are tied to defined milestones achieved through prescribed actions, the in-class interactions previously described are never routine. I find studio teaching to be exhilarating as well, however. With practice, I have built confidence in my ability to respond to whatever comes up without having to respond with a solution. In fact, while it requires great effort, I do relax into the reactive nature of this form of teaching and experience the effort as a positive flow of action.
>
> (Boling 2016:98–99)

The description of studio teaching highlights the constant evaluation and judgements made by the teacher in relation to students as individual learners. She notes that the students' progress may be unexpected and faster than anticipated. The student and tutor relationship lies at the heart of the learning experience, and for the student it is a relationship in which emotions are integral (Austerlitz and Aravot 2006). The exchanges between student and tutor are influenced by the affective response elicited in the student, and this will be influenced by the goals and perceptions of the student: 'students constantly evaluate their successes and particularly, their status, according to the tutor's reactions. They do that before, during and after any dialogue, and dwell on it extensively' (Austerlitz and Aravot 2006:94). These authors claim that student emotional responses are some of the most important ways students evaluate their studio encounters and 'interpret the meaning of dialogue with tutors' (p. 95). The affective is always present in the learning environment but seldom acknowledged, certainly not in any reified form. Emotions are linked to expectations and stances underlying goals or objectives and can reveal deeply held values such as justice or fairness. Each encounter may have an emotional response, and each requires adjustment to the sense of self and the relationships with others in a dynamic interplay amongst the participants in studio learning.

A small-scale study identified just how complex the student-tutor relationship might be, with some students finding relationships with some tutors difficult to manage, whilst others identified when the relationship worked really well and the borderline between friend and friendly was exactly right, enabling students to grow as individuals:

> I think my tutors have got it right. They know what they're doing; they've done it for a while. They are experienced and talk to you like adults and will debate with you but it's also like with a learning curve you can talk to your tutors and can have a debate as long as it's in a polite manner and you're not being rude or anything, it is that sort of growing up that you personally have to do in order to understand your tutors properly so it's definitely a two way thing, you have to do some growing up before you can understand them but I think they have got it right and talk to you in the way you expect to be talked to and they talk to you with respect. You do develop a relationship with your tutors but it's a healthy working relationship. They don't become scary, they come like work colleagues in a way, they're someone you can ask questions with and someone you work with because you are both working to the same thing, they are working to you coming out with the best degree you can. Interesting.
>
> Your tutors are there to help you grow and will teach you a lot if you let them and work with them.
>
> (Student cited in Shreeve and Batchelor 2012:24)

Tutors in this study also recognised that the relationship, based on an equitable respect on both sides, was an ideal which they aspired to, but within the interviews with tutors, there was evidence of carefully managed boundaries and control which maintained a 'professional distance' (p. 23). Barriers to good learning relations from the tutor's perspective included: the pressure of workloads with constraints placed on the time they had in face-to-face contact with students and increasing administrative workloads; poor teaching and tutorial spaces; different cultural expectations of the learning relationship within the discipline; students wanting their work to be liked by the tutor rather than have an honest critique or students appearing to be uninterested in their studies. The gender of the tutor and the imbalance of one gender or another in certain disciplines (e.g., in the UK textiles is predominantly female and industrial design predominantly male) was also felt to be a factor in learning relations; female tutors were perceived as more sympathetic and caring. This could be an advantage or not, but female students in a primarily male discipline reported that it was definitely an advantage to have a female tutor. Female tutors, on the other hand, felt that they could be perceived to have a different role to their male colleagues, particularly if they were in a predominantly male discipline; they felt as if they were more likely to be perceived as caring and to take on those personas rather than those of professional expert (Shreeve and Batchelor, unpublished outcomes from the same research project). The researchers also felt that there were some instances of tutors adopting parental roles (maternal or paternal) within the relationship where in extremes, they were positioning students as children, creating stickiness which students resented and potential dependencies which were alien to the independent working and development of neophyte professionals which underpins higher education learning (Shreeve and Batchelor 2012).

The curriculum as a sticky site of engagement is subject to the individual tutor's encounters with students within a particular time frame and is also influenced by the way they perceive the relationship between their practice and teaching roles. The interactions between the tutor and the student in a learning environment are negotiated and sometimes limited by the tutor's experiences, which might lead to them withholding certain kinds of experiential information (Shreeve 2011; Shreeve 2009) or conversely facilitate access to the way in which they experience their creative practice – knowing when to be a friend, but not be too friendly (Shreeve and Batchelor 2012), being an authority figure, an expert, being ignorant or a counsellor. Supporting learning is a performative act and an act of translation from professional sphere to university. The identity of the tutor is complex, and the relations with students in the process of learning calls on different aspects of their identity at different times or an ongoing adjustment to their persona. As a conduit to the world beyond the university (the creative practice), the tutor has a very distinctive agency on the curriculum for their students, but the sticky curriculum in the studio is a state of flux in terms of roles and identity construction for all participants. Decisions have to be made and courses of action determined, frequently in challenging, ambiguous situations entailing difficult evaluations. Knowledge is emergent, dynamic and newly created and is not the sole province of the tutor. The act of teaching might be perceived as a 'performative paradox' (Buckley and Conomos 2009:17) in which the actions of the tutor are obscured as they appear not to be teaching.

The tutor however is placed in a position which requires a professional response to teaching. There is a great deal of autonomy still within the studio environment, where tutors are positioned and largely in control of what and how they teach. This is a position of trust. It demands appropriate translation of creative practice into learning activities which will enable students to become or to identify as a creative practitioner.

The tripartite teaching team

There are other critical contributors to student learning in art and design. There are those working in the 'third space' (Whitchurch 2013), brokering learning opportunities perhaps, or in outreach work enabling access to university or in supporting learning through the development of study skills. The latter are most likely to be working on writing practices and academic conventions for the art and design student (see, e.g., the Writing PAD website, http://writing-pad.org/HomePage). However, the most important group of staff, about whom very little is known, are the technicians who frequently constitute the stable and accessible aspects of learning, more likely to be present and available than tutors, who have multiple calls on their time at the university, including admissions, research and administration. The technicians are likely to be based in a workshop or technical resources environment, with a home base which provides assistance with making skills, whether using digital tools, textiles, metal or other materials. The technical teams support student access to processes and making, enabling learning in a less formal way than with tutors. They are more likely to be available on an ad hoc basis throughout the week; they do not form part of the assessment process and therefore have different power relations with students (Blythman et al. 2008). As part of the support teams within creative learning environments, technicians also partly inhabit the 'third space' or a sticky space, where there is ambiguity and conflicting identity work also taking place (Whitchurch 2013).

The relationship between technicians and academics, as anyone who has worked in higher education art and design will know, can be fraught with difficulties and challenges about boundaries between teaching and technical roles and responsibilities. Where good working relationships exist, the technical team becomes part of a constructive, albeit mutable, relationship in which the objective is helping students to learn. In this kind of environment, there is no doubt about the technician's role in supporting and helping students. In the following example the technician clearly has similar conceptions of their role in student learning to many tutors; they are part of a mutual learning relationship or 'partners in a learning community' (Little et al. 2009:7). They are undertaking 'a kind of exchange' which might be considered to be teaching by a different technician in a different institution or a different time.

> Their [students'] relationship to us or the technical resources is obviously about equipment and processes but it's also about conversation and about dialogue and about learning together . . . you're learning about how people approach things, how they think about things.
>
> (Technician quoted in Blythman et al. 2008:517)

The equipment which enables production of student ideas is also important to the technical teams. With more access to state-of-the-art, professional-level equipment, technicians felt more able to help students and felt valued within the organisation. With investment in equipment technician confidence in their role increased (Blythman et al. 2008).

Technicians are increasingly the more stable part of a relationship in learning, consisting of student, tutor and technician. Peer learning, the mutable and multiple roles of the tutor in studio based learning and the access to process, materials and advice frequently provided by the technical support teams are all part of what might be termed a 'tripartite teaching team' in art and design. In the example of co-construction of curriculum cited earlier in the chapter (Smith 2015), the technicians identify that the increased autonomy they experienced through a student-led project also helped them feel part of the learning team. Increased partnership or collaboration in learning may lead to more stickiness in the curriculum, but it also leads to greater learning for all participants with an increased sense of autonomy for all at various times in the relationship.

Student identity

Identity is always present for students. This is linked to the roles and perceptions of the roles they undertake, but for the student the curriculum is the vehicle for a process of becoming a creative practitioner (see Chapter 7 for further explanation). They are learning to think and act as professionals (Shulman 2005), but they are there to create their own versions of knowledge fashioned from the dialogic exchange present in the studio, online and with peers. The ability to articulate a critical view and to defend one's own work are the key factors which demonstrate the ability to be a creative professional, that and the production of the 'work'. Inherent within this are facets of identity work (Taylor and Littleton 2006) which are ongoing projects of the self (Giddens 1991). Within the actions and interactions of learning, students are working out new forms of identity as knowledge, practices, beliefs and values are presented through engagement in learning. This is expressed by a student who took part in a series of workshops exploring emotions in learning creative subjects where she positions the artist self as a decidedly sticky project with positive and negative aspects to becoming:

> The artist self could be defined as the intangible aspect of the artist. It is in a state of dynamic flux. In order to grow, the artist self has to develop an openness and flexibility of mind and spirit to constantly construct and reconstruct meanings about concepts, processes and ideas regarding developing visual language within art practice. The artist self is mutable and fluid. In my case, it was experienced as elusive and mercurial, exciting and equally frustrating. It could be argued that this constant reconstruction and reframing of the learning experience that defines the artist self as opposed to other student learning experiences.
>
> (Okuleye 2008:194)

In spite of this idea of exclusivity around the constant reframing and reconstruction work which engages the learner in fine art practice, we would argue that a similar situation exists for design students (and possibly many other disciplines). The 'exciting and equally frustrating' aspects of this ongoing project of learning to become are characteristic of the sticky curriculum. Affordances mean that knowledge, attributes and beliefs are there to be taken up or rejected or modified to suit previously held positions. All of this is in pursuit of the student's individual version of a professional identity within a wider social and political arena which may construct similar or different forms of creative identity.

The purpose of higher education changes with historical time and perspectives. The current climate of instrumental economics claims the dominant ground in political discourse around universities. However, it was not always so and is not always so for students. Many will be going through higher education with different and sticky notions of the purpose of being there. The majority may well be attracted by the intrinsic rewards of a creative activity with an increasing awareness of the public-facing role of the artist and designer (Daniel and

Johnstone 2015). It was reported to one of the authors that a small group of fine art students held three distinctive reasons for being at university: firstly to become a practising artist (a view we predominantly take in this volume looking at the art and design higher education curriculum); secondly to work in some way associated with art practice, not necessarily as a practising artist and finally to simply study the subject for its own sake but also to credentialise the study with a degree title, the focus being to obtain a degree in a subject which the student enjoys. Underlying this are different conceptions of projected identity, and this potentially makes study sticky for students. If you have conflicting, unformed or uninformed projections of your future identity, it becomes more challenging to become a member of the group or to develop an aligned vision to the community of practice in the university where a predominant view of the purpose of higher education may not be the same as that held by individual students.

Different reasons for undertaking a degree in art and design might also entail parental pressure (I always wanted to be a designer, and my daughter is so talented!); the progress through formal schooling in which art and design was the subject in which a student excelled or a view of being an artist or designer which is perhaps romanticised or mythologised as a way of life which beckons or calls in a particular way. These perceptions may not always be borne out by study at university level (Austerlitz et al. 2008). Students always bring with them their own histories as learners and individuals. By the time they successfully complete an undergraduate degree, they have become socialised into a way of being and acting which is shaped by their tutors and others in the learning environment and beyond it in the world of practice (Hockey 2007).

A student's 'learning power' (Deakin Crick 2012) is also linked to the difficult, liminal space of not knowing, of ambiguity and stickiness likely to be encountered in higher education art and design, and discussed in previous chapters. Students who develop an identity as practitioners early in their course, as well as a learner identity, are likely to be those who succeed. They learn to manage the ambiguity; it becomes a part of their identity or a threshold over which they have crossed (Osmond 2009). They have to become independent learners but also peer learners, engaged in the collective responsibility of the learning environment (Logan 2013). Dialogue is the glue which holds this environment together and enables students to practise the critical language of the discipline with tutors, peers and frequently students in different year groups engaging in critical evaluation of their own and others' work. The use of dialogue in the sticky curriculum is where the construction of identity is acted out (Mitchell 1996).

Language use is crucial to an identity of becoming. Students begin to acquire the right kind of terminology (Shreeve 1998) and the metaphors which are used by professional practitioners (Logan 2008). Behind this lie the concepts, beliefs, histories and technologies of the creative subject, the discourse of being a particular creative practitioner. Articulating is demonstrating or 'professing' the language of the professional. The language currency within the studio or online is also a visual language, material in form, and this too is central to student identity. Students studied on entering a doctoral programme in practice based creative subjects brought with them already formed identities as creative people (Hockey and Allen-Collinson 2005; Hockey 2007; Hockey 2003). This study indicates that socialisation through their undergraduate degree programmes form creative identities which are based on the subject specialism studied: for example, artist, photographer, print-maker or ceramicist. These forms of making are central to the creative identity of students in which the materials and processes of their practice are inextricably linked to their sense of self. Making or practising their subject is the central core of their creative identity and important for the 'ongoing validation of the creative self' (Hockey 2003:84). '"Making", whether producing artefacts in the form of ceramics, glass, print or furniture, was an activity that the students felt to be central to their identity. In the words of one interviewee: "I am what I make"' (Hockey and Allen-Collinson 2005:82). In doctoral study this particular self was frequently at odds with the new demands of the PhD, which required systematic analytical review of the making process and a form of writing which many students did not feel to be in line with their current identity, although engagement with the demands of doctoral study could change the way that they saw themselves and the research process.

Identity work is then an ongoing part of studying in higher education. As skills, attributes and preferences emerge, students are encouraged to become creative individuals with their own values, beliefs and ambitions. The focus on a personalised practice is also a site of stickiness as relations with tutors and the perceived roles fluctuate. The tutor becomes a guide, or a mentor, required to encourage or offer up possibilities which the student may or may not follow. Ambiguity and diversity mean that the responsibility for development is positioned with the student, but the tutor still holds the position of power in this relationship, for the assessment is usually controlled by the tutor. This paradox in creative learning in higher education lies at the heart of the sticky curriculum; the tutor requires autonomy from the student but ultimately passes judgement on the particular form of autonomy constructed by the student as 'the work' is assessed (see Chapter 8).

To summarise the complexity of the sticky curriculum we offer the reader Figure 5.1. The student sits at the centre of a curriculum consisting of knowledge, practices, processes and materials. These are mediated through pedagogies (see Chapter 6) with their associated relationships, and these sit within the cultural practices of the individual course, the learning communities and teams formed within the university's overarching culture. This sits within the dominant sociocultural and political discourses of the time and geographic location. Running through the curriculum are the prevalent values discussed in Chapter 3 and the digital practices which increasingly mediate the pedagogic and sociocultural environments.

Conclusion

The curriculum in art and design is a space providing affordances for learning. Because of the ambiguity present and underlying learning activities, there are potential negative or positive responses by students to engage in these kinds of activities. Negotiating the curriculum is an act of engagement, but stickiness

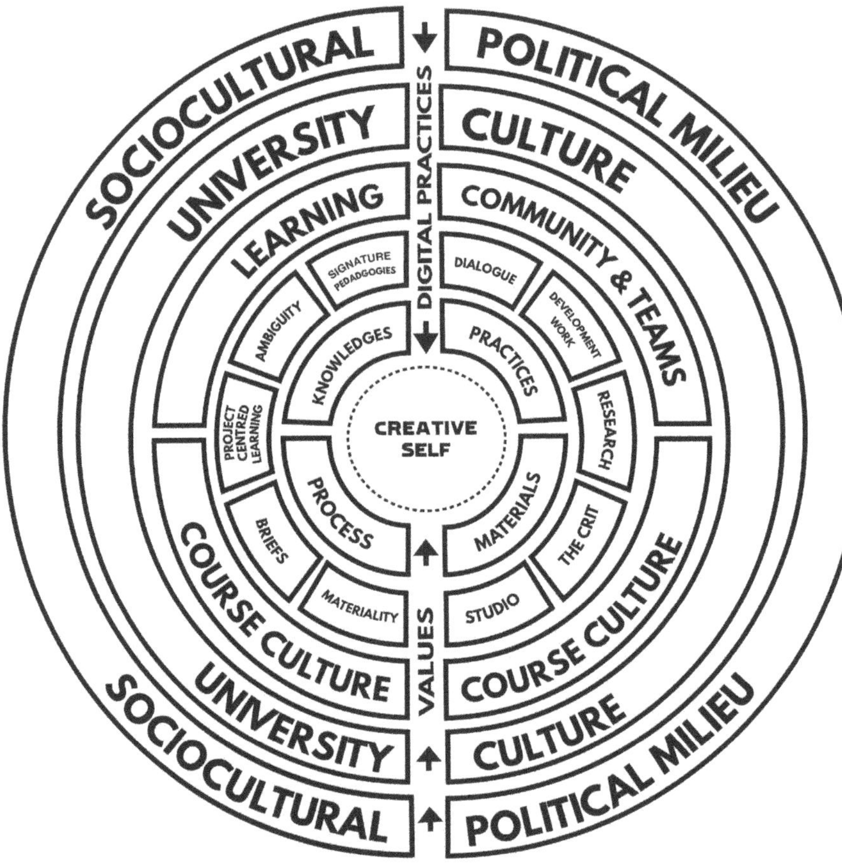

Figure 5.1 The sticky curriculum in art and design

pervades all kinds of engagement, those with formal or informal aspects of curricula, in relationships with others engaged in learning and teaching and above all with work on the 'ongoing project of the creative self' (Hockey 2003:84).

The materiality of the 'work' produced by students, the outcomes of their engagement in creative practice, is a manifestation of their achievement and therefore a measure of their success in becoming a creative practitioner. The work becomes a part of who they are and central to their sense of self and also of their confidence and self-efficacy. If they successfully negotiate the sticky curriculum, learn to manage and work through uncertainty, the work demonstrates that confidence and a mastery of ambiguity. The outcome of learning is to develop certainty within 'the work' and, therefore, the self, even though this may not be stable but will require ongoing identity work to engage with new possibilities within the curriculum and later with the world of creative practice.

References

Ashwin, P., 2009. *Analysing Teaching-Learning Interactions in Higher Education: Accounting for Structure and Agency.* London and New York: Continuum.

Ashwin, P., 2014. Knowledge, Curriculum and Student Understanding in Higher Education. *Higher Education*, 67(2), pp. 123–126.

Atkinson, D., 2015. The Adventure of Pedagogy, Learning and the Not-known. *Subjectivity*, 8(1), pp. 43–56.

Austerlitz, N. and Aravot, I., 2006. The Emotional Structure of the Student-tutor Relationship in the Design Studio. In A. Davies, ed. *Enhancing Curricula: Contributing to the Future, Meeting the Challenges of the 21st Century in the Disciplines of Art, Design and Communication.* London: The Centre for Learning and Teaching in Art and Design. University of the Arts London, pp. 91–106.

Austerlitz, N., Blythman, M., Grove-White, A., Jones, B. A., Jones, C. A., Morgan, S., Orr, S. and Shreeve, A., 2008. Mind the Gap: Expectations, Ambiguity and Pedagogy Within Art and Design Education. In L. Drew, ed. *The Student Experience in Art and Design Higher Education: Drivers for Change.* Cambridge: Jill Rogers Associates Ltd Publishers, pp. 125–148.

Barnett, R. and Coate, K., 2005. *Engaging the Curriculum in Higher Education.* Maidenhead and New York: Open University Press/SRHE.

Belluigi, D. Z., 2016. Constructions of Roles in Studio Teaching and Learning. *International Journal of Art & Design Education*, 35(1), pp. 21–35.

Bergmark, U. and Westman, S., 2016. Co-creating Curriculum in Higher Education: Promoting Democratic Values and a Multidimensional View on Learning. *International Journal for Academic Development*, 21(1), pp. 28–40.

Blythman, M., Parker, B. and Tiffin, S., 2008. Forget the Academic Staff! The Contribution to Creative Learning in Practice of Technical Staff and Equipment. In N. Houghton, ed. *Enhancing Curricula: Using Research and Enquiry to Inform Student Learning in the Disciplines.* London: Centre for Learning and Teaching in Art and Design, pp. 512–523.

Boling, E., 2016. How I Learned, Unlearned, and Learned Studio Again. In E. Boling, R. A. Schwier, C. M. Gray, K. M. Smith and K. Campbell, eds. *Studio Teaching in Higher Education: Selected Design Cases.* London and New York: Routledge, pp. 88–100.

Bovill, C., 2013. Students and Staff Co-creating Curricula: A New Trend or an Old Idea We Never Got Around to Implementing? In C. Rust, ed. *Improving Student Learning Through Research and Scholarship: 20 Years of ISL.* Oxford: Oxford Centre for Staff and Learning Development, pp. 96–108.

Bovill, C., 2014. An Investigation of Co-created Curricula Within Higher Education in the UK, Ireland and the USA. *Innovations in Education and Teaching International*, 51(1), pp. 15–25.

Buckley, B. and Conomos, J., eds., 2009. *Rethinking the Contemporary Art School: The Artist, the PhD and the Academy.* Halifax: The Press of the Nova Scotia College of Art and Design.

Cennamo, C., 2016. What Is Studio? In E. Boling, R. A. Schwier, C. M. Gray, K. M. Smith and K. Campbell, eds. *Studio Teaching in Higher Education: Selected Design Cases.* London and New York: Routledge, pp. 248–259.

Cocchiarella, F. and Booth, P., 2015. Students as Producers: An 'X' Disciplinary Client-Based Approach to Collaborative Art, Design and Media Pedagogy. *International Journal of Art & Design Education*, 34(3), pp. 326–335.

Dall'Alba, G. and Barnacle, R., 2007. An Ontological Turn for Higher Education. *Studies in Higher Education*, 32(6), pp. 679–691.
Daniel, R. and Johnstone, R., 2015. Becoming an Artist: Exploring the Motivations of Undergraduate Students at a Regional Australian University. *Studies in Higher Education*, pp. 1–18. Online. Available from: http://srhe.tandfonline.com/doi/abs/10.1080/03075079.2015.1075196.
Deakin Crick, R., 2012. Deep Engagement as a Complex System: Identity, Learning Power and Authentic Enquiry. In C. S. Reschly and C. A. Wylie, eds. *Handbook of Research on Student Engagement*. New York: Springer US, pp. 675–694.
Eraut, M., 2000. Non-formal Learning and Tacit Knowledge in Professional Work. *Journal of Educational Psychology*, 70(1), pp. 113–136.
Ghassan, A. and Bohemia, E., 2015. Amplifying Learners' Voices Through the Global Studio. In M. Tovey, ed. *Design Pedagogy*. Farnham and Burlington: Gower, pp. 215–236.
Giddens, A., 1991. *Modernity and Self-identity: Self and Society in the Late Modern Age*. Stanford: Stanford University Press.
Hockey, J., 2003. Art and Design Practice-Based Research Degree Supervision Some Empirical Findings. *Arts and Humanities in Higher Education*, 2(2), pp. 173–185.
Hockey, J., 2007. United Kingdom Art and Design Practice-based PhDs: Evidence From Students and Their Supervisors. *Studies in Art Education*, 48(2), pp. 155–171.
Hockey, J. and Allen-Collinson, J., 2005. Identity Change: Doctoral Students in Art and Design. *Arts and Humanities in Higher Education*, 4(1), pp. 77–93.
Little, B., Locke, W., Scesa, A. and Williams, R., 2009. *Report to HEFCE on Student Engagement*. HEFCE, Bristol. Available at: http://oro.open.ac.uk/15281/1/Report_to_HEFCE_on_student_engagement.pdf [Accessed December 12, 2016].
Logan, C., 2008. Metaphor and Pedagogy in the Design Practicum. *International Journal of Technology and Design Education*, 18(1), pp. 1–17.
Logan, C., 2013. Living Artists: Identity, Independence and Engagement in Fine Art Learning. *Art, Design & Communication in Higher Education*, 12(1), pp. 33–48.
Mann, S. J., 2001. Alternative Perspectives on the Student Experience: Alienation and Engagement. *Studies in Higher Education*, 26(1), pp. 7–19.
Mitchell, S. E., 1996. Institutions, Individuals and Talk: The Construction of Identity in Fine Art. *Journal of Art & Design Education*, 15(2), pp. 143–154.
Okuleye, Y., 2008. Alchemy of Happiness: Transformative Conversations in Art School. In N. Austerlitz, ed. *Unspoken Interactions: Exploring the Unspoken Dimension of Learning and Teaching in Creative Subjects*. London: The Centre for Learning and Teaching in Art and Design. University of the Arts London, pp. 191–203.
Orr, S., 2010. Collaborating or Fighting for the Marks? Students' Experiences of Group Work Assessment in the Creative Arts. *Assessment & Evaluation in Higher Education*, 35(3), pp. 301–313.
Osmond, J., 2009. 'Stuck in a Bubble': Identifying Threshold Concepts in Design. In D. Clews, ed. *Dialogues in Art and Design: Promoting and Sharing Excellence*. York: ADM HEA/GLAD, pp. 130–135.
Polanyi, M., 1967. *The Tacit Dimension*. London: Routledge & Kegan Paul.
Rancière, J., 1991. *The Ignorant Schoolmaster: Five Lessons in Intellectual Emancipation*. Stanford: Stanford University Press.
Shreeve, A., 1998. Material Girls. In P. Johnson, ed. *Ideas in the Making: Practice in Theory*. London: Crafts Council, pp. 41–48.

Shreeve, A., 2009. 'I'd Rather Be Seen as a Practitioner, Come in to Teach My Subject': Identity Work in Part-time Art and Design Tutors. *International Journal of Art and Design Education*, 28(2), pp. 151–159.

Shreeve, A., 2011. Being in Two Camps: Conflicting Experiences for Practice-based Academics. *Studies in Continuing Education*, 33(1), pp. 79–91.

Shreeve, A. and Batchelor, R., 2012. Designing Relations in the Studio: Dealing With Ambiguity and Uncertainty in One to One Exchanges. *Design and Technology Education: An International Journal*, 17(3), pp. 20–26.

Shreeve, A., Sims, E. and Trowler, P., 2010. 'A Kind of Exchange': Learning From Art and Design Teaching. *Higher Education Research & Development*, 29(2), pp. 125–138.

Shulman, L. S., 2005. Signature Pedagogies in the Professions. *Daedalus*, 134(3), pp. 52–59.

Smith, C., 2015. *'Between the Institutional Cracks': An Evaluative Case Study of a Student-staff Co-production Project.* Unpublished MA Dissertation. University of the Arts London.

Taylor, S. and Littleton, K., 2006. Biographies in Talk: A Narrative-discursive Research Approach. *Qualitative Sociology Review*, 2(1), pp. 22–38.

Trowler, P. and Cooper, A., 2002. Teaching and Learning Regimes: Implicit Theories and Recurrent Practices in the Enhancement of Teaching and Learning Through Educational Development Programmes. *Higher Education Research & Development*, 21(3), pp. 221–240.

Weller, S., 2012. Achieving Curriculum Coherence: Curriculum Design and Delivery as Social Practice. In P. Blackmore and C. B. Kandiko, eds. *Strategic Curriculum Change*. London and New York: Routledge/SRHE, pp. 21–23.

Wenger, E., 1998. *Communities of Practice*. Cambridge: Cambridge University Press.

Whitchurch, C., 2013. *Reconstructing Identities in Higher Education: The Rise of 'Third Space' Professionals*. Abingdon and New York: Routledge/SRHE.

Zimmerman, B. J., Bandura, A. and Martinez-Pons, M., 1992. Self-motivation for Academic Attainment: The Role of Self-efficacy Beliefs and Personal Goal Setting. *American Educational Research Journal*, 29(3), pp. 663–676.

6 Teaching practices for creative practitioners

Introduction

This chapter draws largely on the idea of signature pedagogies (Shulman 2005) to explore the teaching practices likely to be encountered in creative arts disciplines. We believe these approaches to the curriculum and learning are significant ways that denote the nature of teaching and learning in the subjects and groupings which make up the art and design area but also contribute to stickiness in the curriculum. They are indicators of the way in which practices beyond the university, in creative industries, are translated or made available to learners through recontextualised learning activities (Bernstein 2000) which help students to act, behave and think like practitioners, albeit within the structures, constraints and affordances of a pedagogic university environment.

From a disciplinary point of view, one might take an ethnographic or epistemic viewpoint to categorise the sub-disciplines (Biglan 1973; Becher 1989; Becher and Trowler 2001), but one might also look at the learning and teaching strategies and approaches to identify very distinctive differences amongst subject areas. Such an approach has been identified by Shulman (2005), who states that professions have particular pedagogic approaches which enable students to learn to think and act as a professional would. These he called signature pedagogies, and subsequent studies have identified signature pedagogies in a range of subjects (Gurung et al. 2009; Chick et al. 2012). For example, Shulman identified law, which used mooting in order that students learn to present an argument and debate in public. Law also has an emphasis on the precision of language use and definition and the need to identify and remember salient facts and issues. Teachers who are also trained professionals identify ways of learning which help students operate in similar ways that they understand in their professional lives outside the university, but within any subject there are differences in the way it is taught and the emphasis on the kind of skills and knowledge deemed significant.

One might argue that being an artist is not a profession or that designers are not a specific profession. However, there are distinctive pedagogies which are shared by many art and design subject areas. Klebesedal and Kornetsky (2009) identified 'the Crit' as a signature pedagogy for the arts (see Chapters 3 and 8 for more information about the Crit). The salient point here is that when practised well, the Crit is a pedagogic tool which helps students to develop a critical and evaluative approach to creative work (see Figure 6.1). Students are also

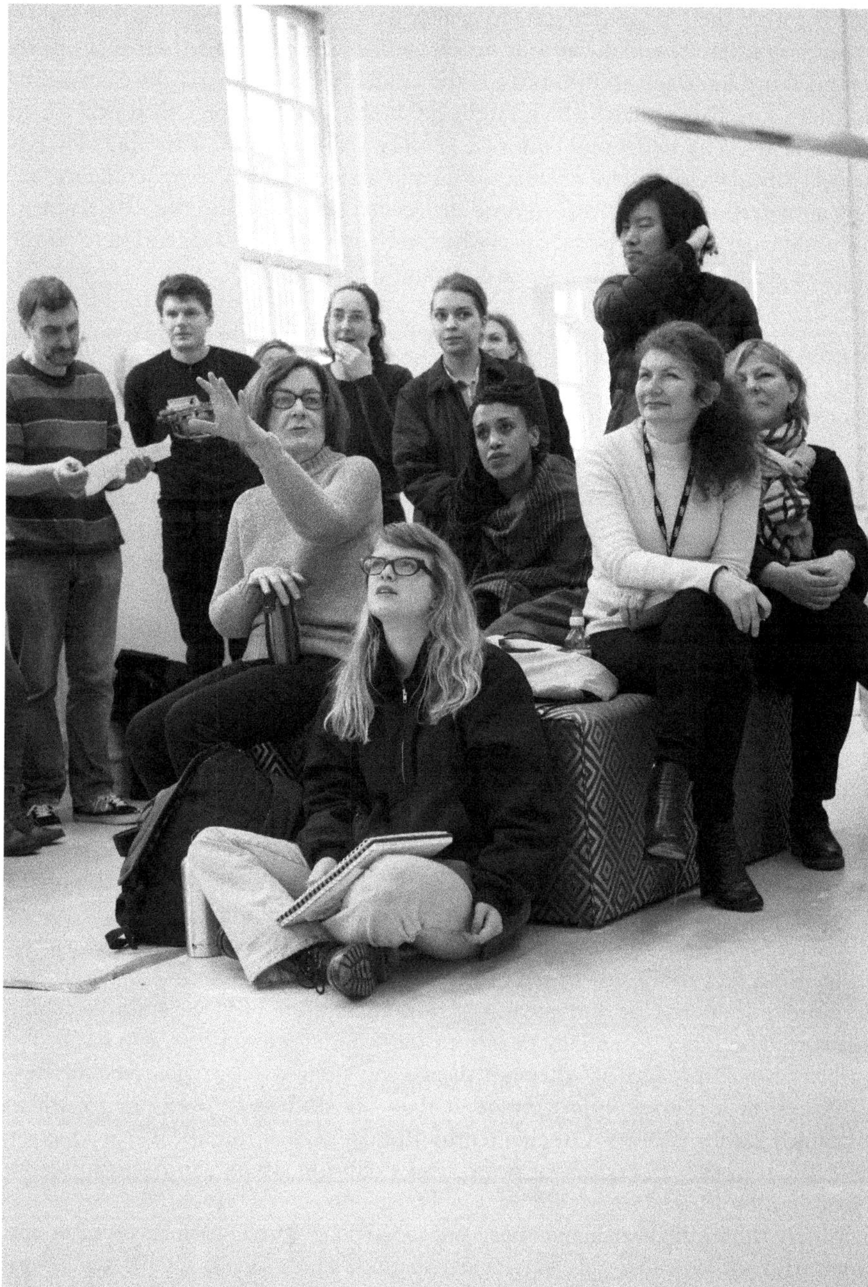

Figure 6.1 The Crit is a signature pedagogy
Photograph by Valentina Schivardi

able through the Crit to defend and evaluate their own work, a trait that will be important when operating in a professional context. The Crit itself is probably not practised in design studios outside the academy, but there may be elements of practice (e.g., like a pitch) which might be similar to the way a Crit is performed in university. The pedagogy is not necessarily a direct copy of the practice but designed to develop useful characteristics and abilities which are essential to successful operation in a context beyond university. Sims and Shreeve (2012) identify additional signature pedagogies which we summarise and extend here. Some of these are independent and some codependent.

Signature pedagogies

The studio

The space where learning occurs is usually referred to as the studio, but there may also be associated resources where technical processes take place, such as workshops. These physical spaces are important in helping structure the kinds of learning which we describe in this volume. A space may not seem like pedagogy, but in its widest sense the studio helps structure what can and does take place when students learn, and it has been a central part of organised learning in visual arts for more than a century. This space also echoes those found in professional working environments. A seminal study of the professional architect's studio (Schön 1985) identifies that there are cultures residing in the studio with discussion and the artefacts associated with the design or art activity present. This is a space which helps structure learning (Smith-Taylor 2009). There is usually no central focus for the lecturer to hold forth, but rather students create a social learning environment discussing amongst peers and enabling the tutor to explore progress and work and to hold group or individual tutorials. Shulman's observation of the design studio provides a perspective of the learning space from one who is external to the discipline. He highlights the centrality of the artefact in learning and the fluid nature of the tutor's exchanges, noting that they are 'not the only source for that pedagogy' (Shulman 2005:54). The studio teaching structure also has a potentially negative side, where criticism has been levelled at tutors who simply 'cruise' through dispensing their wisdom (Davies and Reid 2000), a tutor centred approach rather than the student centred one identified by Smith Taylor (2009). Others identify the dangers of uncritical reproduction of cultural norms and issues of power and exclusion which can occur in studio (Gray and Smith 2016).

Ideally the studio is an active, busy and social place where learning is visible and open to discussion through active participation. Traditionally in the Art School students would have access to an individual space where they worked, pinning up the ongoing explorations and visual stimuli relating to the project brief or to their own interests, leaving out work in progress and accessing the space for as long as they wished. The studio has been identified by Brandt et al. (2013) as a place which prepares students for the professional world. The studio remains the ideal social space in which to work and learn for most tutors, although it is increasingly under pressure by universities counting the amount of resources allocated to each student (Boling et al. 2016) and increasingly may be time limited in its accessibility to students. Many students will be migrants across campus without their own dedicated studio space, and strategies to create communal shared learning are increasingly likely to be digital, online spaces. As Marshalsey (2015) states, the changes to learning in communication design mean that learning is perhaps more likely 'to be dispersed between studio, home and non-owned spaces, and across physical, digital and hybridised forms of learning space' (p. 340). She goes on to explore how individual sensory experiences of space affect everyone working in them and may potentially affect learning within the studio, depending on particular local conditions and their impact on individuals. The specific physical space of the studio may also impact on and influence the learning process and the actual artefacts which emerge from the studio, depending on local conditions (see materiality, which follows).

An extension of the expanded studio, using multiple spaces, has been suggested by Australian academic Associate Professor Fiona Peterson (personal communication, 2015), who suggests that studio has become or is becoming a metaphor for the approaches to thinking and practising which pervade design pedagogies. She asks: is the studio more 'a state of mind' than a particular physical space? Studio as a state of mind demands that learners engage in collaborative and community learning, using available spaces, whether physical, online, inside or outside the university. The shared experiences, linked by attitudes expected in the studio, of risk taking and experimentation, may be demonstrated by learners and teachers as an evolving space.

Ironically, as pressure builds to reduce access to the studio for art and design students, it is increasingly recognised as an innovative and engaging way to learn and is being adopted, with variations, by other disciplines, often incorporating learning technologies (Brown 2006; Boling et al. 2016). Work by Lange and Smith (2014) indicates that art and design pedagogies are not only appropriate within creative industries subjects but can be transposed into science learning as well, suggesting that it is largely tradition or culture which shapes the way that learning and teaching are undertaken within subjects as well as the influence of ways of thinking and acting happening beyond the university, as Shulman (2005) suggests.

Pedagogies of ambiguity

We have explored in some depth earlier in Chapter 4 the notion of the complex and ambiguous territory which constitutes learning in creative practice. Where no known specific factual outcomes are envisaged at the start of the learning journey, the engagement in learning is a process of discovery and creation by individuals. Students must learn to manage and work through ambiguity to succeed in creative practice. This is deemed to be a threshold concept for design students (Osmond et al. 2010; Osmond and Tovey 2015) and is a familiar situation for tutors who need to reassure students that it is acceptable to not know what the end goal might be.

The brief

The brief is described elsewhere in this volume (Chapter 7) as the vehicle which launches the project based learning embodying the curriculum. The written brief presents the learning task or project which students undertake and by which their learning is structured. Universities may require tutors to use templates to ensure that all relevant information is included in a project brief, including dates, learning outcomes and assessment requirements. In the context of art and design, tutors may demand that their briefs have a particular designed look to them rather than use a university-generated template which offends their design sensibilities. Even in the way learning tasks as texts are presented, tutors frequently try to inculcate visual aesthetic design awareness and sensitivity in their students. Thus tensions can be set up between competing expectations, which makes the curriculum and learning sticky, requiring negotiation by tutors.

The live project

In the context of design, the brief is often written to read like a professional design task and frequently is drafted in consultation with industry partners who will 'set' the brief (project) within a framework of their own company, thus simulating the kinds of parameters they encounter for design work. This type of assignment is called a live brief. There can be conflicts arising between industry representatives' aims and the requirements of higher education, creating stickiness for students and tutors in fulfilling the brief.

The live brief describes a situation which is positioned in the world beyond the university. Ideally students will engage with a company or with people at different levels in the community to design or make products, artefacts or services which fulfil a need. This includes fine art students who might be asked to work with a local gallery or create a site-specific work for a community. Situated within wider communities the live project represents the kind of work which students will encounter on graduation. This is the pinnacle of learning: to become a professional, as the live project is 'real' although scaffolded by the lecturers who provide support, advice and encouragement whilst the work is being carried out. This boundary between learning and creative practice is however somewhat contested in terms of just how 'real' the experience is and can be when the objective is to enable students to learn; see Harriss and Widder (2014) for a discussion of the live project as a pedagogic tool in architecture. The live project may be introduced at any stage of the learning cycle but often after the student has had a basic introductory period of learning in university and is considered ready and prepared to tackle more complex issues.

Some projects are more live than others. The title may be given to a project that is actually one of the lecturer's own creation. The lecturer may simulate a work context for a project that has no actual linkage with the industry in question. At the other end of the scale, an authentic live project may result in the company using the students' work in production. Clearly in these examples an awareness of intellectual property rights is essential to ensure that students are protected from exploitation.

Development work

This is evidence of development of ideas and is normally required, not necessarily a sketchbook, but sometimes a collection of loose-leaf workings or a blog which traces the thought processes and evolution of thinking, thus making visible the ways in which students locate and explore ideas. The visible format is important and centres the discussions held by tutors and by fellow students about the work. This enables ongoing feedback and critique to take place and helps develop the critical stance required in the disciplines. The thought made visible provides a trace, connections, diversions and convolutions which are essential for creative thinking enabling the student to return to or explore new avenues previously discarded. Such reification is an important part of the learning process and fundamental to the pedagogic process. It is here that the tutor will expect to see the outcomes of research undertaken around the topic of the project brief.

Research

Research is a term used in a specific way in art and design but which lacks clear definition. It refers to a process of finding and exploring information on which to base the generation of conceptual, visual and material ideas. The way research is undertaken is seldom articulated, but expectations of what constitutes good research certainly exist within course groups, usually as tacit knowledge emphasising the ambiguity of the learning environment (Kjølberg 2012). In each course and subject culture, there will be an expectation or cultural configuration of what constitutes good research. A small-scale study explored the variation in ways students approached the research component of a fashion/textiles project and identified that it was possible to do this in increasingly complex ways, from reproducing elements of the visual material studied in the designed artefact to embodying abstract ideas and concepts in the designed artefact (Shreeve et al. 2004). Further research would be useful to understand more fully how and what constitutes research processes in undergraduate learning across different sub-disciplines and where there are commonalities. There are certainly distinct cultural differences in expectations of research (Kjølberg 2012) but usually consensus that merely collating information from the Internet does not constitute sufficient research on which to base a creative project. There may be some requirements to 'read' around a subject area as well as generate visual materials and explore these to generate new products and artefacts. In many cases research is generated by the students' own interests and subjective responses to the world (Barrett 2007), particularly within the later stages of a design course. Research is also required for theoretical or cultural and historical studies which are part of the degree programme. This kind of research may encompass critical reading, the construction of arguments or points of view and, in the final year, is likely to value primary research which contributes to a dissertation on a subject or question of the student's own choice. This might correspond more closely to academic research in other disciplines; although the subject of the study is most likely to relate to artists, designers and their outputs, it usually does not preclude any other subject of interest to the individual student.

Dialogic exchange

The kinds of questioning, discussion and debate which characterise learning in art and design is fundamental to enabling students to develop their work. Exchanges may take place amongst peers or students at different levels of experience as well as with tutors. These discursive situations prompt critical thinking and self-evaluation and develop the language of the discipline. The fundamental role of language in the learning process runs parallel to the visual and material world in which ideas emerge as finished products (Logan 2006; Shreeve et al. 2010).

Materiality

Discussions are situated within a very material world, even if this might include online or digital learning environments. The 'work' produced by the student, whether digitally or in small experimental material samples, drawings, sketchbooks, maquettes or finished products, enable discussion and questioning. This is in distinct contrast to the written components of the curriculum which normally are constructed individually, handed in, marked in private by the tutor and handed back with grades and comments. The work and its development in art and design is present and central to an exchange of views. The material dimension carries the significance of the work and its meaning to be apprehended by the viewer and/ or the user. This dimension is significant because everything in our manufactured and commercialised world is designed and accessed through experience.

There are however courses which now teach only through computer-aided design and no longer manufacture physical artefacts. This goes to the heart of our Western higher educational values evolved from William Morris and the Arts and Crafts movement in the latter part of the nineteenth century. He believed that to know a craft, you had to experience it with your own hands. The embodied knowledge which physical engagement with materials provides is distinctive. It enables one to imagine or project the behaviour of materials when they are constructed. For example, in fashion design the drape or the stretch properties of the fabric will behave in a particular way, and this should be incorporated into the design. Embodied knowledge is part of a skilled production; it is tacit and hard to describe to a learner (Dormer 1997). The importance of physical experience in developing knowledge and understanding of creative practice is exemplified by a first-year graphic design tutor, Nigel Bents, at Chelsea College of Art: University of the Arts London, who manages ways to ensure that students physically encounter letter forms, in print, or three dimensions through many different embodied experiences, an example of the high tech, low tech, no tech approach common in the contemporary Art School. Actually experiencing the materiality of paper, ink, space and letter form is, he believes, providing an understanding which the digital design world no longer offers a student and which is essential to becoming a professional practitioner. Learning in a material world is different to learning to design solely on screen; although if the medium of your craft is digital, this would no longer apply! The materiality of digital devices is a medium in itself, and if you communicate through the screen, you design through the screen. However, the digital, nondigital, multiple modes debates are ongoing, and many viewpoints coexist in the university. Where technologies are useful and available, they are generally incorporated into learning opportunities, with students often determining what kind of approach they wish to take in terms of the materiality of creation.

Another specific area of material learning is through 'object based learning' which puts an artefact at the centre of the learning process. Frequently used in association with museum collections and material culture, the artefact offers a multisensory experience and a window into others' cultural lives (Chatterjee and Hannan 2015). The object, though, might also be used as a tool to support learning in manufacturing processes and techniques or to illustrate alternatives within the studio and workshop environment. Many teaching collections were established in the early years of Art Schools and have been retained and augmented as a teaching resource (Willcocks 2015).

Most of these signature pedagogy characteristics were originally identified through examining four broadly defined subject areas in art and design – design for performance, fashion product design, graphic design and fine art – and were by no means inclusive of the many variations in practice within the discipline as a whole (Shreeve et al. 2010). Individual courses also develop distinctive ways of working to prepare students for the world of work. For example, in advertising, courses might build in the possibility of students working as creative teams, that is, one person specialising in copy writing and another in creative generation of visual ideas. The practice of employing such creative teams is prevalent in the industry, and course teams have capitalised on this practice by enabling students to develop partnerships which often persist for the majority of the working lives of the individuals concerned. Assessment practices, learning activities and opportunities are all designed to encourage partnership collaboration, with creative teams progressing through higher education and entering the workplace together. This is a distinctive signature pedagogy for advertising, not universally adopted in every course. There may be many more examples of specifically designed signature pedagogies in the various sub-disciplines of art and design, and this requires further investigation.

An intriguing report of artists' interventions in compulsory-level schooling (Thomson et al. 2012) identified what the authors describe as signature pedagogies, that is, the attributes which practising artists bring to learning situations within the schools sector which are distinctive from 'pedagogies of the mainstream' (p. 9). They identified also that the constraints teachers are under from sociopolitical structures alter the way that teachers who are also artists behave. This is illustrated by Atkinson's (2002:4) 'pedagogised identities', which are constructed by the social norms of many schools and the examination system, bringing particular constraints and expectations about art and design to the fore of practice as teachers. Practising artists therefore bring a different set of behaviours and attitudes into the learning environment. The report lists nineteen different and distinctive traits, many of which ring true of art and design in the university but only one explicitly identified here – the use of artefacts (materiality). In summary the authors of the artists' intervention report (Thomson et al. 2012) state:

> It was observable across all of the sessions that the practitioners were at pains to stress to the students that there was no definitive right or wrong answer to artistic problems. The emphasis was on whether the work looked and/or felt right to the student in the context of what else was happening in the class. So standards were apparent and applied, but individuals were expected to develop their own skills of discrimination and judgement. There was therefore a stronger orientation towards intrinsic rather than extrinsic motivation and evaluation in the artists' sessions.
>
> (p. 44)

Like the authors of this volume, the report also takes the view that learning is a holistic function with ontological and epistemological dimensions, or as Dall'Alba and Barnacle (2007) phrase it, an ontological turn characterises the kind of learning which takes place when artists are involved, and this, as described earlier in this volume, is the prevailing approach in higher education. Many of the characteristics of learning activities the report's authors observed are recognisable to us as common-sense truths based on our own experiences. The pedagogic practices identified in the report include the open-ended challenge, which was described as 'not so much about following a road map as journeying together and seeing where the group arrived' (p. 44); 'permission to play', which involved disrupting the 'taken for granted ways of school thinking and doing', provocation used as a stimulus for meaning making and the generation of ideas and possibilities; taking learning out of the classroom; using the self as a teaching resource and referring to professional norms. The report provides an external frame of reference which identifies some of the taken-for-granted aspects of higher education in which the authors have been long embedded. Signature pedagogies in art and design are therefore extended through this external focus on the compulsory education sector to include those pedagogic practices which we recognise from their report.

The ways that artists and designers approach learning is something which they bring with them from their own learning situations and knowledge, which they have developed on the job in their own practices. However, when practitioners become teachers in higher education, often as part-time or fractional appointments, they are juggling the two different worlds of practice and teaching, even though they are teaching others about their practice world. There are variable ways to experience this relationship (Shreeve 2008), and although they bring value and values into the university (Budge 2014), they are subject to norms and structures which require some kind of adjustment or even translation of their practice into the university working environment (Bernstein 2000).

Teaching strategies

A repertoire of teaching strategies was identified by Shreeve (2008), which elucidates some of the ways in which practitioners help students become creative practitioners. These are similar to the pedagogic practices identified by Thomson et al. (2012) but are perhaps more specific than those observed in schools. The strategies identified form a hierarchical list of ways to help students become practitioners which moves from the basic to the more complex.

1. ***Passing on your knowledge***. This is a skills based approach which is more or less show and tell and expects students to perform to a similar standard. This limits the ontological aspects of learning for students because an emphasis only on performance offers no associated development of the context or emotional aspects of being a practitioner. Where skills alone are emphasised in the curriculum, it is possible that the associated stickiness (as in challenges) or breadth of complexity associated with practice is limited.
2. ***Using examples from practice***, or bringing in objects and artefacts, or examining finished or partially completed artefacts is a strategy which helps illustrate the outcomes and, in the case of partially finished work, also the processes of professional practice. Here students are encouraged to analyse and understand processes and completed artefacts to gain insights into the world of the practitioner through the products made.
3. A more sophisticated variant of bringing in artefacts is to ***bring in your own work*** as a basis of discussion or learning. Here tutors are able to provide the insight into thinking which went into the development and creation of the artefact and to illustrate the kinds of decisions and questions they posed themselves during the process of creation to help students understand how it is to be and think like a practitioner. This was mirrored in the school study where they identified the self as a teaching resource.
4. ***Learning whilst teaching or specifically for teaching*** is a way in which practitioners balance their two roles. Using this strategy is a way to exchange knowledge between the two different social worlds they inhabit, between being a practitioner and being a teacher. Learning from students while teaching is common, and tutors may learn specific or new theories or approaches for their students which enrich both their teaching and their own practice.
5. Closely allied to this strategy is ***the removal of boundaries to both practice and teaching***. Whilst engaged in one activity, it is feasible to think of the

other and to be influenced by what is happening to the benefit of both teaching and practice. Students thus benefit from thinking which is current and based in the actual experience of the practitioner teacher. They are able to access the world of practice through the tutor's flow or exchange of knowledge, and the tutor benefits from the learning environment too.

6 ***Paralleling*** is a way for the tutor to simultaneously engage in their practice and in teaching related activities. For example, a tutor may design a project which is virtually the same as her own creative work. Here the tutor is demonstrating that it is possible to engage students in similar conversations, questions and activities as those that constitute her own creative practice. Students here are more likely to be perceived as co-constructors of learning rather than recipients.

7 ***Dovetailing*** is where the roles of teaching and practicing begin to merge. One activity can fulfil purposes in both education and practice worlds. This is illustrated by a tutor on a foundation art and design programme (a one-year pre-degree course in parts of the UK) who is also a curator. In visiting end-of-year shows she identifies recent graduates to put together an exhibition of work. At the same time she is generating information for her students on the foundation course about different degree programmes so that they can make informed decisions about where to study.

8 ***Collaborating*** is a teaching strategy which brings the students and tutors together in their learning activities. The tutor perceives little difference between themselves and their students, both of them together on a journey of discovery within the practice. For tutors there is no boundary between their practice and teaching worlds, and they are keen to enable students to see the similarities between themselves and their teachers. Students are also a part of the world of practice, or as Lave and Wenger (1991) might say, they are on the periphery of the community of practice, engaging in legitimate peripheral participation with the old timers or tutors.

9 Two other strategies were identified in this study but were deemed to be associated only with practitioners who aligned more fully with academia than with practice worlds. They are interesting in that they have a distinctive dimension which allies the tutor (still a practitioner) with the activities of the university. The first of these is ***to engage in your subject but within an academic framework***. This is to engage in study to develop your own understanding of the subject or to take a more 'academic' approach to what has hitherto been a primarily economic engagement. This is not to abandon the practice that is something which is an engrained part of your identity but possibly to see it in a different light, using theory or others' points of view, or to develop the practice with the help of others. Although this could be argued to be outside of the signature pedagogies framework, the strategy is also one which helps bring new points of view or new dimensions to the practice for students. It is possible to view this as a means to develop the subject area or the practice. Where practitioners engage in academic development of their subjects, students should benefit from a broader engagement and debate which practitioner tutors can bring to the learning environment.

10 The second strategy associated only with practitioner tutors experiencing a closer relationship to academia is perhaps more surprising as one might expect it to underpin all practitioners' teaching strategies, that is, ***to recreate the experience of practice within the teaching environment.*** This is possibly a limitation of the research approach used in this study where interviews to recall the teaching experience limits the recall to significant instances and does not explore all the intentions or practicalities of the teaching situation. However, the emphasis on recreating both the structure of the practice context, as in the physical environment, and the way of working with customers in design, and the emotional and cultural expectation, as in the speed at which teams work in broadcasting, were evident in the study.

These strategies which link practice and teaching help illustrate the potential richness of the learning environment and the variety of ways in which it is possible to begin to learn to think and act like a professional or to learn through signature pedagogies which enable students to become professional.

The 'real-life' problematic

There are, however, issues with creating or recreating the environments of working life within an educational setting. The distinction between 'real life' and education is always present in some form in spite of individual tutor's actions to develop approaches to teaching which seek to convey or inculcate disciplinary ways of thinking and being. They are two distinct spheres of activity. Cultural Historical Activity Theory (Engeström et al. 1999; Engeström 1990) is one way to understand this, and it is explained by the difference in the object of the activity. In education the object is to enable learning, whilst in creative industries, the object is to produce a product, performance, artwork or service. This object of activity in higher education helps structure the emphasis of the activity on the learning taking place rather than the outcome or product of creative practice. However, one has also to bear in mind the notion that the object is always contested; that is, it is often more complex or nuanced than it first appears, and therefore any activity system could be argued to be inherently sticky. There may indeed be different objects of activity present and vying for supremacy; for some tutors the designed object or artefact may be the primary goal or object, as it is in the professional world, thus setting up a tension in conflict with the need to learn through mistakes. Competing objects and intentions serve to create stickiness around the goals of learning and the curriculum. The emphasis on the object of activity also changes the way that mediating artefacts are used in learning and in professional practice. Different communities and divisions of labour within the two different spheres of activity create different tensions and intentions behind people's actions within each sphere, thus setting up different cultural configurations, however hard the teaching team tries to make learning relevant and 'real' for students.

When referred to as 'real life', the social world of practice is set in opposition to the lived life of the students, tutors, technicians and others who work to support and create learning environments in university. Clearly there is a commonly held view that education is somehow 'unreal', and in some respects it is! The environment is created specifically to provide a place to learn and to develop aspects of the subject through research activities. There are a host of rules, regulations, cultural practices and expectations which differentiate practising in university to practising in another cultural sphere of activity. Even when students are performing a paid job as part of their course, for example, filming an event, putting on an exhibition or designing public seating for a shopping centre, they are still working within the social setting of the university *at the same time* as operating outside it.

This specifically designed location requires a pedagogic, that is, learning, focus to be present rather than simply a reconstruction of the world of creative practice, which might be the case in a training venue. When practitioners teach in university, they are required to make an act of translation and to reframe the practice so that its key components become accessible to those learning it (Bernstein 2000). The access to the tacit, professional knowledge of procedures and rules of practice requires enabling by the tutor, or 'recontextualisation' of practice. Recontextualised practice principles are made available to students through learning activities tutors generate. Within the pedagogic activity internal and continuous evaluation of learning establishes pathways that render tacit and explicit rules or principles of practice accessible (Colwell 2014). Within the project brief certain exercises or activities will be designed to enable learning. Sometimes these work and other times not. This may be dependent on individual's participation, the number of students in relation to the activity may hinder apprehension or the activity will only mirror practice and not enable access to understanding practice principles. The positioning of the tutor and the design of learning activities which encourage appropriate ways of engaging with ideas and principles of practice require a creative reading of the learning activity and an articulation or dialogue about what is happening to support the development of practice identities in students. Within learning activities it is important for students to access the underlying reasons why certain things are done rather than only access the processes. Simply using the references to the practice actually excludes the students from developing an understanding; they require access or the 'routes of development' to fully understand the practice principles to contextualise the broader framework of practice as a lived experience. Colwell (2014) uses Social Activity Method schema (Dowling 1998; Dowling 2013) to reveal student learning pathways through expression (dialogic) and descriptive (textual) categories that are generated, like the learning activity, by recontextualised practice principles. It is debatable whether practice principles can always be accessed through higher education; it is possible that each individual working context will require renegotiation and regeneration of understanding and knowledge to fully engage with practice as it is found outside academia, for as argued earlier in this volume, knowledge is mutable, contested and definitely sticky in its cultural settings.

Colwell (2014) also argues that teachers need to access different languages or to develop new languages of description from those of both the practice and academic worlds to build confidence in mediating practice for learners. Here too in media it is essential to develop the process, not simply concentrate on the product when learning. Students have to create an artefact such as a script because, if there is no evidence of practising during the learning process, there is no access to a critique with the student to develop their understanding and ability to practice. Learning is therefore embodied in an artefact, performance or piece of writing which is 'out there' and central to tutors' and students' evaluation and critique. Inevitably the social practices of the university begin to structure the ways that teachers develop learning activities and conform to, disrupt or subvert the rules of the activity of learning in higher education. This is a sticky combination in which curriculum, a translation of practice into education, requires sensitivity and creativity to enable learning with a deep approach to practice subjects and the development of ownership of esoteric knowledge by students.

A study of the discourses used by academics in media studies (Dean 2015) also identifies the use of 'real life' as an opposition to university life in relation to the subject. This commonly articulated discourse is frequently aired, but the rationale for its prevalence is debatable. Interestingly Dean sees it as potentially keeping education in its (more subservient) place. No longer does the university hold the higher ground socially; it has become subject to the more powerful discourses of industry, employability and accountability, and it is the practice arena which is authentic and valued:

> This relationship between industry, wider society and the academy is very clearly denoted by a discourse of 'out there in the real world'. Widely used both inside and outside the academy as evidenced by the participant responses, this denotes a clear hierarchy with education portrayed as artificial, a simulation and subservient. A discursive practice is created that mitigates [sic] against collaboration. The widespread use of this phrasing amongst media lecturers is significant as it is one area of the analysis which suggests that academic staff are not balancing an oppositional discourse but are comfortable using language that keeps education 'in its place'.
>
> (Dean 2015:280)

Attempts to blur the boundaries between the 'real world' and academia are the essential characteristic of signature pedagogies, but moving into and operating within the world beyond the university whilst being a student is not solely the province of the tutor structuring learning activities; sometimes it is volunteering or self-identified placements which offer opportunities to cross the boundary into the 'real world'. Students are negotiating and learning from multiple contexts which are not always recognised through assessment.

In a study of students transferring creative learning to work-related, voluntary sector environments, Shreeve and Smith (2012) identified that students were drawing on not only the taught subject-related skills but were extending these in work situations. They might be using problem solving and creative approaches to tackle new and unforeseen challenges. They were drawing on the skills they brought with them from their life-wide experiences, adapting approaches to teaching which they had experienced as learners and transferring skills learnt beyond the university back into their own learning environments. These forms of boundary crossing or blurring of the boundaries between education and work contexts were also dependent on the opportunities each individual student perceived within the working environment. Where they felt that they had freedom and responsibility, and where this also enabled the development or alignment of personal philosophies, there was more likelihood of multiple transfer or more transition between the boundary of work and education and more stickiness and stretching of the creative curriculum for individuals. In the most intensive cases learning and the value placed in learning opportunities provided by experiences beyond the university resulted in the broadening of subject-related skills, world viewpoints and future opportunities for paid working. In such cases students felt able to contribute and to have an impact on society through their work-related learning. Where opportunities for engagement in learning in wider situations beyond the university can be provided, the curriculum is capable of being stretched to the life-wide opportunities which individuals, with support, can make relevant to their subject-specific learning. Such opportunities for a stretchy view of curriculum also help increase students' self-efficacy, enabling them to use and recognise skills evolving through their university education and moving them from a position of novice to expert.

The signature pedagogies, the approaches to learning and teaching which inculcate the nature of being in the profession, and by extension in art and design, the discipline, sub-discipline or subject area, are of course modified by continuous change and development. This may be triggered by political change, for example, the emphasis in the UK on employability in higher education or the emphasis on reflective thinking in learning processes in higher education bringing in the idea of explicit reflection, usually through journals or blogs, by changes to local knowledge with the introduction of a new member of the teaching team bringing in different approaches from her creative practice or by technologies. Most disciplines will now use digital for many creative practices, and pedagogies have changed to incorporate these using digital blended spaces for many aspects of learning and teaching. Whether digital approaches constitute or are on their way to becoming signature pedagogies is arguable; they are a tool or medium, and in some cases the very nature of the creative discipline, and in the latter case the use of digital teaching and learning, could be argued to be a signature pedagogy. For example, an online course in photojournalism uses a variety of e-learning modes to enable professional practitioners to undertake study whilst they are located in dispersed locations throughout the world (Lowe and Blythman 2009). The blogs are described as the 'glue' which holds all together and helps create a community of professional learners, increasing their knowledge and understanding of their profession within an existing wider community of professional photojournalists. The exchanges and sharing of reflections online could be argued to demonstrate a digital version of a signature pedagogy which develops critical evaluation skills for the profession and enables dialogue to take place on a one-to-one basis using the shared visual medium online.

In another example where digital is the medium, students who are learning to render three-dimensional objects on the screen are encouraged through the setting of professional standards and expectations to achieve proficiency in mastering a challenging process (Paquette et al. 2016). The authors postulate that it is the acquisition of key threshold concepts (Meyer and Land 2006), particularly structural visualisation, together with an awareness of a professional standard (a qualitative judgement and also expectation of what constitutes good working approaches) rather than simply knowledge of the technical software tools, which enables students to achieve mastery in a relatively short space of time. This is in opposition to the notion that proficiency is something which takes repeated and lengthy practice. This chimes with the idea of signature pedagogies which enable students to think and act like professionals, providing they can move across the key threshold concepts associated with being professional – not simply a matter of acquiring skills but of thinking and acting like a professional digital artist.

The idea of professionalism is implied by the term signature pedagogy; professionalism is the ability to make the transition from higher education into practice. In Paquette et al.'s (2016) study graduates now employed in the global computer graphics industry were asked to reflect on their learning experience and their current position of expertise. They recognised their ability to 'visualize the instructions as they are read' (p. 25); that is, they were able to plan, to foresee potential solutions and likely problems and challenges and to set about the task in a more informed way than those less competent. The definition of professionalism used in this study was that it made graduates able 'to evaluate their own work and behaviour in the context of a work-place environment and the demands of the industry' (p. 25).

For an art student, however, there is no industry rather a range of practices into which they will establish their own version of art practice or practices. Hughes (2014) states, 'Artistic practice has developed a problematic relation to knowledge' (p. 73). In this article he cites the almost mantra of 'not-knowing' (p. 75), tacit knowledge and intuition as the guiding principles of art pedagogy, an alignment with commercialised art practice beyond the university and a current position of artistic practice being in a state of constant change. In opposition to this constant change, he posits a pedagogy of 'dwelling' (p. 77), that is, existing in long term and repetitive involvement with certain ideas, citing artists Ackling and Charlton as progenitors of this approach. Importantly for our argument that signature pedagogies are significant means to apprehend the multifaceted knowledge of art and design, he states, 'More than most subjects within Higher Education, Fine Art making and teaching have the same genesis' (p. 79); that is, practice and the way that students learn to practice are inextricably linked through reproduction of practice principles. Inherent in this example is the potential variation for many differently validated signature pedagogies across the multitude of subject areas making up art and design.

Conclusion

The complexity of art and design disciplines offers up a wide variation and local practices, making monolithic claims for a signature pedagogy rather a sticky problem to pin down. We have offered here an insight into those that we believe are pervasive in the university but also instances of highly specialised signature pedagogies. We suspect there are many more out there waiting to be identified. The signature pedagogies and the strategies practitioner tutors use to help students learn are ways to develop multiple knowledges about practising in creative industries. Students are supported to not only learn about the discipline but learn to think and behave like creative practitioners in their own right.

The idea of signature pedagogies helps create the link between university education and the professions, but as ever, the relationship is sticky. Practice has to be mediated and structured to support learning and to accommodate the expectations of the university and of many of the political discourses prevalent in society. These discourses also have a tendency to position learning in university as 'other' than the 'real world' however imaginative and creative tutors are in helping students learn. In many respects university learning has more critical views of practice to offer, and graduates in art and design are in a position to enter the 'real world' with a range of varied attributes acquired through engagement in creative pedagogies from within the university.

References

Atkinson, D., 2002. *Art in Education: Identity and Practice.* Dordrecht, Boston and London: Kluwer Academic Publishers.

Barrett, E., 2007. Experiential Learning in Practice as Research: Context, Method, Knowledge. *Journal of Visual Art Practice*, 6(2), pp. 115–124.

Becher, T., 1989. *Academic Tribes and Territories: Intellectual Enquiry and the Culture of Disciplines.* Buckingham: Open University Press.

Becher, T. and Trowler, P., 2001. *Academic Tribes and Territories: Intellectual Enquiry and the Culture of Disciplines.* 2nd ed. Buckingham: Open University Press/SRHE.

Bernstein, B., 2000. *Pedagogy, Symbolic Control and Identity: Theory, Research, Critique.* Lanham and Oxford: Rowman & Littlefield.

Biglan, A., 1973. The Characteristics of Subject Matter in Different Academic Areas. *Journal of Applied Psychology*, 57(3), pp. 195–203.

Boling, E., Schwier, R. A., Gray, C. M., Smith, K. M. and Campbell, K., eds., 2016. *Studio Teaching in Higher Education: Selected Design Cases.* London and New York: Routledge.

Brandt, C.Cennamo, K., Douglas, S., Vernon, M., McGrath, M. and Reimer, Y., 2013. A Theoretical Framework for the Studio as a Learning Environment. *International Journal of Technology and Design Education*, 23(2), pp. 329–348.

Brown, J. S., 2006. New Learning Environments for the 21st Century: Exploring the Edge. *Change: The Magazine of Higher Learning*, 38(5), pp. 18–24.

Budge, K., 2014. *Creative Practice, Value, and the Teaching of Art and Design in Higher Education.* Unpublished PhD Thesis. The University of Melbourne.

Chatterjee, H. J. and Hannan, L. eds., 2015. *Engaging the Senses: Object-based Learning in Higher Education.* Farnham and Burlington: Ashgate Publishing Ltd.

Chick, N., Haynie, A. and Gurung, R., 2012. *Exploring More Signature Pedagogies: Approaches to Teaching Disciplinary Habits of Mind*. Sterling, VA: Stylus Publishing.

Colwell, S., 2014. Scriptwriting as Pedagogy: Vocational Education for Media Production and the Recontextualisation of Practice. *Journal of Media Practice*, 15(2), pp.107–122.

Dall'Alba, G. and Barnacle, R., 2007. An Ontological Turn for Higher Education. *Studies in Higher Education*, 32(6), pp.679–691.

Davies, A. and Reid, A., 2000. Uncovering Problematics in Design Education: Learning and the Design Entity. In C. Swann, ed. *Re-inventing Design Education in the University*. Perth: Curtin University, pp.178–184.

Dean, P., 2015. *Undergraduate Media Studies in England: A Discourse Analysis*. Unpublished EdD Thesis. University of Bedfordshire.

Dormer, P., 1997. *The Culture of Craft*. Manchester: Manchester University Press.

Dowling, P., 1998. *The Sociology of Mathematics Education*. Abingdon: Routledge.

Dowling, P., 2013. Social Activity Method (SAM): A Fractal Language for Mathematics. *Mathematics Education Research Journal*, 25(3), pp. 317–340.

Engeström, Y., 1990. Learning, Working and Imagining: Twelve Studies in Activity Theory. Helsinki: Orienta-Konsultit Oy.

Engeström, Y., Miettinen, R. and Punamaki, R., 1999. *Perspectives on Activity Theory*. Cambridge: Cambridge University Press.

Gray, C. and Smith, K., 2016. Critical Views of Studio. In E. Boling, R. A. Schwier, C. M. Gray, K. M. Smith and K. Campbell, eds. *Studio Teaching in Higher Education: Selected Design Cases*. London and New York: Routledge, pp.260–270.

Gurung, R., Chick, N. and Haynie, A., 2009. *Exploring Signature Pedagogies: Approaches to Teaching Disciplinary Habits of Mind*. Sterling, VA: Stylus Publishing.

Harriss, H. and Widder, L. eds., 2014. *Architecture Live Projects: Pedagogy Into Practice*. Abingdon, Oxon: Routledge.

Hughes, D., 2014. Dwelling as an Approach to Creative Pedagogy. *Art, Design & Communication in Higher Education*, 13(1), pp. 73–87.

Kjølberg, T., 2012. *Visual Research Practice in Fashion and Textile Design Higher Education*. Unpublished PhD Thesis. University of Brighton.

Klebesedal, H. and Kornetsky, L., 2009. Critique as Signature Pedagogy in the Arts. In R. Gurung, N. Chick and A. Haynie, eds. *Exploring Signature Pedagogies: Approaches to Teaching Disciplinary Habits of Mind*. Sterling, VA: Stylus Publishing, pp. 99–120.

Lange, S. and Smith, J. R. A., 2014. Promoting Collaborative and Interdisciplinary Learning via Migration Between Different Learning Spaces. In C. Nygaard, J. Branch, L. Scott-Webber and P. Bartholomew, eds. *Learning Space Design in Higher Education*. Oxford: LIBRI Publishing.

Lave, J. and Wenger, E., 1991. *Situated Learning: Legitimate Peripheral Participation*. Cambridge: Cambridge University Press.

Logan, C., 2006. Circles of Practice: Educational and Professional Graphic Design. *Journal of Workplace Learning*, 18(6), pp. 331–343.

Lowe, P. and Blythman, M., 2009. Blogs and the e-Flective Practitioner: Professional, Not Confessional. In J. O'Donaghue, ed. *Technology-Supported Environments for Personalized Learning: Methods and Case Studies*. Hershey and New York: IGI Global, pp. 149–166.

Marshalsey, L., 2015. Investigating the Experiential Impact of Sensory Affect in Contemporary Communication Design Studio Education. *International Journal of Art & Design Education*, 34(3), pp. 336–348.

Meyer, J. and Land, R., 2006. *Overcoming Barriers to Student Understanding: Threshold Concepts and Troublesome Knowledge*. London and New York: Routledge.
Osmond, J., Bull, K. and Tovey, M., 2010. Threshold Concepts and the Transport and Product Design Curriculum. *Art, Design and Communication in Higher Education*, 8(2), pp. 169–175.
Osmond, J. and Tovey, M., 2015. The Threshold of Uncertaintly in Teaching Design. *Design and Technology Education: An International Journal*, 20(2), pp. 50–57.
Paquette, A., Reedy, G. and Hatzipanagos, S., 2016. Race Cars and the Hellbox: Understanding the Development of Proficiency Among Digital Art Students. *Art, Design & Communication in Higher Education*, 15(1), pp. 7–34.
Schön, D. A., 1985. *The Design Studio*. London: RIBA Publications.
Shreeve, A., 2008. *Transitions: Variation in Tutors' Experience of Practice and Teaching Relations in Art and Design*. Unpublished PhD Thesis. Lancaster University.
Shreeve, A., Bailey, S. and Drew, L., 2004. Students Approaches to the 'Research' Component in the Fashion Design Project: Variation in Students' Experience of the Research Process. *Art, Design and Communication in Higher Education*, 2(3), pp. 113–130.
Shreeve, A., Sims, E. and Trowler, P., 2010. 'A Kind of Exchange': Learning From Art and Design Teaching. *Higher Education Research & Development*, 29(2), pp. 125–138.
Shreeve, A. and Smith, C., 2012. Multi-directional Creative Transfer Between Practice-based Arts Education and Work. *British Educational Research Journal*, 38(4), pp. 539–556.
Shulman, L. S., 2005. Signature Pedagogies in the Professions. *Daedalus*, 134(3), pp. 52–59.
Sims, E. and Shreeve, A., 2012. Signature Pedagogies in Art and Design. In N. Chick, A. Haynie and R. Gurung, eds. *Exploring More Signature Pedagogies: Approaches to Teaching Disciplinary Habits of Mind*. Sterling, VA: Stylus, pp. 55–67.
Smith-Taylor, S., 2009. Effects of Studio Space on Teaching and Learning: Preliminary Findings From Two Case Studies. *Innovative Higher Education*, 33(4), p. 217–228.
Thomson, P., Hall, C., Jones, K. and Sefton Green, J., 2012. *The Signature Pedagogies Project: Final Report*. Available at: www.creativetallis.com/uploads/2/2/8/7/2287089/signature_pedagogies_report_final_version_11.3.12.pdf [Accessed February 25, 2016].
Willcocks, J., 2015. The Power of Concrete Experience: Museum Collections, Touch and Meaning Making in Art and Design Pedagogy. In H. Chatterjee and L. Hannan, eds. *Engaging the Senses: Object Based Learning in Higher Education*. Farnham and Burlington: Ashgate Publishing Ltd., pp. 43–56.

7 Realising the curriculum in art and design

The role of the project

Introduction

In the previous chapter we looked briefly at the role of the studio and the project in our articulation of art and design signature pedagogies. Here we return to the pedagogy of the project to unpack this important aspect of creative educational practice. This is a chapter that surfaces key differences between art and design. Whilst project centred approaches to teaching are commonplace in design education (Swann 1986, 2002), in fine art their position is more contested. In some fine art courses, there are no set projects or assignments as such, and the focus is on the development of students' individual work and practice, whilst in other fine art courses, projects are deployed to support learning. Sometimes this is as much about nomenclature as pedagogy; the fine art example given may be seen by some to be a form of project, whilst other fine artists would reject the term outright. The elasticity of the term project can embrace most assignment based teaching approaches, but it would be wrong to imply that the pedagogic approaches outlined in this chapter are universal. As a result of these debates, much of this chapter focuses on the project in the context of design in higher education.

If you walk into a university lecture hall while a lecture is being delivered, you can usually work out who the teacher is. It is likely that the teacher could be identified even if the class was being delivered in another country in a language and discipline that was unfamiliar. In contrast, when you walk into an art and design studio while a class is happening, it is a lot less clear who the teacher is. Students who have recently arrived to study art and design at university may struggle to recognise the studio as a rich teaching and learning space. On the surface the pedagogy in the studio can look like it lacks purpose or direction. If we are to observe studio based teaching and learning, we might end up asking: where is the curriculum? In this chapter we locate the sticky curriculum in the studio by unpacking the pedagogy of the project. Brief based or project centred learning is the 'backbone of . . . art and design education'(Dineen and Collins 2005:47).

The project 'is the container for debate, learning, practice, development and research' (Blair et al. 2008:82). Essentially it is a written learning task which sets out a challenge and the parameters for learning through undertaking the task. The scope of a brief might draw upon the natural world, the community, real world challenges, manufacturing processes, market segments, the artistic/ designed world, social, historical or political contexts.

Tutors will set out a time frame within which students are expected to present work for interim Crits and final submission. In the contemporary university the brief is also likely to include information such as how the assignment will be assessed, the learning outcomes, assessment criteria and submission guidelines.

The brief is not formulaic or prescriptive; there will be an openness that allows students to respond in diverse and innovative ways. This enables students to co-create a personalised curriculum that supports their individual learning goals. The students are offered a set of signposts to help them journey through a largely independent learning activity. In Orr et al. (2014:34) one student reports that 'you choose your own brief, you make it your own'.

There are many different approaches to project based studio teaching, but typically students will attend 'a briefing' with the course team near the start of the project. This briefing is an important pedagogic ritual, and the lecturer will commonly introduce an assignment by setting out the project requirements to the students and offering them a chance to ask questions. The written brief may be accompanied by visuals which set the context or illustrate the kind of designs, designers, artists or images which help illustrate the context and history relating to the brief.

Most student projects will position somewhere on a spectrum of openness and constraint. The degree of openness in any given project might be thought of as the project's elasticity. Some projects are more stretchy than others. Thus at the open end of the spectrum, an undergraduate fine art project may simply exhort the student to 'continue to experiment with focus and purpose producing new art work',[1] which is only a project in the loosest sense of the word, whilst at the more constrained end of the spectrum, a first-year product design project may specify that the task is to design a specific lighting solution for a new product design agency. Some argue that open-ended briefs open up more affordances for the development of a student's creativity because the student has to do more work to identify the opportunities for divergent thinking. In opposition to this view, Bell (2013) argues that constraint rather than openness supports creativity. Freeman (2006) develops this argument further when he points out that the key spectrum is not one of openness and constraint; rather it is connected to the nature of the problem set and how it can be responded to:

> The weakest act of 'successful creativity' does little more than simply solve the problem to which the student has been directed. The strongest creative work, however, is able to open up a range of problems and possibilities.
>
> (Freeman 2006:99)

Relating these ideas about the project to the concept of the sticky curriculum explored in Chapter 5, we note that the studio project mediates the curriculum. The project triangulates the knowledges, skills and practices that students develop with the support of their tutors. A pedagogically rich project will offer stickiness that supports learning; it will ensure that the students encounter sticking points that they need to traverse; it will allow for play; it will give the students challenges they will struggle with and there may be sticky situations that need to be addressed.

The pedagogy of the project

It is important to note that even a tightly constrained project is not concerned with setting out a problem that has a single answer which all the students are expected to identify. Swann (1986, 2002:51) notes that art and design students 'take off in different directions once they have been briefed with a problem'. We might think of the project brief as a human cannon at a circus that has been calibrated so that students, when loaded into the same cannon, all get pushed out in different directions and different velocities. Crucially, the student is more than a passive body being propelled by a human cannon. Once released the students need to learn to fly by themselves. The information in the brief will only get a student a short distance in the learning journey. The project is written to encourage a rich diversity of response. A first-year fine art student cited in Logan (2013:39) describes this well; 'we all do something different, the only thing in common is the creativeness'. The key point to recognise is that student goals are individualised (Svennson and Edstrom 2011). Researching higher education fine art in South Africa Belluigi (2013) calls for projects that 'allow for asimilar ways of coming to a certain goal or that allow for divergent solutions' (p. 9). Looking at the project from this perspective, one might conceptualise it as a catalyst that activates learning. A good brief 'stimulates the will to learn' (Connolly and Silen 2011:217) and can be the starting point for the creative process (Dineen and Collins 2005). This forward-facing generative approach to the curriculum stands in contrast to assignments in some disciplines which ask students to present learning in a synoptic fashion drawing on what *has* been learnt rather than what *is* to be learnt.

A typology of the brief

Having noted the disciplinary contexts of fine art and design earlier in the chapter, we now draw out a general typology of briefs.

Process-focused briefs

Early in any programme of undergraduate creative study, the brief given is likely to encourage the student to focus on the *process* of making, and the grading scheme will support risk taking with priority given to the process rather than the artefact or object produced. Thus a process-rich project that enabled substantial learning to take place will be welcomed even if it results in a poorly resolved product or artefact. A focus on process is also a feature of some enquiry based learning pedagogies (Aditomo et al. 2013).

Often the briefs given at the start of a course will be more prescribed and/or scaffolded. As the term suggests scaffolded learning (drawing on Vygotskian theories of learning) relates to the ways teachers can vary the support given to students. Thus the teaching scaffold around the student is tightly or loosely structured dependent on learning needs. There are sound pedagogic reasons for this. The aim is to help students bridge the gap between school and university (Austerlitz et al. 2008). As students move through to graduation, the briefs will become more open ended to allow students' work to respond to their own interests, intentions and learning goals. In some contexts students may, towards the end of their programme of study, design their own briefs and be encouraged to set out their own learning outcomes; indeed this is one way to understand the capstone special project or summer show that is a common part of an undergraduate art and design degree. The brief's elasticity increases throughout the course. For Dineen and Collins (2005) this is the key difference between an imposed project (early in a course) and a self-set project (at the latter end of a course).

Immersive briefs

An immersive brief is one that is set over a short period of time and is usually associated with the suspension of other elements of the course. A group of students may be set a four-day project that is the only work set for this period of time. These projects may be part of the core curriculum, or they may be set as extracurricular activity. Immersive briefs lend themselves well to interdisciplinary practice. In a chapter that explores art and design for radical times, Courchesne (2009:136) comments: 'Structuring education in relation to projects that invite a multi-trans-inter-non-disciplinarity has spread . . . the idea of thinking-in-action is more than ever at the heart of leading universities' strategies for education, research and creation'. Immersive projects offer an intensity of experience, and these briefs are usually very sticky. By this we mean that engagement is hard to resist, there will be few distractions and the project, in a short period of time, offers an intense learning experience.

Group brief

Group or collaborative projects are increasingly common in art and design. Many educators include group projects to help students become familiar with ways of working that are common in creative industries. A group project can be part of an employability curriculum that helps prepare students for ways of working post graduation, building teamwork and negotiation skills. Alternatively group projects may be set to promote a sense of community amongst a student body to address a sense of student belonging that aims to enhance retention. Collaborative briefs can support the development of interdisciplinary practice, which is increasingly important in a world where boundaries between subjects are becoming more and more sticky. Group projects may also be introduced as a means to manage the large teaching workloads and assessment requirements that tutors encounter in the face of increasing student numbers.

Live briefs

Live briefs, introduced in Chapter 5, are projects that are set by, or in conjunction with, an external party (Roworth-Stokes and Ball 2015). Typically a live project might take the form of a design company that wants help with a new product range, and they may work with the course team to commission a brief that requires students to carry out research and development. This approach to giving students access to authentic professional practice has merit and is valued by students. The live brief has parallels with the practices associated with client briefs that design students will encounter post graduation. The live project offers an equality of opportunity (unlike internships that often rely on personal networks that are differentially available to students) where all students have access to industry and the staff can shape the project to maximise the learning for both industry and the students. This is an important point; industry needs a reason to work with the university. Access to a pool of talented creatives is enough of a driver for many, and industry feedback is usually positive.

As discussed in Chapter 6 in these contexts the course team has to mediate the space between industry and academia. Typically industry personnel will offer formative Crits and may offer prizes, but the final educational grading will be carried out by academic colleagues who understand assessment frameworks. This approach can lead to occasions where there are differing views of quality. For example, a company may select a student for a prize where that same student has not done well when graded against the stated learning outcomes. These situations can be managed with tact and sensitivity. An example arose for one of the authors where a tourist board selected a student design that received very poor marks from the course team. The design aesthetic requirements of the tourist board were deemed to be old-fashioned by the design lecturers.

When industry colleagues or artists lead Crits, the feedback may be more robust than students are used to, and this can prepare them for the realities of practice post graduation. This kind of feedback has also been used in the past as an excuse for industry-hardened tutors to provide damaging feedback to students, destroying confidence and often creating a climate of fear (Blair 2007). Part-time tutors who are also industry practitioners need to remember that they are working with novices, not professionals, as this tutor realised:

> I got complaints because I was so harsh . . . with them, I was very tough, um, I still am, but in a different way. But I now realise that the reason I was getting complaints and because I was so harsh was because I was still a television producer, I wasn't a teacher, and I was teaching, I was treating my students as if they were a particularly *dozy* and recalcitrant production team! It was really *unfair* you know and so I feel bad about it!
>
> (Shreeve 2008:115, emphasis in original)

The value of taking part in live briefs enables students not only to experience a very close approximation of professional life but to be able to include the companies that they have worked with on their CVs, which offers an effective way to enhance their employability.

Another type of live brief is a competition brief. This may be as part of the course for all students, or it may be a brief set as an extracurricular project. Many companies and organisations will set a competitive brief to promote their products and services as well as provide opportunities for students to offer up new approaches.

The 'no brief' brief

Acknowledgement is needed that some creative practitioners (particularly in fine art) rail against the brief and are more interested in giving students space and access to materials and ideas so that they can develop their work. Others worry that the sheer overwhelming open-endedness of this would be too much for some students. In today's massified, fee-paying university environment, students expect more than access to space. The 'no brief' brief approach may leave too much to chance. Instead it is commonplace to give students studying art and design some kind of brief or assignment title. A form of the 'no brief' brief can be found towards the end of a given course of study, when students are given very broad parameters within which to produce work and they develop their own brief.

Dystopian or utopian brief

Many design educators see the authenticity of a project as key, but it is important to note that the utopian or dystopian brief can also be found in the Art School. These briefs have no basis in current practices found post graduation but are offered to promote creativity and innovation. For example, in one university fashion students designed for alien dystopian bodies as a way to make body shape strange and to heighten awareness of shape and form. In another university students are given information about a future post-climate change dystopia as a means to encourage students to think about sustainable practice. These briefs offer a complex set of dilemmas for students to engage with to support learning. Jonassen and Hung (2008) remind us that ill-structured dilemmas afford rich learning opportunities.

Wider debates

The assignment or project brief is a taken-for-granted element of design studio education, so much so that it is barely noteworthy, and this means that there is very little scholarship on the subject. Many tutors will have experienced some form of studio based, brief-led pedagogy when they were students 'if they were fish, the norms of the studio practice would be their water' (Cennamo et al. 2011:33). However, a key difference between the experience for students now compared to students' experiences thirty years ago is that in the twenty-first century, it is likely that the brief will be written down, and there will be more detail given about how it will be graded and assessed. This change reflects the greater need for tutor accountability and quality assurance that are key tropes in the twenty-first-century university landscape.

The brief is a mediating artefact that transforms the studio into a learning space, and this approach to learning is firmly established in the Art School. This is a worthy topic for further examination in a higher education sector that is increasingly interested in non-transmission based approaches to teaching that promote student creativity and resilience.

Interest in student centred pedagogies in higher education is reflected in the increasing profile given to problem based learning and enquiry based learning. Problem based learning and enquiry based learning approaches have been established in universities to counter traditional transmission teacher-led pedagogic approaches (Lee et al. 2014; Armitage 2013). Problem based learning came to international attention as a result of the work at McMaster School of Medicine in Canada in the 1960s. Within this context problem based learning can be characterised by the following:

- a group based approach to learning;
- self-directed learning; and
- the setting of an authentic task or real-life scenario.

(Higgs and McCarthy 2008)

There is literature that explores a range of subtle differences between enquiry based learning and problem based learning (Healey 2005; Higgs and McCarthy 2008; Aditomo et al. 2013), but this is not our focus. At its simplest the difference relates to the degree to which the tutor sets or defines the problem that the students will address. In enquiry based learning there is an expectation that the students will have a role in the identification of the problem.

In subjects *outside* of art and design, problem based learning and enquiry based learning are frequently referred to as being very different from traditional forms of teaching, whilst in the Art School project centred learning *is* a traditional form of teaching. The sizeable literature emerging from proponents of problem based learning working in other disciplines has a campaigning tone that seeks to challenge and change practices in the academy (see, e.g., Barrett and Moore 2012; Lee et al. 2014). A lecturer employing problem based learning approaches today may not have been taught like this as a student, and she is unlikely to feel like a fish in water using this approach in non-art and design disciplines.

Unsurprisingly, given its roots in medical education, early problem based learning scholarship did not refer at all to creative studio based education. A list of eleven enquiry based learning goals cited in Aditomo et al. (2013) did not reference the development of creativity as a learning goal. This means that there are some key differences about how the project is understood and applied in creative practice in contrast to other subjects. Firstly, the studio set brief, whilst it may be collaborative and set for a group, is more typically, certainly in fine art, primarily a vehicle for individual study and enquiry. Secondly, a brief may pose a problem, but the use of the word problem implies that what is being asked for from the student is a solution, and a creative response is not usually conceived of in this way; 'design is no normal problem solving where the problem and the solution are seen as separate entities that are bridged by a linear process' (Cassim 2013:193). Design students can be set assignments where the key challenge might be to identify what the problem is (Cennamo et al. 2011). Belluigi (2009), writing about fine art, and Valentine and Ivey (2009), writing about design, remind us that there is as much skill in identifying the possibilities inherent in the problem set as there is in simply addressing the problem.

Creativity is at the heart of the art and design brief. It is a vehicle to promote, extend and sustain students' creativity, and this is not the central aim of the problem in problem based learning. In more recent problem based learning literature (Higgs and McCarthy 2008), there is recognition that today's graduates need to be comfortable with uncertainty, and there is an interest in design thinking that encourages creative and critical thinking. The promotion of design thinking is evident in some of the problem based learning literature. For example, Jackson and Buining's (2011) chapter explores the ways that design thinking can bring creative approaches into problem based learning. Design thinking (in common with Art School pedagogy, see Danvers 2003) promotes the use of nonlinear divergent thinking tools (i.e., open-ended play) to aid problem setting and problem solving. Within a design thinking approach the initial focus is on the rapid and extensive production of ideas (ideation) rather than the evaluation of these ideas that comes at a later stage (Brown and Katz 2009; Cassim 2013).

Some problem based learning researchers adopt the use of the phrase 'ill-defined problem'. This term usefully encompasses some of the messiness of real-world problems that do not have easily determined or precise parameters; however, the expression does not sit well in the context of art and design. Whilst it is easy to say that the art and design brief does not seek to pose an ill-defined problem, it is harder to state with any degree of clarity what it *does* pose. It is probably most useful to think of the brief as a project or an imperative that propels learning.

Studio based learning is another variant of problem based learning, and it does address creative learning. As a term it has some purchase in pedagogic literature, particularly in the United States. Its origins are in architectural education, where lecturers have been writing about project pedagogy since the 1970s (Morgan 1976). For Schön (1987) studio based learning describes an approach to education in which groups of design students are given a project under the supervision of an expert designer. Schön premised much of his reflective practitioner scholarship on what he learnt from studying studio based architectural education.

The term project centred learning (rather than problem based learning) accommodates the breadth of assignment types encountered in art and design. Whilst assignments are diverse they commonly focus on making as a form of enquiry (Hall 2010), so perhaps the **p** in project centred learning can stand for project and practice; thus project centred learning in the studio can also be understood as *practice* based enquiry. The brief itself is just one aspect of project centred learning. Here we turn to what unfolds once the brief is given to students. What do they do, and how is their learning supported by their tutors?

The role of the student in project centred learning

The research that students will carry out in response to a brief will be very wide ranging, and often there are no set key texts. The role of the technicians and the workshop facilities will be crucial. Technicians (and in some countries lecturers) will have a key role supporting students' skill development. For example, a sportswear project in fashion will offer workshops that help students to handle stretch fabrics; a student working with ceramics will have access to a kiln and specialist technical expertise. The objects of the students' research may be visual, conceptual or practical, to do with intellectual territory or to do with researching materials or workshop processes. This points to the way that projects can be designed to help students link theory and practice together (Pearson 2009).

The process of undertaking research in response to a project brief can be a mystery to students new to the process. It is often a tacitly learnt approach where tutors may be reluctant to be too explicit for fear of narrowing the creative potential within the brief (Kjølberg 2012). Art and design research requires ingenuity, developing a broad understanding of the meanings and potential inherent within the brief and an active engagement with visual, physical and conceptual material to explore and generate ideas. In the following extract, a third-year design student shares his experiences of the course:

> [the lecturers] told you what they needed you to hand in, but never really went into as much depth about what they wanted so people kind of had to discover that, people were handing in totally different things to what other people were handing in, so we had to discuss amongst ourselves what we were going to do, sort of thing, and, like, someone would hand in something that's totally different, and we'd go heck, well, what's that? We did know about that, but they didn't explain about it. People were just going off on *their own initiative and doing stuff* which is obviously, what we should be doing, really.
>
> (Cited in Orr et al. 2014:24, emphasis added)

Barnett (2013) writes that the will to learn is a key driver for students developing a tolerance for uncertainty in the twenty-first-century university. This view of the student stands in sharp and welcome relief against popular, more instrumental consumerist views of today's students. In art and design this will to learn can be connected to a creative curiosity that drives students' learning. When students are given a brief, they are placed in the driving seat of their learning. This gives them an opportunity to claim their education and fashion it to their interests and needs. This approach demands active learning from the students (Salama 2015). They have to self-direct their learning with a huge degree of autonomy and independence at the start of a course, which is in contrast to some disciplines where learning autonomy only comes towards the end of the course in the form of a self-managed dissertation. Students are forced to take a stance from the earliest stages in an art and design course. In design education enquiry based approaches position 'students as active definers of the discipline' (Walliss and Greig 2009).

Schrand and Eliason (2012:52) researched the nature of design studio pedagogy, and they compared it to liberal arts pedagogy. They were 'struck by the level of student engagement' and the students' 'active learning approach[es]' in the context of design education. These approaches to learning develop student autonomy and resilience, which are attributes that will support graduates in their professional careers.

Student centred approaches to learning can lead some students to misrecognise the role of the teaching that is inherent in project centred pedagogy. Project centred learning may make teaching invisible. In the words of one student, 'We are not actually taught anything. It is very self directed' (Orr et al. 2014:35).

What is the role of the teacher?

In Chapter 6 we explored signature pedagogies in art and design. Building on these ideas we now unpack the tutor's role, specifically in the context of project centred learning. If students report to us that 'you are kind of teaching yourself almost' (cited in Orr et al. 2014:35), then it raises the question of what the role of the tutor is in the context of project centred learning.

Project centred learning is a student centred pedagogic approach. As such there is, appropriately, a focus on the student's activity and behaviour. However, it is essential that this focus on the student does not mask the key role of the teacher. It is very common for lecturers and researchers to talk about establishing and fostering an environment that supports creativity (Belluigi 2013; Williamson 2009; Corner 2005; Budge et al. 2013). Jackson and Buining (2011) argue that the lecturer needs to design a set of rich learning experiences for students. The idea that the lecturer's role is to set up the right conditions for students offers up the lecturer as a gardener tending to the studio to ensure that it provides a fertile environment for creativity. This conception of the lecturers' role ignores their active teaching role. The pedagogies the tutors deploy are a key part of the environment (Hickman 2008). Might it be more useful to think of the tutor as a midwife helping the students give birth to their own practice as presented by Graham (2009)? This brings to mind the ancient Chinese philosopher Lau Tzu's writing on styles of leadership (cited in Shinagel n.d.). Lau Tzu wrote that the result of successful leadership will be people saying they did it themselves. As Shinagel (n.d:1) comments, 'this is the art of leadership at its best: the art that conceals art'. This is similar to the role of the tutor in art and design. In the following extract the audio visual artist, Muda Mathis describes art teaching: 'You are the observer, the recipient, and the one who pays attention and shows recognition, the one who holds hands and provides support. Essentially, it is about attention and support' (cited in Bourgeois 2007:58). There is a paucity of language to articulate the skills and approaches deployed by the artful studio lecturer. The role of the teacher in art and design is elusive and sometimes contradictory. Whilst much is written about transmission based teaching, there is a much smaller research base to draw on that articulates the tutor's role in project based studio education. Shreeve and Batchelor (2012) interviewed students and tutors, asking them to report on what made for successful learning in the studio. Their findings suggest that tutors needed to 'tune in' to each student's learning needs. As discussed in Chapter 5 this requires skills of negotiation and a reliance on the tutor's awareness of individual learning needs.

The goal or ideal for most students and staff interviewed in this study was for equality in the relationship where there was an adult-to-adult exchange supporting learning. However, the fine line between the roles adopted by tutors in different circumstances and with different students at different phases of the project was also evident. In some cases tutors might be called on to present a more authoritative position or one of leadership, setting examples and reassuring. In others the balance of professionalism with friendliness and enabling qualities was important to support learning to help students become independent practitioners through project work.

A key challenge with project centred learning, as it is delivered in today's massified education, relates to the ways that lecturers need to respond to the learning needs of each individual student as opposed to the collective learning needs of a large cohort of students. Individualised support that relies on understanding and responding to every single student's project gets harder to deliver as the number of students increases and the levels of funding and staffing resource stay fixed. Brief based education in the studio is underpinned by rich interim feedback, and this gets more difficult in large groups. Lecturers have to reconsider the traditional, serial, one-to-one tutorial model where a lecturer does her best to interact with every student because this may amount to a mere few minutes for some students. An experienced tutor will be able to identify shared learning points that can be discussed in the larger group (rather than repeating points made to every student on an individual level). Project centred pedagogies also need to adapt to digital environments and contexts where students are less likely to make work in the studio.

Briefs can be well written, or they can be sloppy and confusing. Writing a good brief that supports creative learning requires considerable expertise and imagination. Lecturers have to manage carefully what information they put in and what they leave out so that students have just enough information to take the work forward but not so much that the creative potential of the brief is destroyed by overspecificity.

Expertise

When students embark on a project in response to a brief, they can find themselves in territory uncharted by the teacher. This raises interesting questions about the locus of expertise that has parallels in PhD supervision. In Orr et al. (2014:6) students reported that they held the knowledge about their work, which they explained to the tutors. In the words of one student: 'For our course it would be explaining [to the tutor] *what do we think our work means, or what it relates to*' (emphasis in original). In this study this was called 'reverse transmission' because the students appear to be transmitting the knowledge they have created to the lecturer rather than vice versa. This presents a shaky basis for the teacher's authority. Project centred learning destabilises common conceptions of expertise. Recasting the nature of expertise the teacher needs to encourage enquiry and stimulate reflection (Cennamo et al. 2011). In the wider context of problem based learning, Barrett and Moore (2012) propose that the following lecturer skills are essential. The ability to:

- facilitate,
- listen,
- observe,
- intervene,
- ask questions, and
- challenge.

Blair et al. (2008) highlight the importance of listening in studio teaching, not a skill set that comes easily to some tutors! Related to this is the important skill of knowing when *not* to intervene to make sure that one does not over contribute. At the centre of this is the importance of tutors being interested in the students' work.

This list appears to offer a somewhat quiet and rather self-effacing skill set. This view is supported when a design lecturer comments to the researchers Harman and McDowell (2011:43): 'it's almost like tapping [the students] in the right direction. We're not really lecturers in that sense, we just sort of guide them'. Harman and McDowell present the design lecturer as 'the expert guide' (p. 43). In their study another tutor elaborates:

> I feel a bit like as if there's water flowing down a river and hits a rock and we're helping them get around the rock and flow on. And often, they're hitting rocks and don't quite know how to get around them and with experience we can just help them move round a problem so they're free to move onto the next crit.
>
> (Harman and McDowell 2011:43/44)

Returning to the work of Rancière (1991), it could be argued that the art and design lecturer needs to be able to follow rather than lead the student. The teacher guides the students' own learning processes (Barrett and Moore 2012). The ability to improvise in the context of an emergent and uncertain learning environment is key (Peters 2012). Belluigi (2013) sees the fine art teacher as a facilitator who focuses on creating environments and relations that support creativity. She reminds us that as well as supporting divergent thinking, the tutor needs to encourage convergence as well. After all, choices have to be made, and deadlines are set and met.

Cennamo et al. (2011) write in detail about the skills needed by studio based design tutors, these include the following:

- giving students assignments,
- the use of open-ended questioning,

- placing student knowledge in public view,
- revoicing (i.e., drawing out key points to share),
- modelling evaluative language, and
- giving prompts or reminders.

Cennamo et al. note that some tutors view themselves as expert coaches leading learning, whilst others feel more comfortable in a role where they defer to the students. One way or another the Art School tutor 'orchestrates experiences' (2011:14), deploying variously the roles of 'instructor, mentor, exemplar, agitator or demonstrator' (Llewellyn and Williamson 2015:11).

Power relations

Project centred learning in art and design creates a complex web of power relations between students and tutors. The ways that power is co-constructed, constrained and enabled means that it is useful to think of power as liquid and mobile. Problem based learning literature (outside of the discipline of art and design) casts traditional lecture based teaching and learning as being concerned with the flow of knowledge from the lecturer to the student (Lee et al. 2014; Armitage 2013). In this model of pedagogy the lecturer holds the power. This is then contrasted with the way that power is conceived of in problem based learning, where students are viewed as moving from a position of powerlessness and tutors are deemed to cede power. There is an assumption that problem based learning is more democratic than traditional (i.e., lecture based) forms of pedagogy, and there is also the view that problem based learning is empowering for lecturers (Barrett and Moore 2012). Starting from this confusing position at the key intersection between the students and their tutors, we want to explore the ways that students and tutors shift in subtle ways between positions of power and powerlessness throughout the course of study.

Many creative educators working in higher education view themselves first and foremost as art and design practitioners rather than educators, and they sometimes resist the idea that they are holders of knowledge and power. There is a conflict at the heart of the creative educator's identity. This idea is entwined with the idea of art education as transgressive and rule breaking (Danvers 2003; Belluigi 2013). Students are actively encouraged to break the rules, and lecturers will sometimes tell students to ignore their advice. Tutor feedback to students can sometimes be signposted as just another view rather than as an authoritative voice. This aligns with the view of teaching that focusses on the educator as first and foremost an artist or designer who is working side by side with the students (see Chapter 6). However, at the same time students are expected to respond to feedback. Students who do less well in relation to grades sometimes are those who refuse to (or don't know how to) be shaped by tutor feedback.

In art and design education it is common for teachers to resist the authority invested in their role as teacher; however, research suggests that there is a didactic element to teaching in this discipline (Strickfaden and Heylighen 2010). In the context of the sticky ambiguous studio, we see the tutor as disappearing; power is liquid and movable; it goes between the student and the tutor. Tutors flip between positions of authority to positions of co-learning. They will be directive and non-directive dependent on circumstances and learning needs. There is a potential mismatch between espoused and in-practice views of power relations. What this means is that narratives about teaching can focus on the equality of tutor/student relationships without acknowledging the power relations at play in practice. Ultimately the teachers are invested with authority because they make decisions about the marks and grades students receive. Grades have value and currency in universities, and the tutors hold the key.

Whilst project centred learning might concern itself with guidance rather than leadership, power is capillary; it works on a micro level (Morley 2003). As we explored in Chapter 3 the questions a tutor asks the student about the work in a Crit, and the grades the work is awarded will influence the work in a range of subtle ways. Power is present. Lecturers may share a dominant discourse of freedom of expression, and 'anything goes', but this is framed within a set of expectations and values about student behaviour and art and design practices. The point at which a tutor decides what grade the student's work receives is a key moment of powerlessness for students. Interestingly after the marks are awarded and the summer show is exhibited, power flows back to the students; the work is theirs, and the lecturer's role can become invisible again. The lecturer moves from the centre to the periphery (Orr and Hind 2009). As Graham (2009) observes in her research into her role as a dramaturge/educator in which she compares her role as dramaturge to that of a midwife, the role of the midwife is sometimes forgotten once the baby is born. When the student work is in the show, it is all about the work. It is all about the student.

Power relations are also connected to ideas concerning expertise. Rancière (1991) observes there is no hierarchy amongst the ignorant. This view is nuanced by Harman and McDowell (2011:8, emphasis in the original), who cite a design lecturer: 'You get to the point where you're *almost* like, there's *almost* like real equality in third year when you're discussing projects, though obviously I've got a lot more years of experience in industry and in teaching'. Harman and McDowell (2011) point out that the frequent use of the word almost serves to underline in a subtle way the absence of equality. Often studio based teaching is connected to the idea of guidance, which links to the idea of facilitating learning. This connotes a powerless position that does not have the status or recognition of being a full teaching academic.

Conclusion

Ewing (2009:160) captures the characteristics of the contemporary student:

> The twenty-first century art student is a browser, inter-actor, co-author, producer, and nomad just like every active cultural participant in an information or knowledge economy. They have grown up in a performative culture where active participation is learning.

In this chapter we have discussed the brief based pedagogies that support students' learning. For Blair et al. 'the project is an established and universal vehicle used by tutors to teach and for the student to explore studio curriculum agendas in art, design, media and communication' and as such it is the 'primary curriculum vehicle' (2008:81). However, it is important to note that there are dissenting voices that reject the project as a pedagogic tool because it is deemed to be, even at its most elastic, an approach to pedagogy that 'contradicts the philosophy underlining an open-forum, open-ended learning approach' (Pearson 2009:173). Whilst recognising this dissent we view the project as a pedagogic tool well suited to practice based visual disciplines, particularly as it allows the tutor to scaffold learning for students over the course of study.

This chapter emphasises the individuality of students' learning goals, but elsewhere in this book we are reminded that there are wider knowledges that are shared across the cohort of students in the studio. There are practices, ways of doing and being that are inculcated in the studio, so it is important not to imply that the sticky curriculum is solely individualised. Groups of students working on their practice within particular studio milieu will acquire (or indeed reject) the dominant values and practices that they are exposed to.

Rich (1977:1) exhorts her students 'to claim an education . . . to be the rightful owner of that information'. Project centred and brief based education offer students a chance to claim their education. It provokes engagement. Participation is unavoidable. The project's stickiness means that passivity is not an option. The well-written brief offers students the chance to shape a curriculum and to develop, bend and grow with their interests and aspirations. It is opportunistic and generative. Both staff and students animate the curriculum. This offers a model for the co-production of curriculum and the elastic canon. Situating creative enquiry led pedagogy within a wider social and political context, Cassim (2013) recognises that the active learning supported by this approach to pedagogy offers a way to prepare students to engage with the wider social and environmental challenges encountered in the twenty-first century (Cassim 2013). A good project will inspire and motivate students, and the work they develop in response will prepare them for uncertain futures.

The pedagogy of Art School project centred learning has great relevance to higher education beyond the confines of art and design. Working in this way demands a lot from students, and the skills and knowledges acquired are well suited to the contemporary workplace where flexibility, creativity, agility and resilience are key attributes.

Note

1 Wimbledon College of Arts; University of the Arts London, BA Fine Art: Painting Brief. Cited with permission.

References

Aditomo, A., Goodyear, P., Bluic, A. M. and Ellis, R., 2013. Inquiry-based Learning in Higher Education: Principal Forms, Educational Objectives, and Disciplinary Variations. *Studies in Higher Education*, 38(9), pp. 1239–1258.

Armitage, A., 2013. Conscientization, Dialogue and Collaborative Problem Based Learning. *Journal of Problem Based Learning in Higher Education*, 1(1), pp. 1–18.

Austerlitz, N., Blythman, M., Grove-White, A., Jones, B. A., Jones, C. A., Morgan, S., Orr, S., Shreeve, A. and Vaughan, S., 2008. Mind the Gap: Expectations, Ambiguity and Pedagogy Within Art and Design Education. In L. Drew, ed. *The Student Experience in Art and Design Higher Education: Drivers for Change*. Cambridge: Jill Rogers Associates Ltd Publishers, pp. 125–148.

Barnett, R., 2013. *Imagining the University*. London: Routledge.

Barrett, T. and Moore, S., 2012. *New Approaches to Problem-based Learning: Revitalising Your Practice in Higher Education*. Oxon: Routledge.

Bell, S., 2013. *The Promise of the Short Text: Writing Risk Into Visual Arts Practice*. Unpublished PhD Thesis. Coventry University.

Belluigi, D. Z., 2009. Exploring the Discourses Around 'Creativity' and 'Critical Thinking' in a South African Creative Arts Curriculum. *Studies in Higher Education*, 34(6), pp. 699–717.

Belluigi, D. Z., 2013. A Proposed Schema for the Conditions of Creativity in Fine Art Studio Practice. *International Journal of Education & the Arts*, 14(19), pp. 1–22.

Blair, B., 2007. At the End of a Huge Crit in the Summer, It Was Crap, I'd Worked Really Hard But All She Said Was Fine and I Was Gutted. *Art, Design & Communication in Higher Education*, 5(2), pp. 83–95.

Blair, B., Cummings, A., Dunbar, T., Hayward, D. and Woodman, J., 2008. BAU-WOW! A Model for Creative Practice, Thinking, Learning, Research and Innovation in the 21st Century. In L. Drew, ed. *The Student Experience in Art and Design Higher Education: Drivers for Change*. Cambridge: Jill Rogers Associates Ltd Publishers, pp. 65–98.

Bourgeois, V., 2007. *Art Mistresses: Between Classrooms and Studio*. Germany: Salon-Verl.

Brown, T. and Katz, B., 2009. *Change by Design: How Design Thinking Transforms Organizations and Inspires Innovation*. New York: Harper Business.

Budge, K., Beale, C. and Lynas, E., 2013. A Chaotic Intervention: Creativity and Peer Learning in Design Education. *International Journal of Art & Design Education*, 32(2), pp. 146–156.

Cassim, F., 2013. Hands On, Hearts On, Minds On: Design Thinking Within an Education Context. *International Journal of Art & Design Education*, 32(2), pp. 190–202.

Cennamo, K., Brant, C., Scott, B., Douglas, S., McGrath, M. and Reimer, Y., 2011. Managing the Complexity of Design Problems Through Studio-based Learning. *Interdisciplinary Journal of Problem-based Learning*, 5(2), pp. 12–36.

Connolly, D. and Silen, C., 2011. Empowering Tutors. In T. Barrett and S. Moore, eds. *New Approaches to Problem-based Learning: Revitalising Your Practice in Higher Education*. Oxford: Taylor & Francis, pp. 215–228.

Corner, F., 2005. Identifying the Core in the Subject of Fine Art. *International Journal of Art & Design Education*, 24(3), pp. 334–342.

Courchesne, L., 2009. Art, Design, and Beyond. In B. Buckley and J. Conomos, eds. *Rethinking the Contemporary Art School: The Artist, the PhD and the Academy*. Halifax: The Press of the Nova Scotia College of Art and Design, pp. 136–144.

Danvers, J., 2003. Towards a Radical Pedagogy: Provisional Notes on Learning and Teaching in Art & Design. *International Journal of Art and Design Education*, 22(1), pp. 47–57.

Dineen, R. and Collins, E., 2005. Killing the Goose: Conflicts Between Pedagogy and Politics in the Delivery of a Creative Education. *International Journal of Art & Design Education*, 24(1), pp. 43–52.

Ewing, L., 2009. Remixing the Hive. In B. Buckley and J. Conomos, eds. *Rethinking the Contemporary Art School: The Artist, the PhD and the Academy*. Halifax: The Press of the Nova Scotia College of Art and Design, pp. 159–163.

Freeman, J., 2006. First Insights: Fostering Creativity in University Performance. *Arts and Humanities in Higher Education*, 5(1), pp. 91–103.

Graham, F., 2009. Dramaturge as Midwife: The Writing Process Within a New Zealand Community Theatre Project. *Journal of Writing in Creative Practice*, 2(2), pp. 209–216.

Hall, J., 2010. Making Art, Teaching Art, Learning Art: Exploring the Concept of the Artist Teacher. *International Journal of Art & Design Education*, 29(2), pp. 103–110.

Harman, K. and McDowell, L., 2011. Assessment Talk in Design: The Multiple Purposes of Assessment in HE. *Teaching in Higher Education*, 16(1), pp. 41–52.

Healey, M., 2005. Linking Research and Teaching: Exploring Disciplinary Spaces and the Role of Inquiry. In R. Barnett, ed. *Reshaping the University: New Relationships Between Research, Scholarship and Teaching*. Milton Keynes: Open University Press, pp. 67–78.

Hickman, R. ed., 2008. *Research in Art and Design Education: Issues and Exemplars*. Bristol: Intellect.

Higgs, B. and McCarthy, M., 2008. *Emerging Issues II: The Changing Roles and Identities of Teachers and Learners in Higher Education*. Cork, Ireland: National Academy for Integration of Research & Teaching & Learning.

Jackson, N. and Buining, F., 2011. Enriching Problem Based Learning Through Design Thinking. In T. Barrett and M. McCarthy, eds. *New Approaches to Problem-based Learning: Revitalising Your Practice in Higher Education*. Oxford: Routledge, pp. 158–170.

Jonassen, D. H. and Hung, W., 2008. All Problems Are Not Equal: Implications for Problem-Based Learning. *Interdisciplinary Journal of Problem-Based Learning*, 2(2), pp. 6–28.

Kjølberg, T., 2012. *Visual Research Practice in Fashion and Textile Design Higher Education*. Unpublished PhD Thesis. University of Brighton.

Lee, J. S., Blackwell, S., Drake, J. and Moran, K. A., 2014. Taking a Leap of Faith: Redefining Teaching and Learning in Higher Education Through Project-Based Learning. *Interdisciplinary Journal of Problem-Based Learning*, 8(2).

Llewellyn, N. and Williamson, B., eds., 2015. *The London Art Schools*. London: Tate Publishing.

Logan, C., 2013. Living Artists: Identity, Independence and Engagement in Fine Art Learning. *Art, Design & Communication in Higher Education*, 12(1), pp. 33–48.

Morgan, A. S., 1976. Learning Through Projects. *Studies in Higher Education*, 1(1), pp. 63–68.

Morley, L., 2003. *Quality and Power in Higher Education*. Maidenhead: McGraw-Hill Education (UK).

Orr, S. and Hind, C., 2009. Space and Place: Writing Encounters Self. *Journal of Writing in Creative Practice*, 2(2), pp. 133–138.

Orr, S., Yorke, M. and Blair, B., 2014. 'The Answer Is Brought About From Within You': A Student-Centred Perspective on Pedagogy in Art and Design. *International Journal of Art & Design Education*, 33(1), pp. 32–45.

Pearson, G., 2009. The Outskirts of Town: A Peripheral Centre for Art, Agency, and Academia. In B. Buckley and J. Conomos, eds. *Rethinking the Contemporary Art School: The Artist, the PhD and the Academy*. Halifax: The Press of the Nova Scotia College of Art and Design, pp. 164–181.

Peters, G., 2012. Certainty, Contingency, and Improvisation. *Critical Studies in Improvisation*, 8(2), pp. 1–8.

Rancière, J., 1991. *The Ignorant Schoolmaster: Five Lessons in Intellectual Emancipation*. Redwood: Stanford University Press.

Rich, A., 1977. *Claiming an Education: Speech Delivered at the Convocation of Douglass College*. Available at: http://isites.harvard.edu/fs/docs/icb.topic469725.files/Rich-ClaimingганEducation-1.pdf [Accessed February 3, 2017].

Roworth-Stokes, S. and Ball, T., 2015. The Use of Design Case Studies in Design Education. In M. Tovey, ed. *Design Pedagogy*. Farnham: Routledge, pp. 181–213.

Salama, A., 2015. *Spatial Design Education: New Directions for Pedagogy in Architecture and Beyond*. Farnham: Ashgate.

Schön, D., 1987. *Educating the Reflective Practitioner*: Toward a New Design for Teaching and Learning in the Professions. San Francisco: Jossey-Bass.

Schrand, T. and Eliason, J., 2012. Feedback Practices and Signature Pedagogies: What Can the Liberal Arts Learn From the Design Critique? *Teaching in Higher Education*, 17(1), pp. 51–62.

Shinagel, M., n.d. *The Paradox of Leadership | Harvard Professional Development | Harvard DCE*. Available at: www.extension.harvard.edu/professional-development/blog/paradox-leadership [Accessed December 27, 2016].

Shreeve, A., 2008. *Transitions: Variation in Tutors' Experience of Practice and Teaching Relations in Art and Design*. Unpublished PhD Thesis. Lancaster University.

Shreeve, A. and Batchelor, R., 2012. Designing Relations in the Studio: Ambiguity and Uncertainty in One to One Exchanges. *Design and Technology Education: An International Journal*, 17(3), pp. 20–26.

Strickfaden, M. and Heylighen, A., 2010. Cultural Capital: A Thesaurus for Teaching Design. *International Journal of Art & Design Education*, 29(2), pp. 121–133.

Svennson, L. and Edstrom, A. M., 2011. The Function of Art Students' Use of Studio Conversations in Relation to Their Artwork. *International Journal of Education and the Arts*, 12(5), pp. 1–29.

Swann, C., 2002. Nellie Is Dead. 1986. Designer; Reprinted. *Art, Design & Communication in Higher Education*, 1(1), pp. 50–58.

Valentine, L. and Ivey, M., 2009. Sustaining Ambiguity and Fostering Openness in the (Design) Learning Environment. *Art, Design & Communication in Higher Education*, 7(3), pp. 155–167.

Walliss, J. and Greig, J., 2009. Graduate Design Education: The Case for an Accretive Model. *International Journal of Art & Design Education*, 28(3), pp. 287–295.

Williamson, B., 2009. Paint and Pedagogy: Anton Ehrenzweig and the Aesthetics of Art Education. *International Journal of Art & Design Education*, 28(3), pp. 237–248.

8 Art School evaluation

Process, product and person

Introduction

The sticky curriculum and project centred pedagogies help students develop and respond to their own lines of enquiry. Work produced by a student might require the lecturer to visually apprehend the work, smell the work, touch the work, participate in the work, click through the work, listen to the work, experience the work or watch the work unfold. The work might be huge, tiny, heavy, strange, temporal, digital, analogue or elusive; in other words the output forms will be hugely diverse. Grading student work is a multisensory practice.

In this volume we have explored the ways that stickiness is at the core of the creative curriculum. The sticky curriculum is not delivered to the students; instead it is co-constructed with the students, and the individuality of final-year undergraduate work reminds us that there is very little consensus about a common 'core' or canon in art and design (Elkins 2001; Llewellyn and Williamson 2015). The concept of curriculum in art and design encompasses tacit and explicit practices, theories and skills. How then do we grade student work? Clearly, in the context of the creative sticky curriculum, this is not about assessing[1] the reproduction of a given body of knowledge (Payne 2015).

Over the years many art and design lecturers have reported to us that they would prefer not to grade student work at all. They find the assessment requirements of higher education constraining and poorly matched to the needs of creative practice (Vidokle 2009). This relates to the rejection by some practitioners of the academisation of art and design education that we explored in Chapter 1. There are alternative models that resist classificatory assessment (see, e.g., early days in California Institute of the Arts, the Black Mountain College history or the alternative Art School movement), but for the purposes of this chapter, the assumption is that students are studying in higher education and that they receive marks in the form of letters and/or numbers as well as written and oral feedback. Universities and Art Schools have policies that set out the assessment regulations, and we explore the ways that assessment practices comply with, subvert and respond to these policies.

As discussed in Chapter 1, art and design is increasingly taught within a university context, so it is important to consider assessment in the context of wider educational debates. There is a tension at the heart of assessment. This results from its dual focus on assessment for learning and assessment of learning. Assessment for learning (known as A4L) seeks to foster learning by offering formative feedback to students so that they can act to improve their work and enhance their learning (Assessment Reform Group 1999). The focus on A4L emerged from school education and has a degree of purchase in university educational discourse. This understanding of assessment contrasts with assessment of learning. This is concerned with deploying assessment as a means to classify student attainment. Thus assessment is part of the experience of learning, but it is also a process that divides and categorises students at stages throughout their programme of study, culminating at the point of graduation. The Crit (see Figure 8.1) embodies assessment for and assessment of learning; tutors give feedback to students, and they make suggestions about how the work might develop. In this mode the tutors are working side by side with students. When final work is submitted, the tutors move to the role of gatekeeper, deciding who gets what final grade. This can be uncomfortable for art and design tutors who have to shift roles from peer reviewer to assessor.

In today's universities it is common for written policy documents to present assessment as a simple transaction in which documents set out clearly what the student needs to learn (written as learning outcomes), and then the student work is measured to judge the extent to which this learning is achieved. This model of assessment has been influenced by Biggs and Tang's (2011) concept of constructive alignment, which seeks to align teaching approaches to intended learning outcomes for students. The influence of Biggs and Tang's ideas on higher education policy coincides with an increased focus on how students learn. This commitment to student centred learning has resulted in outcome based assessment (OBA), which has been a mainstay in higher education for nearly twenty years (Ecclestone 1999). OBA aims to set out in writing the required student learning outcomes with the idea that this removes the hidden curriculum. Proponents of OBA argue that it makes assessment fair and transparent. OBA and the focus on setting out the assessment requirements in writing links to contemporary concerns about transparency, public accountability and the idea of the student as a consumer. It also connects to a widening participation agenda where universities are keen to make the 'rules of the game' clear to students. These agendas collide to create a dominant narrative around assessment that focuses almost exclusively on the written artefacts of assessment (i.e., the assessment regulations, the policies, the learning outcomes and the assessment criteria). There is much that is laudable about OBA, but as early as 1999, Ecclestone (1999, 2004) argued that it had over-promised and under-delivered. There is an overemphasis on what Wenger (1998) would call the reified objects (the various documents) of assessment and a lack of focus on the practice of assessment, that is, how it is experienced by tutors and students.

OBA resides within a techno-rationalist paradigm that concerns itself with the tidy delivery of objective assessment processes. The idea that we can set out intended learning in an unproblematic way in the form of learning outcomes presupposes that language carries meaning in a straightforward way. At this point it is useful to bring in two key terms used by educational researchers who have written extensively about assessment. The first is 'fuzzy standards', a term used by Yorke (2007) to explain the imprecision at the heart of assessment practices and professional judgement. For Yorke 'fuzziness . . . is inherent in most assessments in higher education' (p. 172). Yorke points out that across all disciplines (not just art and design), it is 'difficult to mark with precision' (p. 180) even when the learning outcomes and assessment criteria have been tightly defined. The second term is 'elasticity', used in relation to assessment codifications (the so-called assessment artefacts) introduced by Sadler (2013). Like Yorke, Sadler is using the term elastic to explore the lack of precision in learning outcomes and assessment standards. He argues that assessment artefacts 'fail to convey standards' (p. 283). Crucially both Sadler and Yorke remind us that this lack of precision is not because there is a need to offer increased granularity; instead this is an ontological gap. Language is fuzzy and elastic. Many lecturers will tell you of the numerous emails and questions they will receive from students after a briefing that ask the lecturer to further clarify meaning. What can be 'clear' to a tutor may be opaque to a student. We take one word to illustrate this point; if a learning outcome asks students to demonstrate criticality, then what precisely does that mean? Does criticality mean the same thing in graphic design and ceramics? Does it mean the same thing at master's and undergraduate levels?

Eisner's (1983) critique of educational objectives as a foundation for both curriculum building and assessment counters the rational arguments for using objectives. He highlights the artfulness of teaching and its potential spontaneity in variable social groups and therefore the impossibility of being able to accurately predict the outcomes of teaching and learning activities, which are too numerous to identify with precision. Subject matter is more or less amenable to predictive outcomes, and he specifically cites the arts as those which demand the unpredictable:

> In the arts and in subject matters where, for example, novel or creative responses are desired, the particular behaviors [sic] to be developed cannot easily be identified. Here curriculum and instruction should yield behaviors [sic] and products which are unpredictable.
>
> (pp. 554/5)

The use of objectives to assess is based on a belief that they represent standards against which outcomes can be measured, but Eisner argues that this fails to distinguish between applying a standard and making a judgement. Standards are invariable, but outcomes of learning are multiple and complex, requiring an artful application of judgement in the light of values held by the assessor.

Unsurprisingly there is widespread concern about the implications of OBA in the context of creative education (Pearson 2009). In Europe this approach to assessment is associated with the constraints and bureaucracy placed upon higher education by the 1999 Bologna Declaration (Buckley and Conomos 2009). In Australia there has been a strong university focus on competency based

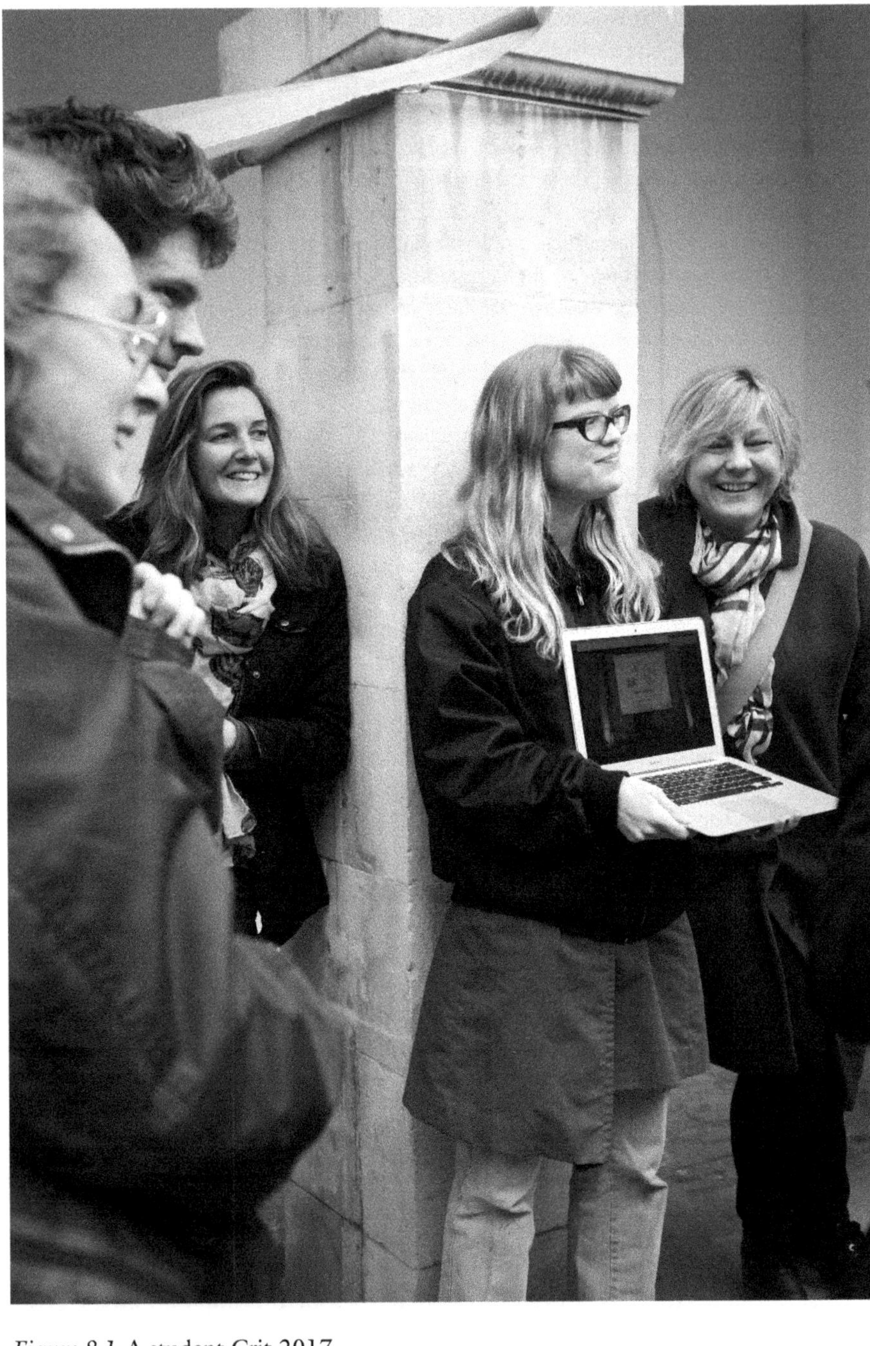

Figure 8.1 A student Crit 2017

Photograph by Valentina Schivardi

assessment, and universities' approaches to quality assurance are felt to clash with the design education ethos (Cowdroy and Williams 2007). Dixon (2000), cited in Fryer (2010:561), argues that tutors are required to suspend disbelief and can feel forced into 'using an inappropriate rational, objective, quasi-scientific model to assess a largely irrational spontaneous and subjective art'. Creativity as a concept does not lend itself to the idea of tightly defined learning outcomes. Fryer notes that 'prescriptive assessment criteria may seem to fit particularly awkwardly with creative work which is inevitably about outcomes that cannot be predicted in advance' Fryer (2010:549).

In Orr and Bloxham (2012) we report that lecturers struggle to verbalise the ambiguity of high-quality creative work, and we cite a lecturer who reports that he is looking for work that has what he refers to as 'zing', which he admits is a very stretchy and elusive term. This lecturer is articulating the idea that there is something unknowable about high-quality creative work. Zing is not the kind of word one finds in a learning outcome. It is a sticky term. Davies, writing about learning outcomes in art and design, talks about how important it is that students have the ability to visualise. He comments, 'This concept is not easily captured in learning outcome form. It's not the kind of thing that can be measured easily. It is, in fact, developed within a whole process of the practice over time' Davies (2012:3). In Addison's (2014) critique of learning outcomes in art and design education (an article playfully presented as a series of learning outcomes), he explores the absence of affect in learning outcome parlance. Feelings and ambiguity have no place within an objective learning outcome paradigm. This shows the disjuncture between what might be called warm assessment that embraces the centrality of the affective and the ambiguous with what we might think of as cold assessment, where these views would be seen as transgressive.

However, it is important to note that learning outcomes do have utility if they are written in a fairly loose and generic way. Learning outcomes offer signposts rather than a common destination, and if they embrace a degree of ambiguity or stickiness, they can support the development of creativity, allowing for diversity of output and differentiation.

Art and design assessment works in the sticky space between clarity and creativity, between rules and imagination (Hirst 2013). A creative project will never be a recipe or a formula. As this volume underlines, the studio offers a space to improvise, experiment and take risks, and these spaces defy easy explanation. There is a key sticking point between the needs to make our learning expectations clear to students in the interests of accountability and fairness whilst at the same time allowing students to surprise us with the unanticipated creative work they produce (Gordon 2004; Cannatella 2001). The sticky curriculum fractures the idea of transparency in assessment.

Art and design assessment is more usefully situated in a constructivist interpretive paradigm (Orr 2007a). An interpretive meaning-making conception of language recognises that staff and students need to agree and contest meanings in communities of practice (see Figure 8.2). Interpretation of the written criteria and artefacts of assessment help staff and students develop shared meanings

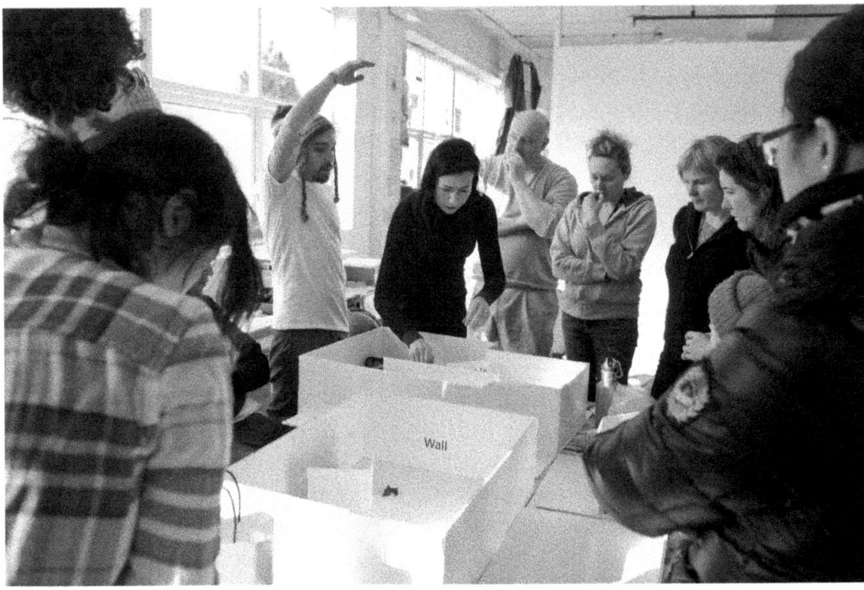

Figure 8.2 MA Art and Science Crit 2017
Photograph by Valentina Schivardi

through the materiality and the oral exchanges which characterise the learning environment. Grading creative work is an act of interpretation (Delandshere 2001). Groups of students and tutors begin to understand through seeing and experiencing the work and its assessment. Our understanding of communities of practice is nuanced in recognition that modular programme structures, and the employment of part-time staff means that the idea of a tight course team community that is in regular contact does not reflect the contemporary Art School. Communities of practice may be dispersed and virtual.

Group marking approaches strengthen the rigour of grading in art and design. Tutors often work together to grade student work in the studio. The need to assess creative practice forces educators to engage with multiple subjectivities, and when lecturers mark work together in the studio, their discussions help establish shared standards. Whilst each tutor will approach assessment with an individual, specialised evaluative gaze (Gilio 2016), working together they can acknowledge their subjectivities, and through dialogue they come to a group subjectivity, what Shay refers to as intersubjectivity; thus 'multiple subjectivities shape assessors' interpretations of student performance' (Shay 2005:663). Shay's study of an engineering community offers a useful window on group assessment. Shay explores the ways that lecturers' personal tastes and individual approaches are socially produced. In Shay's (2005) words 'intuitive judgements are internalisations of the objective regularities of the field they inhabit' (p. 675). This stops any individual from making arbitrary or whimsical assessment decisions. In this way the Crit dialogue is a 'regulating apparatus' (Crippa 2015:140) whilst also offering a space to new lecturers to participate and learn about assessment through engagement and observation.

Within an interpretive paradigm the aim of assessment is to ensure students get a 'good enough' mark (Yorke 2007). There is no correct mark in any absolutist sense; instead there is a mark of best fit. Recognising the role of professional judgement and the ways that tacit values and practices imbue assessment outcomes means that this view of assessment has much in common with the idea of connoisseurship. Eisner (1976) regards connoisseurship as a useful educational concept because it connects our values and experiences in the act of judgement, which he views as the art of appreciation.

The three evaluative Ps

Creative practice assessment recognises the centrality of the student as maker. When lecturers discuss student work in grading meetings, their assessment talk repeatedly slides amongst comments about the work, how the work was made and about the student who made the work. As a consequence there are three critical elements in art and design assessment that we need to consider. These are process, person and product. We refer to these as the 'three evaluative Ps'. The configuration of these elements is similar but not identical to Belluigi's (2013) triad schema for fine art studio assessment.

In a typical Crit all three evaluative Ps may be present. An interim Crit may focus on work in progress, whilst a final Crit may look at the finished product. In both cases the student and his or her approaches to the development of ideas, thinking, and making will be part of the dialogue about the work. Next we discuss each element in turn.

Process

In Western art and design faculties, lecturers are committed to recognising the importance of the process of making work and are keen to reflect this in the ways that they carry out assessment (Orr and Bloxham 2012; Vidokle 2009). For example, Barrow (2006) notes that in the discipline of design, the marking emphasises the way the design process was implemented. Cowdroy and de Graaff (2005) note the same emphasis on process in the grading of fine art.

Lecturers in art and design often use a journey metaphor to describe students' individual learning. As we know from other chapters, this is not about a journey that is fully predetermined by the lecturer or the curriculum. The emphasis is on students' individually negotiated learning trajectories. Johnson (2002:216) says that 'fine art is perhaps unusually dependent on the cognitive and conceptual development of students over time'.

The focus on process means that lecturers want to see evidence of the learning journey to be apparent in the submission. The work should surface the journey towards (process) as well as an arrival point (the product). The way that the work can 'show' the learning is hinted at in the exchange between two tutors marking work in the studio quoted as follows:

Lecturer 1: . . . he's obviously experimenting with different types of media and trying to come in to his own . . . umm . . .
Lecturer 2: . . . yeah he is making some break through there for himself isn't he?
(Design lectuers in dialogue cited in Orr 2007b)

These lecturers are looking for the students' 'path to transformation' (Barrow 2006:358). The focus on the process of art making and the value placed on it reflect the widely held view that this is where the learning is taking place (Orr 2010a). The process of making can offer a story about the arc of learning. Whilst an interest in process resides specifically in studio education, it is reflected more widely in the idea of narrative assessment (see, e.g., the assessment approach adopted at Alverno College), where there is a greater focus on tutors writing transcripts that engage with and evaluate the student learning journey. Having considered the importance of process, we now turn to the role of the product.

Process – product spectrum

Whilst we can see that in the creative educational arena, there is a focus on marking the process of making, in contrast in the professional arena of the arts world or the creative industries post graduation, the focus will be on the final product. Occasionally exhibitions may explore artists' processes, but it is much more typical to exhibit the final product. Students need to make the transition from an educational context to the professional arena. This reflects the journey they make from being a student to being a proto artist or designer to being a professional artist or designer. To support this transition the assessment practices typically focus more and more on the product as a student moves through the course of study. Thus a year-one undergraduate project commonly assigns a significant portion of marks to the process of the making, whilst a third-year project will commonly assign the bulk of the marks to the product. The summer show or graduate show is the point where the work is exhibited in a professional context, and it marks the exit point for students as they move to the professional arena post graduation.

This change of emphasis underlines that process and product are interlinked. Even when lecturers mark work in the final year, they are rewarding traces of the process in the product. We are unable to isolate the development of the work from the final submission, and there is a relationship between the feedback students receive over the term and the marking of the final submission. The student work submitted for assessment should seamlessly offer a product (artefact or design solution) and a story about the journey to that product. We see the development and realisation of the project.

Person and the work: a journey to become

The third P refers to the person whose work is being graded. Rowntree's (1987) seminal book on assessment is titled *Assessment: how shall we know them?*. He writes that assessment offers an opportunity to know the student. The person (i.e., the student) and the work (the product) are intimately connected in art and design assessment practices. Students invest themselves in their practice. Creative students have emotional investment in their work (Behardien 2014), and this enmeshed view of the student and the work offers a fresh take on popular ideas about assessment in other disciplines. In university exam boards lecturers are exhorted to separate the student's work from the student's identity. The idea of this disconnect is that it will help the lecturer look dispassionately at the strengths and weaknesses of student work without feeling like it is the student who is under scrutiny. In universities today there is increasing emphasis on anonymous marking of student work. This separation stands at odds with art and design research into marking and grading. Orr and Bloxham (2012:243) observe that art and design lecturers' Crit discussion 'repeatedly slides between the student work and the students as creators'. The student as maker and the work they make are entwined: the maker and the made. The artwork does not disembody the maker; in fact the artwork offers the assessor clues about the maker.

Journeys offer a way to think about the development of identity and selfhood. Students' learning biographies share journeys of the self. Frayling (1993) argues that art and design education connects to the idea of autobiography and personal development. This is creative practice as a journey to become, as discussed in Chapter 5. Barrow (2006) compares marking practices in the disciplines of design and business, and he notes that this emphasis on the student's biography of learning is not apparent in business education. He draws on Foucault to say that design assessment is a technology of the self. The self is under scrutiny, and the work should offer an autobiographical narrative of learning. This explains why reflective journals and sketchbooks have become common parts of art and design assessment; they offer the lecturer a proxy for the narrative of learning.

Where did you start your journey?

If we are to consider assessment as a journey, our attention is usefully directed to the students' starting points. Lecturers' assessment talk suggests that they recognise the journey travelled by individual students, and they would like the marks to reflect this. What this means in practice is that there is a desire to mark the work in relation to the student's intention and starting point (Crippa 2015). This is known as ipsative assessment. Thus if a student comes in with a low entry profile and makes huge strides (back to the journey metaphor), then their assessment should reflect the distance travelled. Equally if a student sets out with a very ambitious learning goal that is perhaps poor in its final execution, then the marker wants to acknowledge the intent to offset the weakness in the final submission. These are transgressive ideas in the academy where the focus is on transparency, standards and accountability. Ipsative marking does not align with university codes of practice that seek to establish common standards for attainment for all students. Within ipsative assessment students would need to write their own learning outcomes or indeed their learning intentions, which is an approach adopted in some Art Schools, but this can be too restrictive for some educators who want the student to travel in directions they could not anticipate at the onset of a project.

Shaping the sticky curriculum

Assessment serves to create and contest the boundaries of art and design. This is best encapsulated by the phrase 'is it a first or a fail?'. In many subjects a comment such as this would be nonsensical. How can student work be on the boundary of a fail and a first when these two outcomes are so divorced from one another? To understand this comment we need to reflect on the ways that assessment shapes the curriculum. If students are innovating with the very idea of what work is, the tutors will need to decide if they recognise this work as legitimate practice. Students working in art and design globally stretch the frame of reference for what we call fine art and what we call design. One only has to think about the fine art work students were presenting 100 years ago (e.g., the meticulous rendering of statues from antiquity) and compare it to fine art today to recognise that the sticky curriculum is historically referenced and that assessment (usually in the form of the Crit) has become a key site for the boundaries of the discipline to be contested and negotiated (Llewellyn and Williamson 2015). The conceptual turn in fine art over the last twenty years will have been shaped, stretched, and framed within numerous Crits in numerous departments that collectively serve to remap the territory. Assessment serves to discipline the subject by determining what is and what isn't deemed to be art and design; 'assessment institutions' decisions about what value judgements and criteria are used will arguably influence what is taught' (Fryer 2010:551).

The judgements the lecturers make about student work will reflect the values of the studio and the wider values of higher education and the arts arena. Whilst acknowledging the role of connoisseurship, a cautionary note comes from (Lamont 2012:8), who comments that 'connoisseurship (or an ability to discriminate) can easily slide into homophily (an appreciation of work that most resembles one's own)'.

Addressing this challenge means that assessment approaches should challenge the 'pale, male, stale' curriculum by surfacing the ways that values underpinning curriculum and assessments are related (Asquith 2015). In the UK there is concern about attainment differentials between Black, Asian and Minority Ethnic students and white students. These attainment differentials situate within a complex range of social, cultural, political and financial contexts (Steventon et al. 2016). Building on ideas we explore in Chapter 3, we speculate about the ways tutors might approach grading students' creative work when it does not speak to the tutor's cultural frame of reference. Thus when a tutor is looking at fine art that draws in a particular aesthetical reference frame that they are completely unfamiliar with, how do they grade this work? Addressing this, the key challenge is to exploit assessment as a progressive tool to widen our grading reference frames to welcome marginalised voices and global cultural frames. If assessment is to be socially just (McArthur 2015), we need to surface the ways that Art School values may link to its assessment practices.

Experiencing assessment: sticky practices

Assessment in art and design encourages students to adopt meaningful study approaches; they are assessed on project work in which they invest their time and energy to create new products. This is central to their learning, not a test or exam that may inadvertently encourage a surface study approach. However, in a research project asking students to recount their experiences of an assessment recently completed, we found that it was possible for students to experience the same assessment process on one course in variable ways (Shreeve et al. 2004). Shreeve et al.'s research adopted a phenomenographic methodology and was therefore setting out to identify variation in experience. This research indicates that students could feel very differently about assessment in project based art and design subjects. Where students felt that assessment was something 'done to them', the focus was on the quantity of work done and the effort that went into their project rather than the quality of the outcome. There was also a palpable feeling of tutors being in a policing role, there to check and ensure that the students were 'doing it right'. This is at odds with most professed approaches to teaching in the subject where tutors express the open-ended nature of assessment where there are in theory no 'right answers' – only a range of possibilities. Where this kind of experience of assessment predominates, it is unlikely that students will succeed in their project work if the tutor is expecting quality of thought and experimentation; no amount of work will meet their expectations. More complex experiences of assessment from the students' point of view included those of experiencing it as something 'done for the student' with an emphasis on developing the students' skills and abilities. The tutor is perceived as being there to guide students in the appropriate direction and help them. When students experience assessment in this way, they are aware that there are some kinds of criteria, not simply the tutor's likes and dislikes, which come into play. The final category of experience identified in this study was one in which it was possible to see assessment as something 'done with' the student. The emphasis here was on being able to operate in the wider world in a professional manner. The student and tutor were perceived as collaborators enabling students to achieve their own goals and ambitions within the project with a due emphasis on the quality of the outcome. Where assessment in art and design is sticky, students, given the same assessment assignment, will potentially experience it differently. Thus students can conceive of assessment as correction, development, or understanding oneself, positions which suggest that the student may conceive of assessment as being done to them, for them or with them (Shreeve et al. 2004). In phenomenographic approaches it is not possible to identify cause and effect, only to map the differences possible in one particular phenomenon. Other studies have identified influencing factors on approaches to learning (Laurillard 1984) where the assessment task can influence the same student to approach learning in either a meaningful (deep) or memorising (surface) approach.

The reasons why students experience assessment in different ways are likely to relate to their previous experiences of assessment and learning (Prosser and Trigwell 1999); the students' perception and understanding of the task; influences beyond the immediate learning environment where pressures of work, family commitments, emotional stress, cultural capital and other social and emotional factors may be present. Assessment cannot be made to be equal and totally fair when factors beyond the control of the Art School are at play. However, the impact and power of the tutors as gatekeepers in the assessment process are enormous (Mann 2008) and can influence the perceptions and behaviours of students. Students who understand or experience assessment as a process which is done in collaboration with tutors are probably more likely to be those with cultural capital, maturity or self-efficacy, which enables them to experience learning and assessment as a collaborative process with tutors.

Tutors' experiences of assessment are also worthy of consideration. Given the importance of this part of academic work in relation to students' destinations and outcomes, it is interesting to note that it is rare for a university lecturer to receive formal training about assessment before they carry it out. In the absence of formal instruction, Sambell and McDowell (1998) discuss the ways that our intuitive ideas and beliefs about assessment (often gained through our own experience of being assessed) inform our approaches. Typically we learn how to assess student work by assessing alongside other more experienced tutors. This is learning through participation (Wenger 1998).

Jawitz (2009:4) examined new lecturers' 'learning-to-judge trajectories' in social sciences, natural sciences and design, and he notes that design lecturers usually progress to an academic role as a result of their professional practice expertise unlike new academics in the natural sciences who usually progress from junior postdoctoral research assistants posts. Studying the ways that these new lecturers learnt to judge student work, Jawitz notes that the dialogic and public nature of design assessment offered a useful learning space for new academics. The design lecturers in this study understood that the key imperative was to reach grading consensus through dialogue to harmonise grades.

As discussed elsewhere in this volume, the dominance of the oral mode of making judgements and the public nature of the assessment process are common features of studio practice. This provides new academics and students with regular access to the discourse of judging performance and opportunities to observe and listen until they feel ready to contribute. Studio based dialogues help students and tutors develop assessment literacy. Jawitz (2009) suggests that a modification of individual and community habitus needs to take place for harmonisation to occur in evaluation processes. This implies that a group of people can agree, modify, change and evolve assessment practices. Far from being a clear, standard, monolithic entity, assessment appears to be a sticky, mutable and inevitably variable practice. Given this perspective, where academics need to learn and share, it follows that students, if they are to be given the same access to assessment process and understanding of terms such as learning outcomes, grading criteria, ranking and so on should also take part in learning to become part of the assessment practice of a particular course (Drew and Shreeve 2006). As Elwood and Klenowski (2002) argue: '[students] need access to the wide range of assessment activities employed by tutors as assessors as well as access to other members of the community and to our shared understandings of how we make our judgements' (Elwood and Klenowski 2002:246).

Assessment moving forward

The Crit and the approaches adopted to grade work in the studio have not changed in many universities in spite of substantial increases in student numbers over the last decade. For some lecturers there is a sense of loss. There is a way that they want to grade work and the way they have to grade work. It is our view that the most effective way to address the increasing workload associated with evaluating and grading student work is to do more to approach assessment as a partnership between students and staff where there is greater emphasis on peer review. Rather than viewing this as a cynical attempt to ask students to do academic work, it can be viewed as a useful way to bring students into the assessment community of practice. This encourages them to think like a practitioner and to enter the world of practice. It is crucial that our students graduate knowing how to evaluate their own work, so the less we say in Crits and the more the students are given space and time to develop their own evaluative gaze, the better equipped they are to thrive post graduation.

The increase in student numbers also needs to be explored in the context of the digital turn, which is bringing new assessment debates to the surface. In what ways is a digital image of the work different to the work – or does the image of the work become the work to be assessed as such? Are student centred approaches to the Crit made easier in an egalitarian online environment, or do power relations pervade the virtual studio? As art and design faculties are situated in universities where increasingly student written work is submitted anonymously and online, how does visual practice avoid being regarded as an irritating exception to university policy? The digital is a space for assessment that we need to deploy artfully to support student learning.

Conclusion

Fryer captures the challenges of creative assessment when he writes:

> How might I deal with my own 'cultural arbitrary' whilst assessing [creative] practical work when students create moments that have a sense of something I find difficult to understand or measure. These are the moments I treasure

> as a teacher, the moments when I know the students may have found something really exciting and yet they are the moments when my assessment criteria seem redundant.
>
> (2010:538)

Art and design lecturers who were educated in Western Art Schools in the 1960s and 1970s will recall that in these 'good old bad old' days, there was very little written documentation about assessment. Assessment was a mystery. Contemporary art and design education within a university setting is now locked into the conventions of the academy. Tutors and students now encounter reams of written information about the rules and regulations of assessment. One core convention is that students' work is graded against explicit standards, but standards don't leap off the page into tutors' and students' heads; active engagement is needed. Standards need to be constructed and agreed through dialogue in communities of practice.

A constructivist or interpretive view of assessment recognises and welcomes the written guidance and learning outcomes but crucially acknowledges that learning outcomes can only specify learning at a general level. Learning outcomes cannot be, nor would we want them to be, 100 percent explicit about the learning that is required. Local interpretation by students and staff and creative space is needed to allow for divergent learning. There may be no immutable fixed standards, but lecturers are able to agree on marks that are fit for purpose. A good-enough mark is not the act of calculation or measurement; these terms do not convey the practice of professional judgement. Lecturers bring professional, social, cultural and critical knowledge to the practice of assessment that works in conjunction with the written learning outcomes. In this way the grading of creative practice encompasses the subjective and the objective (Orr 2010b).

Assessment that has integrity does not lurk behind the safe veneer of objectivity even in the context of a litigious and consumerist higher educational environment (Gilio 2016). It is essential that there is open honesty about the challenges of assessing creative practice, and that work is done to surface the values that underpin assessment. At its best a Crit provides an opportunity for lecturers and staff, as peers, to practise the exposition of their ideas and to explore, defend and reach agreement about the merits and intentions inherent in the work. At its worst the Crit can be a place where there is a clash between the powerful and the powerless that intersects with issues of privilege and disadvantage.

Students learn to value what lecturers value, so assessment practices need to align with what we hold dear. In art and design, learning, teaching and assessment are entwined. This is at the heart of what we understand by assessment as an artful practice that responds to the contingencies of the sticky curriculum.

Student learning is supported when they are active agents in assessment. Any student studying fine art or design at university will not expect exams or multiple choice to assess their developing practice. Students can be brought into the creative assessment conversation because our overarching learning goal is to help each student develop their own evaluative gaze.

Note

1 The term assessment in the UK is a word that encompasses any aspect of work that is concerned with giving marks, grades or written or oral feedback on student work. In the interests of clarity we will refer when possible to grading and marking, which are terms that are well understood internationally, and when we do use the word assessment, we use it in its UK meaning.

References

Addison, N., 2014. Doubting Learning Outcomes in Higher Education Contexts: From Performativity Towards Emergence and Negotiation. *International Journal of Art & Design Education*, 33(3), pp. 313–325.

Alverno College, n.d. *Alverno's Grading System*. Available at: www.alverno.edu/grades/ [Accessed December 30, 2016].

Asquith, S., 2015. *Art School Curriculum: Pale, Male, Stale?* Available at: http://shellyasquith.tumblr.com/post/108163042838/event-art-school-curriculum-pale-male-stale [Accessed July 3, 2016].

Assessment Reform Group, 1999. *Assessment for Learning: Beyond the Black Box*. Cambridge: University of Cambridge, School of Education.

Barrow, M., 2006. Assessment and Student Transformation: Linking Character and Intellect. *Studies in Higher Education*, 31(3), pp. 357–372.

Behardien, I., 2014. *'Who Are They' or 'What and How They Know': An Investigation by a Fine Art Lecturer Into the Basis of Her Own Legitimacy*. Unpublished MPhil Thesis. University of Cape Town.

Belluigi, D. Z., 2013. A Proposed Schema for the Conditions of Creativity in Fine Art Studio Practice. *International Journal of Education & the Arts*, 14(19), pp. 1–22.

Biggs, J. and Tang, C., 2011. *Teaching for Quality Learning at University What the Student Does*. SRHE. Maidenhead, England: Open University Press.

Buckley, B. and Conomos, J., 2009. Introduction. In B. Buckley and J. Conomos, eds. *Rethinking the Contemporary Art School: The Artist, the PhD and the Academy*. Halifax: The Press of the Nova Scotia College of Art and Design, pp. 2–26.

Cannatella, H., 2001. Art Assessment. *Assessment and Evaluation in Higher Education*, 26(4), pp.319–326.

Cowdroy, R. and de Graaff, E., 2005. Assessing Highly-Creative Ability. *Assessment & Evaluation in Higher Education*, 30(5), pp. 507–518.

Cowdroy, R. and Williams, A., 2007. Assessing Creativity in the Creative Arts. *Art, Design & Communication in Higher Education*, 5(2), pp. 97–117.

Crippa, E., 2015. From 'Crit' to 'Lecture-Performance'. In N. Llewellyn and B. Williamson, eds. *The London Art Schools*. London: Tate Publishing, pp. 133–150.

Davies, A., 2012. Learning Outcomes and Assessment Criteria in Art and Design: What's the Recurring Problem? *Networks*, 18, pp. 1–7.

Delandshere, G., 2001. Implicit Theories, Unexamined Assumptions and the Status Quo of Educational Assessment. *Assessment in Education: Principles, Policy & Practice*, 8(2), pp. 113–133.

Dixon, S., 2000. *Assessing the Performer*. Available at: palatine.ac.ukeventsviewdoc57.pdf [Accessed May 31, 2017].

Drew, L. and Shreeve, A., 2006. Assessment as Participation in Practice. In C. Rust, ed. *Improving Student Learning: Improving Student Learning Through Assessment*.

Oxford: Oxford Brookes University, Oxford Centre for Staff and Learning Development, pp. 81–92.

Ecclestone, K., 1999. Empowering or Ensnaring?: The Implications of Outcome-based Assessment in Higher Education. *Higher Education Quarterly*, 53(1), pp. 29–48.

Ecclestone, K., 2004. Learning in a Comfort Zone: Cultural and Social Capital in Outcome-based Assessment Regimes. *Assessment in Education*, 11(1), pp. 30–47.

Eisner, E. W., 1976. Educational Connoisseurship and Criticism: Their Form and Functions in Educational Evaluation. *Journal of Aesthetic Education*, 10(3/4), p. 135.

Eisner, E. W., 1983. 'Educational Objectives: Help or Hindrance?' Elliott Eisner [1967]. *American Journal of Education*, 91(4), pp. 549–560.

Elkins, J., 2001. *Why Art Cannot Be Taught: A Handbook for Art Students.* Champaign, IL: University of Illinois Press.

Elwood, J. and Klenowski, V., 2002. Creating Communities of Shared Practice: The Challenges of Assessment Use in Learning and Teaching. *Assessment and Evaluation in Higher Education*, 27(3), pp. 243–256.

Frayling, C., 1993. Research in Art and Design. *Royal College of Art Research Papers*, 1, pp. 1–5.

Fryer, N., 2010. From Reproduction to Creativity and the Aesthetic: Towards an Ontological Approach to the Assessment of Devised Performance. *Research in Drama Education: The Journal of Applied Theatre and Performance*, 15(4), pp. 547–562.

Gilio, S., 2016. *The Knowledge-Knower Structures Used in the Assessment of Graphic Design Practical Work in a Multi-Campus Context.* Unpublished PhD Thesis. Rhodes University.

Gordon, J., 2004. The 'Wow' Factors: The Assessment of Practical Media and Creative Arts Subjects. *Art, Design & Communication in Higher Education*, 3(1), pp. 61–72.

Hirst, L., 2013. Groundwork. In R. Somerson, ed. *The Art of Critical Making.* Hoboken, NJ: Wiley, pp. 32–51.

Jawitz, J., 2009. Learning in the Academic Workplace: The Harmonization of the Collective and the Individual Habitus. *Studies in Higher Education*, 34(6), pp. 601–614.

Johnson, C., 2002. The Position of the Fine Art Student in the Context of Public Accountability of Higher Education, With Specific Reference to the Quality Assurance Agency Experience. *Teaching in Higher Education*, 7(2), pp. 215–224.

Lamont, M., 2012. Toward a Comparative Sociology of Valuation and Evaluation. *Annual Review of Sociology*, 38(21), pp. 2–30.

Laurillard, D., 1984. Styles and Approaches in Problem Solving. In F. Marton and N. Entwistle, eds. *The Experience of Learning: Implications for Teaching and Studying in Higher Education.* Edinburgh: Scottish Adademic Press.

Llewellyn, N. and Williamson, B., eds., 2015. *The London Art Schools.* London: Tate Publishing.

Mann, S., 2008. *Study, Power and the University.* Maidenhead: SRHE.

McArthur, J., 2015. Assessment for Social Justice: The Role of Assessment in Achieving Social Justice. *Assessment & Evaluation in Higher Education*, 41(7), pp. 1–15.

Orr, S., 2007a. Assessment Moderation: Constructing the Marks and Constructing the Students. *Assessment & Evaluation in Higher Education*, 32(6), pp. 645–656.

Orr, S., 2007b. *Making Marks: The Artful Practice of Assessment in Fine Art.* Unpublished Doctoral Thesis. Institute of Education, University College London.

Orr, S., 2010a. Collaborating or Fighting for the Marks? Students' Experiences of Group Work Assessment in the Creative Arts. *Assessment & Evaluation in Higher Education*, 35(3), pp. 301–313.

Orr, S., 2010b. We Kind of Try to Merge Our Own Experience With the Objectivity of the Criteria: The Role of Connoisseurship and Tacit Practice in Undergraduate Fine Art Assessment. *Art Design and Communication in Higher Education*, 9(1), pp. 5–19.

Orr, S. and Bloxham, S., 2012. Making Judgements About Students Making Work: Lecturers' Assessment Practices in Art and Design. *Arts and Humanities in Higher Education*, 12(2–3), pp. 234–253.

Payne, J. C., 2015. Investigating the Role of Cultural Capital and Organisational Habitus in Architectural Education: A Case Study Approach. *International Journal of Art & Design Education*, 34(1), pp. 9–24.

Pearson, G., 2009. The Outskirts of Town: A Peripheral Centre for Art, Agency, and Academia. In B. Buckley and J. Conomos, eds. *Rethinking the Contemporary Art School: The Artist, the PhD and the Academy*. Halifax: The Press of the Nova Scotia College of Art and Design, pp. 164–181.

Prosser, M. and Trigwell, K., 1999. *Understanding Learning and Teaching: The Experience in Higher Education*. Buckingham and Philadelphia: SRHE and Open University Press.

Rowntree, D., 1987. *Assessing Students: How Shall We Know Them?* London: Taylor & Francis.

Sadler, R., 2013. The Futility of Attempting to Codify Academic Achievement Standards. *Higher Education*, 67(3), pp. 273–288.

Sambell, K. and McDowell, L., 1998. The Construction of the Hidden Curriculum: Messages and Meanings in the Assessment of Student Learning. *Assessment & Evaluation in Higher Education*, 23(4), pp. 391–402.

Shay, S., 2005. The Assessment of Complex Tasks: A Double Reading. *Studies in Higher Education*, 30(6), pp. 663–679.

Shreeve, A., Baldwin, J. and Farraday, G., 2004. Variation in Students Conceptions of Assessment Using Learning Outcomes. In C. Rust, ed. *Improving Student Learning: Theory, Research and Scholarship*. Oxford: Oxford Centre for Staff Development, pp. 223–234.

Steventon, G., Cureton, D. and Clouder, L., 2016. *Student Attainment in Higher Education: Issues, Controversies and Debates*. London and New York: Routledge.

Vidokle, A., 2009. From Exhibition to School. In S. H. Madoff, ed. *Art School (Propositions for the 21st Century)*. London: MIT Press, pp. 189–200.

Wenger, E., 1998. *Communities of Practice: Learning, Meaning, and Identity*. Cambridge: Cambridge University Press.

Yorke, M., 2007. *Grading Student Achievement in Higher Education: Signals and Shortcomings*. London: Routledge.

9 Drawing conclusions

Introduction

In this volume we have explored and set out our analysis of art and design pedagogy in the university, drawing on our own experience, our research and the literature. We have used this opportunity to explore the stickiness of the curriculum, both to position the discipline in the literature and to enable further discussion about creative practice pedagogies which can help students and tutors manage complex, rich and ambiguous worlds. The sticky curriculum requires work to negotiate it successfully; it presents challenges and asks for a response rather than presenting predetermined solutions. The learning routes are obscured and misty, difficult to follow, and nobody tells you exactly which way to go. You might be stuck for a week or a month, unable to see clearly through the mists, but this sticky and difficult place is where creative outcomes might be found and also much pleasure in the creative process. The paradox of the fog which enables us to 'unsee' and respond or to 'see' in different ways to that which is obvious is essential to support creative development of art and design outcomes. We require the mist to enable new visions. A series of similar paradoxical situations are what makes the curriculum sticky with tensions inherently pervading most aspects of university Art School practice. In Chapter 3 we listed five commonly held values which were paradoxical. Here we return to these and expand on them to link them explicitly to our concept of the sticky curriculum.

Teaching but not teaching

The tutor who is creating conditions for learning in creative practice is drawing on her practice knowledge in all its forms, reified course documents, university practices and pedagogic practices described earlier in this volume. The role of university lecturers in art and design is a sticky one. They need to create conditions for creative learning to take place, providing technical and process information as well as an insight into the community of practice their discipline represents. As knowledge is only partially available and tutors frequently do not directly instruct their students, they can appear not to be teaching. Inherent in the teacher's role is 'the performative paradox' of teaching art (Buckley and Conomos 2009:17).

They are often thinking on their feet, making judgements and evaluations of student work which does not fall neatly into previously validated and valued formats. The tutor needs to be responsive, reflective and innovative as well as being entrepreneurial in using opportunities for learning that arise unexpectedly.

The focus on the project as the vehicle of learning, where the student is required to develop their own response through research and development of ideas and through experiment with materials and processes, obscures the active role of the tutor. For many students the tutor becomes someone who does not teach; they see their learning as self-taught – 'we teach ourselves really', and the teaching becomes invisible.

Unseen learning outcomes

Project centred learning asks what is to be learnt, not what has been learnt, a contested space when the university requirement is for tutors to specify learning outcomes in advance. This is usually circumvented by writing broad and open outcomes which leave space for interpretation rather than precision as well as allowing different forms or expressions of the outcome to emerge in the course of learning. This ambiguity requires work by course teams and tutors to define what their expectations are. It is only through the process of engaging or travelling through the project that learning can be understood. This is learning in the present tense; you cannot undertake last-minute revision in this kind of learning as you might for an exam; it is learning as you go. This is not to say that all subject matter is unknown before the start of the project; there are usually technical processes, particularly in design subjects, which will be clearly set out and mastery expected. However, the precise form of this mastery is frequently the unknown part, and as the course progresses in complexity along with increased independence for the student, there is less clear knowledge about the expected outcome of the project. The work becomes stickier and less prescribed. Learning in art and design has a very particular temporal dimension. The work needs to be current, not backward looking, even though it might be dependent on what has gone before. Working towards the unknown or not-yet-known requires the ability to work in the present and look to the future or create the future. This is a vision held by the student: the tutor must empathise, tune in to the future envisioned by the individual student and support the journey towards it.

In the studio environment this is indicated by tutors who say that they are not 'trying to get students to go there' but helping them realise when they are 'there' (Shreeve et al. 2010:131). This is a form of teaching which guides students from a position of uncertainty to one of certainty and belief in what they are doing. This form of invisible teaching is recognised by many students but not all. As one student says: 'they're not trying to tell us to do anything, they're just trying to give us ideas to do it ourselves in the end' (Orr et al. 2014:35). Art School teachers work hard to create conditions for learning, providing resources and technical information, suggesting alternatives and providing role models, exemplars and project briefs which are vehicles to enable learning (Chapters 5, 6 and 7). They are drawing on their practice knowledge and using a variety of teaching strategies to help students become creative practitioners. They are teaching but not seen to be teaching.

Fluid roles in studio

Fluctuating roles for learners and teachers are present in the community of learning, including technical teams, theory tutors and study support tutors. At any point the role the tutor undertakes may be as co-learner journeying together, learning from students, following students or being an 'ignorant school master' (Rancière 1991). The role of the tutor is sticky, problematic, changing constantly and always in relation to the student they are working with at the moment in that precise place and time. Good teachers perform and adjust their behaviour accordingly. They know when to be a friend but not too friendly, when to be didactic and instruct and when to stand back and admit ignorance (Shreeve and Batchelor 2012). They need to be there and not be there for the student. All this is creative teaching for creative learning.

Reflection – surfacing student learning

Obscuring the nature of teaching in art and design higher education through placing the responsibility for learning with the student helps disguise the active teaching taking place. It may also help obscure learning as the intentions behind teaching are not articulated. Helping students critically reflect can help them recognise what has been learnt (Ellmers 2015). Whilst Ellmers supports the idea of reflection, it is not without problems for art and design students. They are asked to bring in an additional practice, in written form, which is frequently at odds with the decision-making processes they have undergone in making a piece of art or a specific design which is not verbalised. The notion of reflection in action popularised by Schön (1983) is often replaced by demands for reflection post action or in a means at odds with creative practice processes. The deeply rooted, intuitive, affective and nonverbal processes of creative practice have to be translated. This places students in a sticky position, learning another language to make their learning transparent. However, reflecting through the act of writing could be posited to offer another means of creative practice to extend a repertoire of practices (Orr et al. 2010). Practising art and design in the university requires students to be multimodal (Kress and van Leeuwen 2001).

Risk taking

The commonly held tenet in art and design higher education is to celebrate risk taking (Chapter 3). When groups of tutors get together in staff development or in curriculum planning and development, they frequently talk about risk taking being an important attitude in their students, and they exhort their students to take risks in tackling the project brief. This becomes a sticky concept when the hidden values of tutors, the institutional structures and the assessment processes impact on the effect of risk taking. Who bears the cost of failure if the risks go wrong? Where in the assessment criteria or learning outcomes has the tutor explicitly stated that the outcome was not important, but the ability to take a risk has been the desired outcome? This is not impossible to build into assessment criteria or into learning outcomes, but there is an inherent paradox here, for if all risk taking is valued (and we have established that it clearly is not in Chapter 3), then where is the risk in taking a risk? Perhaps the most risky strategy for the student would be to play safe and not take a risk (Bell 2013). For risk perhaps we should be saying exploration, which is not without risk, but risk taking is a sticky concept. The kinds of risks really encouraged are travelling without knowing the end, embracing that which cannot be foreseen, welcoming the accidental, exploiting potential, so perhaps it is impossible to encourage explicitly. These are the risks of engaging with the new and the unexpected and not being afraid to embrace them.

Failure

Failure is valorised by tutors who might celebrate making mistakes or learning through error perhaps as a means to creative generation (Chapter 3). But actually failing to reach a pass mark in assessment is failure which is not valued. The right type of failing is perhaps one of the hidden and socially constructed values in the sticky curriculum which an individual student needs to negotiate. Success might be something to wrestle from failure, or when encountering a sticky situation in the curriculum, but failure is not an outcome to be desired by anyone. Tutors' espoused values concerning risk taking need to be challenged and problematised. Success might be brought forth from 'failure' through creative application of thinking and making. Sticky values conflict the individual and the social in the Art School and require work to make them accessible and visible.

Values can subject students to particular forms of failure through lack of cultural capital or a misrecognition of cultural capital, for example, or through commitments which prevent them being in the studio as frequently as their successful peers and to produce less work than their peers. Art School geographies are linked to hierarchies of value, and location sticks to students and their outputs. Assumptions may be made about standards in smaller, regional places of learning which are at odds with the actual outputs (Elkins 2001; Pearson 2009). Failing is something which is frequently culturally determined and not solely set out by levels or standards in assessment.

Freedom and control – anything goes?

Art School, in the late 1960s carried the flag of the unorthodox, the new, the anything goes freedom to create what you wanted. Rebellion was embodied by the Hornsey School of Art student sit-in (1968) and their demand for a new curriculum (Tickner 2008). An emancipated view of art education, premised on the child centred art movement, and the modernist tendencies of expressionism and abstraction linger still in the approach to pedagogy in the Art School (Houghton 2016). However, the paradox of freedom for students to decide what they will do within the broad structures of a project brief belies the control exerted through powerful discourses and practices which also prevail in the university and in the expectations of the political and social world beyond academia (Chapter 3).

Choice lies at the heart of student actions, but forces which help structure discourse value certain voices or points of view above others, or are ignorant of others' cultural viewpoints, deny to some students the opportunities they have to create their own value systems and their own artistic or design practices. Freedom is always bounded by the legitimisation of practice by those who control access to the practice both within and outside academia.

Disruptive pedagogies

Tutors help create the unexpected and the 'sticky' in their learning activities (Chapter 5). Disruption to 'normal' teaching and learning activities is the realm of the studio, which is more than a physical space and could be described as a state of mind (Peterson, personal communication, 2015). If a graduate is in town, they might be brought in at a moment's notice to contribute to learning. If there's an opportunity to engage in a competition, or a live brief, it might be welcomed. Timetables might be upended so that students can collaborate across years and courses. Opportunities to disrupt create opportunities for learning but may also create disturbance for students struggling to control their own learning in a less than regular world. Perhaps there is no 'normal' in art and design pedagogies? Is there a balanced point between stasis and chaos which is exactly right for learning creatively? Disruption or causing deliberate stickiness in the curriculum is relatively 'normal' for studio learning. There is control but control which asserts freedoms of its own (Chapter 5).

In this shifting and responsive environment, the tutor demands autonomy in the student engaging in the project brief. However, the tutor then (usually) controls the assessment process and determines grades and performance as a social practice or an 'artful practice' (Orr 2007). The tutor also sets out the framework for project briefs which can be on a continuum from highly structured to no structure. The earlier years of study in design subjects are likely to have more structured or controlled project briefs, echoing the Vygotskian approaches to scaffolded learning (van de Pol et al. 2010). However, all briefs control and direct learning, however free their interpretation might be. To challenge and make sticky the learning environment for students, a good brief will have parameters which stimulate students to innovative thinking (Chapter 7).

Deschooling

In a place of learning, Art School in a university context, the belief that students have to 'unlearn' everything that they have learnt before is a confusing paradox.

Most educational texts would argue that you start from the position of the student's knowledge and understanding to build on that (Biggs 2003). Perhaps it is a condition of Art School, but we seldom hear of tutors being exhorted to unlearn anything they know! What the notion of deschooling or unlearning hides is the desire for students to embrace new ways of working and thinking which the Art School hopes to engender. There is also a suspicion that the kind of art and design produced in compulsory schooling is not as valid or authentic as that produced by the Art School, and in some respects this is the case. Schooling is structured by common systems of examination which the Art School left behind in the 1960s (Llewellyn and Williamson 2015) and produces a tendency to particular forms of acceptable work (Atkinson 2002). In seeking to deschool there is a danger of overlooking valuable knowledge students bring with them and a danger of dogma belittling individual achievement.

Transparent opacity

Within the art and design curriculum, there is a dialogue between the transparent and the opaque, which coexist. Tutors need to be clear about those fixed aspects which frame the curriculum experience for students (dates, times and places) but help students to recognise and celebrate the ambiguity at the heart of the curriculum. We need to remove sticky and potentially confusing aspects to enable enjoyment of the sticky, obscure boundaries of the known and unknown, where creativity can happen through experimentation and exploration. Students need to learn to live with and through ambiguous, sticky situations and to look for potential routes through to create new products, processes, communications and services.

The paradox of needing ambiguity in the curriculum and the inability to clarify completely what the curriculum consists of lies at the heart of pedagogic practice situated within the open-ended project brief (Chapter 7). There are increasing demands for clarity and transparency of practices in higher education, but these do not always lead to clarity but to further confusion in an overload of information (O'Neill 2002). Transparency has a limited currency; for us the heart of art and design pedagogy is obscure, ambiguous and sticky. We need the foggy box of ambiguous and responsive pedagogy to enable creative thought. If ambiguity were not present, we would not be developing creative practitioners capable of contributing new viewpoints, ideas, objects, forms and processes to the world of creative practice. Clarity and opacity therefore coexist in the curriculum. There are stubborn areas which will remain in obscurity but are essential to learning, areas where tacit knowledge can be hinted at only obliquely. This stickiness presents a challenge to negotiate the seen and the unseen in the curriculum. Tacit knowledge, essential for learning to become a creative practitioner – understanding the language use, conventions, norms and practices embedded in creative curricula – may be at odds with the formal curriculum, that which is written down and made explicit. We also take the view that meaning is made through the 'kind of exchange' which lies at the heart of a discursive pedagogic practice. The learning of language, whether spoken, material or visual, is not transparent; it is learnt and meanings created through social interaction.

Whilst ambiguity and fogginess are to be welcomed as conditions to create and to celebrate emergent practice, other aspects of the Art School require us to challenge how we construct and play out values. For example, complete acceptance of the obscured values of particular hegemonic practices in the Art School serve to disadvantage students not fitting in to preconceptions and practices of the mainstream. Tutors need to shine a light into the obscurity of cultural values inherent and hidden in their curriculum practices (Behardien 2014). Our students are also rejecting what they find in many Art Schools, using the term the 'pale, male, stale' art and design curriculum (Asquith 2015). Hidden values pervade relations between students and tutors and the expectations of the roles and positions they perform. Even the higher value placed on the 'real world' beyond the university plays out in subtle ways to devalue the voices of those creative practitioners who support students' learning (Dean 2015). We therefore need and do not need the mists of obscurity in the curriculum. Students need to learn to accept and live with and through uncertainty (Barnett 2012) and ambiguity (Osmond and Tovey 2015), which is a prerequisite for creativity and a means to face the unknown and complex futures ahead of us. We do not need, however, the obscured cultural practices which can serve to disadvantage some.

Knowing and not knowing

Teachers are frequently in a position of obscurity in relation to creative knowledge. They must accept that there is the 'not known' and the 'yet to be known' coexisting with all the many forms of knowledge pertaining to creative practices (Chapter 2). To accept that knowledge in art and design is problematic is to accept one's position on a continuum of learning, from complete novice to expert, with students as co-travellers in art and design higher education. Here students are working with the tutor in various relational positions which change frequently depending on circumstances, venue, aims and intentions. It is important 'not to know' to accept the unknown or newly known. When students arrive from some educational cultures where ambiguity might be less tolerated, it requires work to traverse the sticky terrain and accept that there is a voyage of discovery to be made (Austerlitz et al. 2008), one in which students need to develop determination and resilience using the resources (including tutor, technician and study support) to help them through the sticky patches of learning to become creative practitioners.

Knowledge that is tacit, explicit and experiential, including the known, the unknown and the search for the 'not yet known', is sticky knowledge. We cannot know when we set out on the journey exactly where it will end for all students. Art and design knowledge in the university setting is therefore hard to identify and make transparent – how can we fully know what will be learnt when we don't know exactly what direction students will take? There are limitations to our predetermined knowledge base. Where there is explicit knowledge, tutors will use it, but creativity always demands work at the borders and in the void between the arms of the paradox. Tutors can draw out a set of parameters for learning in the project brief, but the curriculum is emergent, responsive and opportunistic, and participants need to engage with the unforeseen and unexpected. The paradoxical tensions between setting out the road map but not knowing where we are going is essentially required to allow creativity and individual learning to occur.

The 'knowledge bank' available to learners is apparently limitless. Individual interests and research can lead in many directions – as many as there are students – but the paradox is that it is also worryingly narrow. This is for two reasons: firstly because learning is linked to students' epistemic access to knowledge and secondly because it is linked to the tutor's own access to knowledge. Looking at each of these in turn, we note Morrow's research in South African education that argues for the recognition that certain student groups have been denied epistemological access to knowledge (Morrow 2009). So widening access to the Art School is the first step towards democratising education; opening up the knowledge of the Art School is the next important step. Discussing Morrow's (2009) work Shay (2012:2) argues that it is essential that students are taught the 'forms of inquiry' for the disciplines they study. So to address inequality in art and design education, we need to recognise the importance of knowledge because to ignore it is to perpetuate disadvantage to those who do not have access to the powerful knowledges that are taken for granted in the Art School. Shay argues that this is particularly important for vocational subjects where a focus on skills can serve to diminish the importance of knowledge, and she offers the example of a design course taught in a South African university:

> The course is designed to give epistemic access to the general field of design as well as to a range of specific design disciplines. What the analysis of the curriculum briefs reveals is that designer 'ways of knowing' develop through the engagement with . . . design problems.
>
> (Shay 2012:17)

Returning to the second point, students' access to an apparently limitless knowledge bank is limited by the size, scope and nature of the tutor's knowledge bank. This will relate to the channelling of tutors' experiences, values and the prevailing culture. Teachers do not know everything, and the teacher questions underlying assumptions and prevailing values – facilitating and enabling, not prescribing. But this is not to deny that there is a performative act of teaching taking place. Recognising the student's journey into unknown territory and individualised learning may be acknowledged through the assessment regime, where research is usually a requirement of portfolio submission and part of the work submitted for assessment. But the nature of research too can be obscured to the student. This is one of the localised practices of the art and design curriculum, with variation in the teachers' expectations and recognition of good practice in research (Kjølberg 2012) and ultimately variation in the ways that students will approach it (Shreeve et al. 2004).

Working through and with ambiguity or with stickiness in the curriculum requires students to create their own outputs, learning to live with the stickiness and to utilise it for creative productivity. Ambiguity may reside in the learning environment but should not be apparent (unless intentionally) in the outcomes of learning. Students must learn to negotiate the ambiguous and deliver conviction in their work, presenting a paradox of ambiguity where learning to live with and through ambiguity results in work or outcomes which demonstrate conviction and certainty of student thinking and acting. 'A work can be about ambiguity but it cannot be ambiguous' (George Percy, artist, in conversation July 2016). This of course is determined by the artist, for if ambiguity is present in the work, it must be by design and not a result of confusion or indecision by the artist. The fog of Gormley's box is a purposeful one, even if Richard Wentworth, cited in Reardon and Mollin (2009:375), might state: 'if you're going to make a work of art you better know how to be decisive at some point, because it isn't about walking in fog'. Clearly Gormley would have us walk in fog (see Chapter 4).

The foggy box of ambiguity also helps hide or obscure the mechanics of social interaction in the studio. Some people feel invisible or are invisible in certain discourses. For example, the technicians who help students to learn are often not mentioned in course documents and might not be part of the planning of curriculum activities. The 'third-space' professionals (Whitchurch 2013), those who have newly created roles, not explicitly tutor or technician, who are increasingly present in the university, might not be visible to students who are unaware of the roles they might play in their journey to become professional practitioners. These roles are increasing in number and can slide between the cracks in the busy university. Issues around identities and subjectivities are often obscured. There is usually no time for tutors to delve into the affective responses and the personal histories of the many students in a course.

Practice and theory in tension

Whilst we acknowledge that theory and practice are under tension in many areas of the Art School, we wish to stress the complementarity of these essential elements of a critical practice. The tension is caused in many instances by those students who have a conflicted relationship with text, who might be dyslexic, for example, or have never grasped the requirements for essay writing and find it challenging. Some studio based academics also find the theoretical components alien to their concept of practice and would rather students concentrated on studio based activities in university. We believe that the presence of theory is important, particularly recognising the epistemic access to knowledge already discussed, and is simply another way of seeing and experiencing creative disciplines. Theory is essential to gain new insights and new understanding of the production and consumption of creative outputs. Theory provides students with more tools to interpret the world or to (re)view and (re)present the world. The disciplines of art and design are very much of the world and engaged in 'society's conversation' (Wheelahan 2010:1), although the primary means of engaging might be through material outputs. These are capable of changing the way we communicate, through environmental graphics for example; the efficiency of our cars may be changed through automotive design; the way we eat, sleep, drink, dress or enjoy our leisure time are all profoundly influenced by graduates of art and design disciplines. In fact every aspect of our world may be addressed by artists and designers, including responses to 'wicked problems', those which change once a solution is applied and which have no definitive ending (Rittel and Webber 1973). Artists and designers are increasingly becoming part of the transdisciplinary teams needed to improve the way we engage in conversations about the world. Considering how integral art, design and communication graduates are to our lived experiences, it is surprising that there is such a dominant discourse in universities and elsewhere about the 'real world' (Dean 2015) and art and design being set in opposition to academic subjects.

The 'real world' as an oppositional space

The explicit presence of theory in the form of an essay is one difference between the 'real world' and the university world. This is a pedagogic device which students will rarely need in practice. However, they will need to draw on theories in carrying out their practice. They need theories to become intellectually agile practitioners, and Art School needs to make theory stick to practice to provide the most rounded individuals capable of developing and extending the practice beyond the university. The university is not seeking to train students to precisely replicate a practice (nor would we want to); it is seeking to produce critical thinkers within the practice who can also stretch the practice. One of the reasons why there is an oppositional rhetoric around the university versus the 'real world' is that universities are configured as places to learn and would not want to replicate precisely the forms of practice existing beyond the university. These are two different social spheres, and teachers configure the curriculum through selecting learning activities and pedagogies and representing them through a recontextualising lens (Bernstein 2000).

Although primarily concerned with 'real world' vocational knowledge in art and design, the learning environment is configured differently. The purpose of higher education is to learn and not simply to make artefacts, hence the role of theory in extending the critical awareness of students in moving the discipline forward. They are not restricted by practices in commercial settings or in particular communities of practice. The university is able to protect students from some of the harsher realities of commercial life and the art market whilst they learn, offering a place of play and experimentation, protecting them from the world whilst preparing them for the world (Chapter 3). The tutor is in a position of having to balance the 'reality' of practice in the world with those of practice learning activities (e.g., using a live brief). They are constrained too by the rules of university life, such as assessment, the values of the university as represented by the course teams and the mechanisms for ensuring parity, for example, through the external examiner system in the UK. The tutor strives to (re)create practice in the learning environment yet will forever be denied the precise reality of the practice.

Discourse around the 'real world' positions the university as an inferior set of practices (Dean 2015). This is likely to undermine the authority of the tutor (frequently also a member of the 'real world' practice community). Students are more likely to see industry voices as authoritative, even though they may lack the critical and theoretical viewpoints an academic view of the subject might offer. In Wheelahan's (2010) view, the emphasis on the vocational represents denial to the student of access to powerful knowledge. The sticky relationship and tensions between the real world and the university world need to be negotiated for the student to view academic knowledge as useful knowledge, enabling not only practice but critical practice to develop.

There is a fundamental relationship between the university or Art School world and the 'real world'. They are of course both 'real', and they are inextricably linked. Our students leave university and move into practice worlds; most Art School tutors are practising artists and designers; they are of the practice or 'real world' and also of the Art School world. Many tutors change the way that practice develops through their engagement with learning (see, e.g., Crippa 2015). There are constant fluid and ongoing relations between the practice worlds of art and design and of creative practices beyond the university; only particular discourses shape prevailing views of what kind of relationship this might be.

The centrality of words in a visual medium

Spoken language is an important factor in learning as it helps mediate a largely visual and material world in art and design education. Written documentation is frequently used as evidence in the increasingly bureaucratic and litigious arena of academia. Written records of tutorials, hand-in dates and assessment feedback provide auditable evidence that teaching practice has been carried out correctly. However, spoken language often works in the art and design curriculum as a suggestion, a hint or a metaphor for much of what is happening (Logan 2006). This kind of exchange is sticky with inherent misunderstandings and pitfalls. Thus language simultaneously serves to fix meanings and create possibilities for new meanings. Art and design language use is a learnt, social practice.

The studio's pedagogic discourse will be experienced differentially by students relating to their prior learning, cultural capital and epistemic access. This is why it is important that Crit pedagogy explicitly scaffolds learning in relation to Art School discourse to ensure that students understand that the studio is a place where they are inculcating designer or artist identities and discourses.

The written word tends to be the primary form of communication when perceived from the university's perspective; there is 'logobias' (Kill 2013:21) at work, and expectations tend towards specific forms of the written word, particularly where theory is taught, though increasingly where reflection is expected in the form of essays or written evaluations. This helps reinforce the perceived split between theory and practice as the medium of communication in practice is not the written word. Language however, as Kill suggests, can be a hybrid or polyglossia, not simply the written version. Students and tutors in art and design need to explore complex modes of communication through symbolic language systems and artefacts. It is developing common polyglossic modes which enable communication in the studio.

The studio, whether digital, material or a state of mind, is the means to the acquisition of discursive practices. Here the exchanges between tutor and student and in peer-to-peer discussions help develop fluency in the languages of the discipline. The development of verbal fluency is made alongside material artefacts, sketchbooks, products, digital images and work in progress. The student is becoming a bilingual or multilingual speaker through words and material outputs. The public practice of their fluency is evidenced in the Crit, and this is central to the art and design curriculum, where students are encouraged constantly to make evaluative judgements about their own and others' work (Percy 2004). However, critique also helps shape and often maintain the value judgements, standards and expectations within the culture of the course, the field and the discipline. Powerful discourses are structured by the tutor, who ultimately validates what counts as current in design and in art practices in that particular space.

The tendency for written language to be the primary vehicle for theory helps maintain distinctions between theory and practice. Mediation of theory is verbal, but so also is mediation of practice in the studio. Theory is associated largely with different pedagogic practices, those of reading, writing and the lecture theatre. When different pedagogic practices are used to link theory to studio practice, for example, or to see and experience writing as the creation of an artefact, the written word can lose its terrors for many students, and they can bring theory to inform their own creative practice (Grove-White 2003; Orr et al. 2010). Linking theory and practice through studio pedagogies is important for the discipline to ensure that the often perceived gap between them does not disadvantage students and they are encouraged to access multiple ways of understanding their creative practice and are therefore able to take control of powerful knowledge in multiple forms.

The individual and the social

Learning in the Art School is always a social practice. The sticky curriculum in art and design (see Figure 5.1) illustrates the diverse social spheres of influence that frame studio learning. The pedagogies which are deployed, the community of students who make up the course and the studio (virtual or face to face), are part of the social engagements of particular communities of practice. These will be influenced by wider political and social agendas and more intimately by the teacher/practitioners who bring their ways of being and knowing into the university from the world of practice. Practice beyond the university is always variable; ways of working, thinking and being are shaped by the people who enact the practice. A 'shared repertoire' (Wenger 1998:82) develops which includes artefacts, discourses, ways of doing things and anecdotes about the practice. Communities can evolve locally distinctive repertoires. Evolution also happens in university courses where each course consists of a small group of tutors and technicians and the nature of learning is influenced by an individual tutor's philosophy and beliefs (Llewellyn and Williamson 2015). The values of individuals will shape how the subject is experienced for students. The conceptions and perceived purpose of higher education in the subject will vary with those individuals who hold the most power within the curriculum, and the course will therefore reflect what is valued within the course culture (Chapter 3). The art and design curriculum requires individuals to construct or determine their own paths through the learning opportunities presented. Culturally, expectations are that the individual will become a creative being offering something new to the world. However, the social world offers up existing frameworks and parameters, ways of being which the student is invited to take up and belong to. The tension lies for the learner in being independent enough to succeed but not too independent in stepping outside the expectations of the social world of the creative practice and failing to demonstrate that they can belong to the community of practice represented by the discipline they are studying.

The curriculum offered to students is sticky; that is, parts of it stick to students through their process of engaging in learning (Chapter 5). Particular attributes stick to them and are valued, or not, by the course tutors. The students become the work they are making, and they identify with it and with the materials and processes they encounter (Hockey and Allen-Collinson 2005; Hockey 2007). Such an intimate positioning of the self with work which is then assessed and evaluated is a very public site for social and individual conflation or confliction. Through the Crit or in summative assessment, the tutor is obliged to differentiate the process of evaluation from the person who has produced it – a sticky, tricky position. Increasingly students are demanding anonymous marking of their work, but how can this divorce of work and persona take place? Tutors must remove likes and dislikes in their evaluation; they must separate the person from the author of the work; they must not let personal qualities get in the way of assessment (Chapter 8). But the qualities they frequently look for in a student's performance are personal qualities (Logan 2013). The personal creation and the social process of assessment are in tension. For some tutors the process of assessment is problematic; the reluctant assessor represents the point where authority invested in the tutor meets a point of resistance in the academy.

Tutors are also under tension in their working lives: they may inhabit two different worlds, those of practice and teaching. These might be in conflict (Shreeve 2011), limiting translation of practice for students and creating an uncomfortable identity for the tutor. There may be conflicting and multiple presences of different intentions and beliefs about the purpose of education for the tutor; there may be conflict in the course team because of differences in belief and intention when teaching. These beliefs and intentions might also be in conflict with those held by students. There are many 'rules' in higher education practices which require tutors to perform in certain ways; there are requirements to meet audit and university-determined formats that might not be sympathetic to a tutor's creative practice. There is identity work and multiple subjectivities at play where tutors' roles and responsibilities might need to vary within the course of one working day (Chapters 5 and 6). This is a sticky position, not static, not clear and not predetermined.

Local and global

The sticky curriculum, a place where complex practices shape learning and teaching (Weller 2015), is forged through a series of networks. These centre on the individual students, the tutors and their relationships to creative practice. Teaching and learning are influenced by dominant discourses in the university and the political and social worlds beyond academia (see Figure 5.1). The global nature of twenty-first-century higher education means that intercultural learning can take place without stepping out of the studio. International students bring the global into the local context of the university. The tutor's role is to help all students engage and develop their own identities as artists or designers. However, it is all too easy to 'other' those from different cultural backgrounds and thus disadvantage them in the studio environment rather than accept each person as an individual (Sovic 2013). Identities are fluid. A UK 'home student' becomes an international student the moment they get on a plane to complete a design exchange in China. A Chinese student is a 'home student' whilst studying in a university in Beijing but 'becomes' an international student when he or she travels to Australia to complete a master's degree. We point this out to underline the importance of avoiding language that essentialises the characteristics of international students. We recognise the fluidity of identity and the social constructions of race, class and gender. So-called home students are also diverse, and the local/global nature of the twenty-first-century Art School offers affordances that we can embrace to support students' global/local citizenship and creative practice. Where Art Schools are located in areas where there is less cultural diversity, then pedagogic approaches can be adopted that bring the global in. For example, tutors can set up online global studios (Ghassan and Bohemia 2015). The studio culture may be localised, but increasingly the movement of students around the world offers opportunities to enable better understanding of cultural plurality. Sonvilla-Weiss (2010) promotes the ideas of mash-up cultures in relation to digital cultural practices, and we seek to extend and apply this term to the global/local Art School. We can delight in the mash-up amongst cultures, practices and ways of doing and being that can be found in some of our global/local studios.

Studio as a space and non-space

There is increasing pressure on the spaces in which creative subjects are taught. Measuring room usage per square foot is a practice which is not sympathetic to the traditional use of studio spaces by art and design students, who could at one time create their own personal environment, enabling the viewer (tutor, peer or visitor) to understand at a glance the interests, skills and expertise of the student. This environment enabled immersion in visual ideas and created possibilities through juxtaposition and through 'making strange' a piece of work which emerged from mind, hand and eye in close contact to the creator. Here viewers were able to immerse themselves in thinking about and discussing the work on show. The studio now is more likely to be a shared space, an online space, a mobile space or combinations of all of these (Marshalsey 2015). The key characteristics of the contemporary studio environment, however, might be said to exist as a state of mind (Peterson, personal communication, 2015) or an approach to learning which positions the student, and their thoughts, interests and creations, at the centre of a discussion. Now that discussion might be through email, blog, Twitter, Facebook, Instagram or more recently Slack, but the kind of exchange central to creative pedagogies is still there. Students must share their work in progress and be able to evaluate and discuss it with others. Studio is no longer solely the province of one particular space but can be conceived as a state of mind and an approach to pedagogy encompassing practices common in art and design, such as setting a brief, discussion and critique. Studio is a pedagogy in its own right, wherever that might be and in however many places it simultaneously needs to exist.

Looking in: looking out

Having looked into the pedagogies of the Art School, we finally look outwards to the future and to other disciplines. In the early years of incorporation into the university, the Art School commonly had to find a way to fit into the academy; now it is timely to think about what the university can learn from the Art School. The Art School's journey into the university has been very challenging, and much has been written about how difficult this has been for Art Schools in relation to agendas of compliance and regulation. But these constraints and difficulties have been mediated and managed, and we are at a place where we can think about what the affordances are.

There have been some benefits for Art Schools moving into the university sector. The key benefit has been that Art School staff have had to articulate to others, which has helped them understand the nature of their pedagogy and practices. This is creating literature about creative, studio based pedagogy that can be shared more widely across the disciplines, promoting interdisciplinary practice by new adjacencies. The tacit practices and internal logics that remain unchallenged within closed educational communities have been blown open by new questions asked by a sector commonly unfamiliar with studio practice. Through justifying art and design practices to the universities, our practices have become more rigorous.

What is academic?

When Art Schools became part of higher education, staff had to explain why their work was academic, fitting into dominant definitions of value, but now Art Schools are thinking about how visual and practice based conceptions of academic work are helping to stretch the frame of discourse more widely about the meaning of *academic* across the disciplines. Practice based conceptions of knowledge help stretch university ideas about what counts as knowledge, and this has relevance across the disciplines. The Research Excellence Framework in the UK accepts practice based research, which has enabled a wide range of visual and practice based outputs to be confidently presented as academic research, and in many cases this has strengthened the position of art and design within the academy. So rather than thinking about how Art School work is academic (i.e., how this fits to an existing offer), which is a form of looking in, we can start a dialogue about stretching the definition of academic to bring in richer creative voices looking out.

Sticky pedagogy

This book has focused on the idea of the sticky curriculum purely in relation to studio based education, but it is our argument that this concept has utility beyond the studio. Art School pedagogies are uncomfortable and destabilising but necessary to equip art and design students for twenty-first-century life. The pedagogy offers a model for a sticky curriculum, one which is global, connected and concerned with social justice with a focus on creativity and resilience.

Student centred learning is easy rhetoric, but arguably the project centred learning discussed within this volume offers the tools that can support its implementation. Problem based learning and enquiry based learning literature has not paid much attention to the need to develop students' creativity, so drawing in studio based and design thinking approaches to these pedagogies will support their evolution. Viewing education as the co-production of knowledge is commonly discussed, and the ways that co-production is approached within art and design offers models of practice for transdisciplinary contexts.

Multimodal and experiential studio based pedagogies support the development of students' creativity and criticality. Recognising that values and epistemologies stick to students through the kinds of pedagogic exchange found in the Art School is a way to conceive of the curriculum in other subjects. The curriculum as a site of sticky learning encounters helps students live with and through uncertainty, learning to adopt creative approaches to life.

University as studio

We propose that it is helpful to consider the contemporary university as a studio. Viewing the entire university as a studio draws attention to the university as a messy and creative environment in which we seek to encourage students 'to become' within the context of their given discipline. The university as studio is a place of uncertainty and ambiguity for students, and this environment and its pedagogies and curriculum should be explicitly harnessed to support the development of students' knowledge, creativity and resilience. Viewing the university as studio surfaces the importance of experiential and tacit knowledge in the academy. The university as sticky studio is concerned with identifying and maximising the learning affordances that can be offered through the physical and digital resources and through individuals and communities in a fluid and creative performativity centred on the discipline.

At this point we link our theory of the sticky curriculum with the concept of 'sticky campus' that is gaining some traction in Australasia (Warren and Mahoney 2015; Madden-Dent 2012). Professor Shirley Alexander at the University of Technology Sydney explains the idea:

> The sticky campus; a campus that students want to come to and it has such a heart and a soul to it they want to stay and have those serendipitous encounters with other people from different cultures, from different discipline areas.
> (Alexander 2009)

Discussion about this approach to campus culture and architecture can be found at University of Wollongong, Queensland University of Technology, and in Scotland, Abertay University is discussing this concept in relation to its campus development. The term 'sticky campus' in the Australasian context focuses on the idea of making the campus attractive to students to encourage students to collaborate, to mix and mingle, so that they spend more time in the physical and digital campus, which will support their learning and levels of engagement. For Madden-Dent (2012:1) the 'sticky campus does not describe a college or university covered in gum'; instead it is 'a term referencing a college or university's ability to engage and involve its students in curricular and extracurricular activities'. The sticky curriculum and the sticky campus are not the same thing, but it is our argument that the approach to curriculum and pedagogy set out in this volume offers a template for practices within the sticky campus.

It is also possible to look at the learning, teaching and assessment practices in the sticky curriculum and think about these being usefully transposed to other disciplines. This act of translation is for others to determine having read our text, but we offer up two possibilities here as enticement to go sticky. Firstly, with assessment practices which are discursive, students and tutors engage in rehearsing the way that designers and artists think. This enables access to powerful knowledge, used within a disciplinary context, and helps a shared social meaning evolve. Students are developing an evaluative gaze in relation to creative work. Secondly, where new and part-time tutors are also included in social practices in learning, teaching and assessment, they too can learn the parameters and rules of the game. Working with both visual and verbal languages in explicit modes enables access to the shared practices, standards and expectations in the community of practice in the discipline.

Conclusion

Although we have presented the sticky curriculum as a series of illustrative paradoxes, we would argue against accepting binary oppositions or struggling to reconcile them or to adopt a position at either end of the spectrum. The rainbow of complexity in learning through creative practice is learning to live with and in complexity and contradiction. The sticky curriculum is to be enjoyed, embraced and encountered with gusto. Through learning to live with ambiguity, uncertainty, difficult decisions and conflicting routes, it is possible to learn to create and to maximise opportunities when they are presented. Simultaneously accepting alternative realities and possibilities is sticky. However it is our key argument that this is the most effective way for our graduates to face unknown futures.

References

Alexander, S., 2009. *Our Future Campus.* Available at: http://newsroom.uts.edu.au/news/2009/04/our-future-campus [Accessed January 14, 2017].

Asquith, S., 2015. *Art School Curriculum: Pale, Male, Stale?* Available at: http://shellyasquith.tumblr.com/post/108163042838/event-art-school-curriculum-pale-male-stale [Accessed July 3, 2016].

Atkinson, D., 2002. *Art in Education: Identity and Practice.* Dordrecht, Boston and London: Kluwer Academic Publishers.

Austerlitz, N., Blythman, M., Grove-White, A., Jones, B. A., Jones, C. A., Morgan, S., Orr, S. and Shreeve, A., 2008. Mind the Gap: Expectations, Ambiguity and Pedagogy Within Art and Design Education. In L. Drew, ed. *The Student Experience in Art and Design Higher Education: Drivers for Change.* Cambridge: Jill Rogers Associates Ltd Publishers, pp. 125–148.

Barnett, R., 2012. Learning for an Unknown Future. *Higher Education Research & Development*, 31(1), pp. 65–77.

Behardien, I., 2014. *'Who Are They' or 'What and How They Know'.* Unpublished M.Phil Thesis. University of Cape Town.

Bell, S., 2013. *The Promise of the Short Text: Writing Risk Into Visual Arts Practice.* Unpublished PhD Thesis. Coventry University.

Bernstein, B., 2000. Pedagogy, Symbolic Control and Identity: Theory, Research, Critique. Lanham and Oxford: Rowman & Littlefield.

Biggs, J., 2003. *Teaching for Quality Learning at University.* Maidenhead: Society for Research into Higher Education/Open University Press.

Buckley, B. and Conomos, J., eds., 2009. *Rethinking the Contemporary Art School: The Artist, the PhD and the Academy.* Halifax: The Press of the Nova Scotia College of Art and Design.

Crippa, E., 2015. From 'Crit' to 'Lecture-Performance'. In N. Llewellyn and B. Williamson, eds. *The London Art Schools.* London: Tate Publishing, pp. 133–150.

Dean, P. J., 2015. *Undergraduate Media Studies in England: A Discourse Analysis.* Unpublished EdD Thesis. University of Bedfordshire.

Elkins, J., 2001. *Why Art Cannot Be Taught: A Handbook for Art Students.* Champaign, IL: University of Illinois Press.

Ellmers, G., 2015. The Graphic Design Project: Employing Structured and Critical Reflection to Guide Student Learning. *Communication Design*, 3(1), pp. 62–79.

Ghassan, A. and Bohemia, E., 2015. Amplifying Learners' Voices Through the Global Studio. In M. Tovey, ed. *Design Pedagogy.* Farnham and Burlington: Gower, pp. 215–236.

Grove-White, A., 2003. Theory and Practice in Photography Students' Understandings and Approaches to Learning. *Active Learning in Higher Education*, 4(1), pp. 56–73.

Hockey, J., 2007. United Kingdom Art and Design Practice-based PhDs: Evidence From Students and Their Supervisors. *Studies in Art Education*, 48(2), pp. 155–171.

Hockey, J. and Allen-Collinson, J., 2005. Identity Change: Doctoral Students in Art and Design. *Arts and Humanities in Higher Education*, 4(1), pp. 77–93.

Houghton, N., 2016. Six Into One: The Contradictory Art School Curriculum and How It Came About. *International Journal of Art & Design Education*, 35(1), pp. 107–120.

Kill, R., 2013. Novel Apprehensions and Hybrid Utterances: Practice, Research, Language. *Art, Design & Communication in Higher Education*, 12(1), pp. 21–31.

Kjølberg, T., 2012. *Visual Research Practice in Fashion and Textile Design Higher Education*. Unpublished PhD Thesis. University of Brighton.

Kress, G. and van Leeuwen, T., 2001. *Multimodal Discourse: The Modes and Media of Contemporary Communication*. London: Hodder Education.

Llewellyn, N. and Williamson, B. eds., 2015. *The London Art Schools*. London: Tate Publishing.

Logan, C., 2006. Circles of Practice: Educational and Professional Graphic Design. *Journal of Workplace Learning*, 18(6), pp. 331–343.

Logan, C., 2013. Living Artists: Identity, Independence and Engagement in Fine Art Learning. *Art, Design & Communication in Higher Education*, 12(1), pp. 33–48.

Madden-Dent, T., 2012. *Sticky Campus*. Available at: https://taramaddendent.com/2012/01/17/sticky-campus/ [Accessed January 14, 2017].

Marshalsey, L., 2015. Investigating the Experiential Impact of Sensory Affect in Contemporary Communication Design Studio Education. *International Journal of Art & Design Education*, 34(3), pp. 336–348.

Morrow, W., 2009. *Bounds of Democracy: Epistemological Access in Higher Education*. Cape Town: HSRC Press.

O'Neill, O., 2002. BBC – Radio 4 – Reith Lectures 2002. *A Question Of Trust*. Available at: www.bbc.co.uk/radio4/reith2002/lecture4.shtml [Accessed July 25, 2014].

Orr, S. K., 2007. *Making Marks: The Artful Practice of Assessment in Fine Art*. Unpublished Doctoral Thesis. Institute of Education, University College London.

Orr, S., Dorey Richmond, J. and Richmond, D., 2010. Reflect on This! *Journal of Writing in Creative Practice*, 3(3), pp. 1–24.

Orr, S., Yorke, M. and Blair, B., 2014. 'The Answer Is Brought About From Within You': A Student-Centred Perspective on Pedagogy in Art and Design. *International Journal of Art & Design Education*, 33(1), pp. 32–45.

Osmond, J. and Tovey, M., 2015. The Threshold of Uncertainty in Teaching Design. *Design and Technology Education: An International Journal*, 20(2), pp. 50–57.

Pearson, G., 2009. The Outskirts of Town: A Peripheral Centre for Art, Agency, and Academia. In B. Buckley and J. Conomos, eds. *Rethinking the Contemporary Art School: The Artist, the PhD and the Academy*. Halifax: The Press of the Nova Scotia College of Art and Design, pp. 164–181.

Percy, C., 2004. Critical Absence Versus Critical Engagement: Problematics of the Crit in Design Learning and Teaching. *Art, Design & Communication in Higher Education*, 2(3), pp. 143–154.

Rancière, J., 1991. *The Ignorant Schoolmaster: Five Lessons in Intellectual Emancipation*. Stanford: Stanford University Press.

Reardon, J. and Mollin, D., 2009. *Ch-ch-ch-changes: Artists Talk About Teaching*. London: Ridinghouse.

Rittel, H. and Webber, M., 1973. Dilemmas in a General Theory of Planning. *Policy Sciences*, 4, pp. 155–169.

Schön, D. A., 1983. *The Reflective Practitioner: How Professionals Think in Action*. New York: Basic Books.

Shay, S., 2012. *Contesting Purposes for Higher Education: A Curriculum Point of View*. Available at: www.srhe.ac.uk/conference2012/download/shay-srhe-arc-2012.pdf [Accessed January 31, 2017].

Shreeve, A., 2011. Being in Two Camps: Conflicting Experiences for Practice-based Academics. *Studies in Continuing Education*, 33(1), pp. 79–91.

Shreeve, A., Bailey, S. and Drew, L., 2004. Students Approaches to the 'Research' Component in the Fashion Design Project: Variation in Students' Experience of the Research Process. *Art, Design and Communication in Higher Education*, 2(3), pp. 113–130.

Shreeve, A. and Batchelor, R., 2012. Designing Relations in the Studio: Dealing With Ambiguity and Uncertainty in One to One Exchanges. *Design and Technology Education: An International Journal*, 17(3), pp. 20–26.

Shreeve, A., Sims, E. and Trowler, P., 2010. 'A Kind of Exchange': Learning From Art and Design Teaching. *Higher Education Research & Development*, 29(2), pp. 125–138.

Sonvilla-Weiss, S., ed., 2010. *Mashup Cultures*. Heidelberg: Springer.

Sovic, S., 2013. Classroom Encounters. In S. Sovic and M. Blythman, eds. *International Students Negotiating Higher Education: Critical Perspectives*. London and New York: Routledge, pp. 87–103.

Tickner, L., 2008. *Hornsey 1968: The Art School Revolution*. London: Frances Lincoln Ltd.

van de Pol, J., Volman, M. and Beishuizen, J., 2010. Scaffolding in Teacher – Student Interaction: A Decade of Research. *Educational Psychology Review*, 22(3), pp. 271–296.

Warren and Mahoney, 2015. *Sticky Campus – Perspectives – Warren and Mahoney Architects – Sydney, Auckland, Wellington, Christchurch and Queenstown*. Available at: www.warrenandmahoney.com/en/perspectives/sticky-campus/ [Accessed January 14, 2017].

Weller, S., 2015. *Academic Practice: Developing as a Professional in Higher Education*. London: SAGE Publications.

Wenger, E., 1998. *Communities of Practice*. Cambridge: Cambridge University Press.

Wheelahan, L., 2010. *Why Knowledge Matters in Curriculum: A Social Realist Argument*. London and New York: Routledge.

Whitchurch, C., 2013. *Reconstructing Identities in Higher Education: The Rise of 'Third Space' Professionals*. Abingdon and New York: Routledge/SRHE.

Index

Note: Page numbers in *italic* indicate figures.

abstract knowledge 23
academic components 11–12
academic knowledge 25
academics/technicians, relationship 80
academic theory 33
academic work, explanation 156–7
active learning approach 116
activity spheres 99
Alverno College, assessment approach 132
ambiguity: antithesis 59; characterisation 14; equality/diversity, relationship 62; exploration 62; foggy box 150; lecturer verbalisation, struggle 129; pedagogy 58–9, 91–2; productive 63; requirement, paradox 147; role of 13; teaching 62–4; term, usage 56–7
"anti" world view 49
Architectural Design Crit, Foucauldian rendering 45
art: abstract knowledge 23; academic turn 10–12; assessment 129; concern 24; curriculum, realisation 107; curriculum, stickiness 7; degree, undertaking (reasons) 82; deschooling 46, 49–50; design, relationship 11–12; epistemologies 19–21; feedback 60; knowledge/knowing *35*; pedagogy 3; practices 5; project 14–15; school, safety 58; school tradition 32; signature pedagogies 107; sticky curriculum 71, *84*; student practices 103; subjective 129; teaching, impossibility 46–7; transgressive 46, 48–49
art education 107; gap 58–9; practices 13–15; territories 12–13
artistic practice, knowledge (relationship) 103
artists: intervention report 96; interventions 95–6; self, defining 81
Art School: attainment differentials 62; cool/paradoxical values 45–50; curriculum, historical analysis (Houghton) 23–4; evaluation 125; learning, social practice 153–5; pedagogy 114; pedagogy, practices (codification) 59–60; possibilities 49; practices 42; purpose 58; real world, distinction 44; reason 58; rules, absence of 46, 48–9; theory/practice, incorporation 32; tutors, public output 32; universities, conjoining (problems) 43; universities, relationship 152; values, problems 39–40
Art School Cool 11
artwork: access to 56; creation of 9
assessment: approach (Alverno College) 132; experiencing 135–7; frameworks 111; future 137; institutions 134; journey 133–4; practices 95; predomination 135; student experiences 136; tutor experiences 136; usage 15
assessment for learning (A4L) 126
assignment, debates 112–14
attainment differentials 62

Basic Design Movement 23
Bauhaus curriculum (Gropius) 20–1, *21*
becoming (identity), language (usage) 82–3
Bents, Nigel 95
Black, Asian and Minority Ethnic (BAME): curriculum 43; students/white students 134–5
Black Mountain College 125

BLIND LIGHT 56, *57*; transparency 58–62
blog post format 40
blogs, usage 102–3
BME students 62
Bologna Process 10–11
brief(s) 47, 92; dystopian 112; group 110; immersive 110; live 74, 92–3, 111–12; 'no brief' 112; open-ended project, focus 14; process-focused 109–10; project, role 63–4; questions 64; response 40, 64; typology 109–12; utopian 112; writing, quality 117
bring your own devices (BYOD), impact 10
Brit Art, rise of 40

California Institute of the Arts 125
Chelsea College of Art 95
clarity, concept (problematisation) 61
Coldstream Report 11–12, 31
collaborative learning, opportunities 75
communication, written word (usage) 152–3
compulsory-level schooling, artist intervention 95–6
computer-aided design 94–5
conflict, practice/theory 31–4
connoisseurship 134
constructive alignment, idea of 19
control 145–7
Council for National Academic Awards (CNAA) 31
creative arts education, purpose 30
creative curriculum (curricula) 6; engagement 72
creative disruption 74–5
creative education: ambiguity, role of 13; ambiguity/uncertainty 56
creative learning/teaching: roles/responsibilities of (fluctuation/elasticity) 76; transfer 101–2
creativeness 109
creative practice 43
creative practitioners, teaching practices 14, 88
creative self, validation 83
creative turn 8–9
creative work, ambiguity (verbalisation difficulty) 129
creativity 8; environment 116–17; importance of 114; location 8; prerequisites for 56–7, 63; process of 8; self-questioning 63–4; society's idea of 39–40
Crit 40; assessment 126; discussion 133; judgements 40–1; leading 111; MA Art and Science *130*; progress 51; signature pedagogy *89*; student *128*
Critical Discourse Theory 45
cross-cultural values, impact 43
Cultural Historical Activity Theory 99
cultural process 42
curriculum/curricula: ambiguity of 61–2; Black, Asian and Minority Ethnic (BAME) 43; clarity/opacity, coexistence 147; co-construction 74, 80; co-creation of 74; complexity of 71; contradictions 2 of 4; creation, opportunities 74–5; creative, engagement 72; design of 42–3; experienced 73; expression 20; learning, non-reified aspects of 76; opportunistic 61–2

deschooling 46, 49–50, 147–8
design: abstract knowledge 23; academic turn 10–12; aesthetic requirements 111; art, relationship 11–12; assessment 129; computer-aided 94–5; concern 24; curriculum, realisation 107; curriculum, stickiness 7; degree, undertaking (reasons) 82; deschooling 46, 49–50; epistemologies 19–21; feedback 60; knowledge/knowing *35*; lecturer, expert guide 118; lecturer, role 47; pedagogy 3; practices 5; project 14–15; signature pedagogies 107; sticky curriculum 71, *84*; studio-based design tutors, skills 118–19; thinking 77, 114; transgressive 46, 48–9
design education 107; assignments 64; gap 58–9; practices 13–15; territories 12–13
Design Studies (publication) 22–3
development: routes 100; work 93
dialogic exchange 94
dialogue, usage 42
difficulty, discourse 33
digital medium 103
digital turn 9–10
Diploma in Art and Design (DipAD), setup 31
disciplinary pedagogy, perspective 9
disciplines: boundaries 134; examination, contextualisation 4; groupings 5; specialism 71
discourse: multimodal 30–1; role/nature, examination of 12–13; study, academics' usage of 101

discrimination, BME student vulnerability to 62
discursive practices, acquisition 153
disruptive pedagogies 146
dissent, self-questioning approach 63–4
diversity, ambiguity (relationship) 62
Dormer, Peter 27
dwelling, pedagogy 103
dystopian brief 112

education: democratisation of 149; real life, distinction 99; society's ideas about 39–40; structuring 110
educational objectives, critique (Eisner) 127
elastic production, landscape 63
embedded knowledge, existence 29
embodied knowledge 94–5; importance of 28–9
encultured knowledge 29
engagement 71, 72–3; sticky site, curriculum 79
epistemologies 19–21
equality, ambiguity (relationship) 62
Europe Art School, education 10–11
(e)valuation system, elements 42
evaluative language, modelling 119
evaluative Ps 131–3
experienced curriculum 73
experiential knowing 26–8, 148–9
experiential studio-based pedagogies 157
expertise 64–5, 117–19; ideas, power relations (connection) 120
explicit knowledge 27–8, 148–9

Failing Students in Higher Education (Peelo) 51
failure: importance, student understanding of 46, 48; valorisation 145
feedback 93; industry 111; written/oral 125
fine art, discipline 4
fogginess 148
formal components (stickiness) 75–6
freedom 145–7

giftedness, ideology 51
Goldsmiths, golden period 40
Gormley, Antony 56, 150; BLIND LIGHT installation *57*; box, impact of 60
Gropius, Walter (Bauhaus curriculum) *21*
group brief 110
group marking, approaches (impact) 130–1
group projects, impact of 110
gut feeling, usage 27

higher education: creative educators, role in 119; curriculum, co-creation 74; identity work in 83; local/global nature of 155; purpose of 81–2; research in 109; student-centred pedagogies 113; values of 94–5
home student, international student status 155
Hornsey School of Art, rebellion 145–6

identity 71; development of 133; transformation of 3; work 14, 83
ignorant school master, idea of 64–5
ill-defined problem, phrase (usage of) 114
immersive briefs 110
indeterminacy, term (usage of) 56–7
individual, social (relationship) 153–5
industry feedback 111
informal components (stickiness) 75–6
interdisciplinary practice 110; promotion of 156
intersubjectivity 130–1
intuitive judgements 130–1
invisible teaching, form 143–4

Jetelová, Magdalena 47
job satisfaction, increase in 75
journey metaphor, lecturer usage of 131–2
judge, identification 42
judicious intervention 40–1

kind of exchange 12–13
know how, characteristics of 24–5
knowing 148–50; experiential 26–8; forms of 26–7; interrelationships 34; multiple modes of 28–31; not knowing 148–50; practice of 19
knowing about 26
knowing how 24
knowing that 25–6
knowing why 25–6
knowledge 148–50; abstract 23; academic 25; bank, availability of 149; bank, student access to 149; bodies, complexity/difficulty 22; codification of 22; complexity of 12, 34; co-production of 157; creation of 30; economy of 28; embedded, existence of 29; embodied 28–9,

94–5; encultured 29; explicit 27–8; focus, change 29–30; mixture 30–1; practice 19; social construction of 29; stickiness 30; sticky 148–9; tacit 27; vocational 22, 151

languages: access to 100–1; meaning-making conception 129–30; stickiness, recognition 60; teacher access to 100–1; usage, importance of 82–3; written, role of 153
learning: collaborative, opportunities for 75; embodiment 101; environment of 136; environment, relations to 76–9; examination of 4; facilitator 74; group-based approach 113; interactions 81; learning-to-judge trajectories 136; material 95; non-reified aspects of 76; object-based 95; opportunities for, offering 74–5; organised 90; outcomes, series (presentation) 129; power 82; problem-based 113; process 25; project-centred 114; scaffolded, Vygotskian approaches to 146; self-directed 113; social constructivist theories of 21–2; space, forms of 91; student 144; studio-based 114; support 79; technicians, stability 80; unlearning, culture of 49–50; unseen learning outcomes 143–4; visibility/openness 90–1
lecture-based teaching, problems 76–7
lecturers: learning-to-judge trajectories 136; skills of 118
Lesbian, Gay, Bisexual, Transgender, Queer (LGBTQ) creative practitioners, role of 42–3
listening, importance of 118
live briefs 74, 92–3, 111–12
live project 92–3
logobias 32, 152–3

magic, idea of 12
making: impact of 83; process of 109
massive open online courses (MOOCs), concern 10
materiality 94–7
material learning 95; opportunities for 7
Mathis, Muda 116
McMaster School of Medicine 113
media: disciplinary position 4–5; masters 26; studies, discourse study (academics' usage of) 101
metaphors, identification of 27–8
Morris, William 94
multidisciplinary universities, art/design departments (location) 43
multimodal discourses 30–1
multimodal studio-based pedagogies 157
mystery, idea of 12

National Diploma in Design (NDD) 31
necessity, practice/theory 31–4
negotiation: skills 110; sticky activity 73
'Nellie Is Dead' (Swann) 20–1
New York Vogue 49
'no brief' brief 112
non-engagement 72–3
non-space (studio) 155–6
non-subject, teaching 46
not knowing 148–50
not-known 23; importance of 76
not yet known, search 148–9

object-based learning 95
objectives: regularities, internalisations 131; usage of 127
one-to-one tutorial model 117
open-ended challenge 96
open-ended questioning, usage of 118
opportunistic curriculum 61–2
oppositional space 151–2
oral feedback 125
organised learning 90
outcome-based assessment (OBA) 126; location 126–7

pedagogy(ies) 112; approaches to 32–3; characteristics of 95; disciplinary, perspective 9; disruptive 146; experiential studio-based 157; multimodal studio-based 157; pedagogic discourse 152; pedagogised identities 96; productive confusion 58; signature 90–7, 102–3, 107; spontaneity, requirement of 9; sticky 157; student-centred 113, 116
pedagogy of ambiguity (Austerlitz) 13
performative paradox 142–3
person, work (relationship) 133
Peterson, Fiona 91
phenomenographic methodology, adoption of 135
Plato 20
portfolio submission, requirement 149
Post Digital Art School, concept of (analysis) 10

power relations 119–20; expertise ideas, relationship to 120
practical subjects 32
practice 150–1; carrying out/practising, difference 33–4; community 142–3; discursive, acquisition of 153; interdisciplinary 110; learning 33; reality of 151–2; recontextualisation of 100; social constructivist theories of 21–2; split 33–4; theory of 31–4; usage 42
practising 33
problem-based learning 113; researchers, ill-defined problem phrase (usage) 114
process 125, 131–2
process-focused briefs 109–10
process, product, person (three Ps) 131–3
process-product spectrum 132
product 125; process-product spectrum 132
productive ambiguity 63
productive confusion 58
professional distance, maintenance of 78
professionalism, idea of 103
project: container 107–8; live 92–3; pedagogy 109; requirements of 108; role of 76, 107; third-space 75
project brief: debates over 112–14; open-endedness of 64; role of 63–4; visual stimuli, relationship to 90–1
project-centred learning 114; challenge of 117; concern for 120; student role in 115–16
prompts, giving 119
Prospero, role of 64

Quality Assurance Agency, requirements of 75

racism, BME student vulnerability to 62
radical openness, space 49
real life 99–100; education, contrast 99; scenario 113; usage 101
real world: discourses 152; oppositional space 151–2; positions, discourse of 152; vocational knowledge of 151
rebellion 145–6
recontextualisation 100
reflection 144
reminders, giving 119
research 93–4; undertaking, process of 115
retention, enhancement 110
risk-averse behaviours 48
risk taking 144–5; effect of 145; idea, prevalence of 47; self-questioning approach to 63–4
Ryle, Gilbert 24

scaffolded learning, Vygotskian approaches to 146
self-directed learning 113
selfhood, development of 133
self-managed dissertation 115
shared repertoire 153–4
signature pedagogies 90–7, 102–3, 107; validation of 103
Social Activity Method schema, usage of 100
social constructivism 22
social convention, gatekeepers 23
social gathering, creation of 6
social, individual (relationship) 153
social practice 153–5
social process 42
society conversation 24; engagement in 150–1
sociocultural perspectives 21–6
space (studio) 155–6
speculation, self-questioning approach to 63–4
stickiness: creation of 74–5; enjoyment of 6; formal/informal components of 75–6
sticky: activity 73; campus, concept of 158; definitions, range of 73; elements 76; knowledge 148–9; pedagogy 157; practices 135–7; term (usage) 5–6
sticky curriculum 5–7, 13–14, 142; assessment, usage 15; shaping 134–5; student offering 154
sticky situations: failure/guilt, attachment 6; outcomes, possibilities 6
students: assignments, giving 118; brief 47; creating learning, transfer of 101–2; curriculum, sticky offering 154; expectation of 112; face-to-face contact with 78; goals/ideals of 117; growth of 78; ideal, stereotype of 51; ideas, production of 80; identity of 81–3; knowledge, public view of 119; learning 144; learning power of 82; numbers, increase in 137; perception of 51; performance, assessor interpretation of 130–1; risk-taking 46, 47–8; role of 115–16; sticky curriculum and 154; student-centred

pedagogies and 113, 116; student-tutor relationship, small-scale study of 77–8; valued 50–2; work production of 94
studio: access to, reduction of 91; curriculum 7; education 3; environment 143–4; experiential studio-based pedagogies 157; function of 157–8; multimodal studio-based pedagogies 157; pedagogic discourse of 152; practice 156; roles, fluidity of 144; signature pedagogies 90–1; space/non-space 155–6; studio-based design tutors 118–19; studio-based design tutors, skills of 118–19; studio-based dialogues 136–7; studio-based learning 114; talk 45; teacher, description of 76–7; teaching, listening (importance of) 118; vertical, creation of 74
Studio 2017 *41*
studio teaching: description of 77; problems of 76–7
subjective art 129
subjects: engagement 98; subject-related skills, teaching 101–2
subjects-yet-to-come 23
successful creativity 108
surfaces, stickiness 6–7

tacit knowledge 27, 148–9; codification, absence of 28; movement 27–8
teachers: authority, basis of 117–18; language access of 100–1; role of 116–20
teaching 142–4; collaborating (strategy) 98; collections, establishment of 95; examination of 4; invisible, form 143–4; lecture-based, problems of 76–7; practices 14, 88; professional response to 79; strategies of 97–9; studio, problems of 76–7; tripartite teaching team 79–80
teamwork, building 110
technicians/academics, relationship 80
techno-rationalist paradigm 126–7
theory 31–4, 150–1; practice, split 33–4; provision 150–1; written language, importance of 153
'third-space' project 75
three Ps (process, product, person) 131–3
transparency 58–62; ambiguity, antithesis of 59; pursuit of 60; tyranny of 60
transparent opacity 147–8
tripartite teaching team 79–80
truths, imparting 25
tutors: activity, absence of 20; experiences of, channelling 149; feedback, impact of 119; professional distance of 78; reactions to 77; role of 13–14, 78; student-tutor relationship, small-scale study of 77–8; studio-based design tutors, skills of 118–19; tension of 154–5; time frame 108

uncertainty 56–8; cunning 65
university: Art School, relationship to 152; studio function 157–8
unlearning, culture 49–50
unseen learning outcomes 143–4
utopian brief 112

valuation, manifestation/enactment 42
valued student 50–2
value(s): construction/meaning of 39; cool/paradoxical 45–50; exchange of 44–5; impact of 12–13
verbal fluency, development of 153
vertical studio, creation of 74
virtual learning environment, assignment 61
visual material, elements of (reproduction) 93
Visual Material Culture (VMC) 34
visual medium: usage of 103; words, centrality of 152–3
vocational knowledge 22, 151

Western Art School: idea(l)s 45–50; machismo 43
Western higher education, values of 94–5
wicked problems, responses to 151
words, centrality of 152–3
work: (e)valuation of 41–2, 137; identity 83; materiality of 84; production of 81, 94; pure response to 40–1; stickiness 143; work-related, voluntary sector environments, creative learning (transfer) 101–2
workload, increase in 137
workplace, student entry into 34
Writing Purposefully in Art and Design (Writing PAD) 33, 79
written feedback 125
written language, role of 153
written policy assessments 126
written word: hegemony 11–12; usage of 152–3

Lightning Source UK Ltd.
Milton Keynes UK
UKHW020604231119
354067UK00007B/165/P

9 780367 192501